Computers and Conversation

Computers and People Series

Edited by

B. R. GAINES and A. MONK

The series is concerned with all aspects of human–computer relationships, including interaction, interfacing modelling and artificial intelligence. Books are interdisciplinary, communicating results derived in one area of study to workers in another. Applied, experimental, theoretical and tutorial studies are included.

MONOGRAPHS

On Becoming a Personal Scientist: Interactive computer elicitation of personal models of the world, *Mildred L. G. Shaw* 1980

Communicating with Microcomputers: An introduction to the technology of man–computer communication, *Ian H. Witten* 1980

The Computer in Experimental Psychology, *R. Bird* 1981

Recent Advances in Personal Construct Technology, *Mildred L. G. Shaw* 1981

Principles of Computer Speech, *I. H. Witten* 1982

Cognitive Psychology of Planning, *J.-M. Hoc*, 1988

EDITED WORKS

Computing Skills and the User Interface, *M. J. Coombs and J. L. Alty (eds)* 1981

Fuzzy Reasoning and Its Applications, *E. H. Mamdani and B. R. Gaines (eds)* 1981

Intelligent Tutoring Systems, *D. Sleeman and J. S. Brown (eds)* 1982 (1986 paperback)

Designing for Human-Computer Communication, *M. E. Sime and M. J. Coombs (eds)* 1983

The Psychology of Computer Use, *T. R. G. Green, S. J. Payne and G. C. van der Veer (eds)* 1983

Fundamentals of Human–Computer Interaction, *Andrew Monk (ed)* 1984, 1985

Working with Computers: Theory versus Outcome, *G. C. van der Veer, T. R. G. Green, J.-M. Hoc and D. Murray (eds)* 1988

Cognitive Engineering in Complex Dynamic Worlds, *E. Hollnagel, G. Mancini and D. D. Woods (eds)* 1988

Computers and Conversation, *P. Luff, N. Gilbert and D. Frohlich (eds)* 1990

EACE Publications (Consulting editors: *Y Waern and J.-M. Hoc*)

Cognitive Ergonomics, *P. Falzon (ed)* 1990

Psychology of Programming, *J.-M. Hoc, T. R. G. Green, R. Samurçay and D. Gilmore* (forthcoming)

Computers and Conversation

Edited by

PAUL LUFF
NIGEL GILBERT
DAVID FROHLICH

Social and Computer Sciences Research Group,
University of Surrey, Guildford, Surrey UK

ACADEMIC PRESS
Harcourt Brace Jovanovich, Publishers
London San Diego New York
Boston Sydney Tokyo Toronto

ACADEMIC PRESS LIMITED
24/28 Oval Road,
LONDON NW1 7DX

United States Edition published by
ACADEMIC PRESS INC.
San Diego, California 92101–4311

British Library Cataloguing in Publication Data
Is available

ISBN 0-12-459560-X

Printed and bound by Hartnolls Limited,
Bodmin, Cornwall

List of Contributors

Graham Button
Department of Social and
Political Studies,
Polytechnic South West,
Plymouth,
United Kingdom.

Alison Cawsey
Department of Artificial
Intelligence,
University of Edinburgh,
United Kingdom.

Anthony Finkelstein
Department of Computing
Imperial College of Science,
Technology and Medicine
University of London,
United Kingdom.

Norman Fraser
Social and Computer Sciences
Research Group,
Department of Sociology ,
University of Surrey,
United Kingdom.

David Frohlich
Social and Computer Sciences
Research Group,
Department of Sociology,
University of Surrey,
United Kingdom,

Hugo Fuks
Department of Computing
Imperial College of Science,
Technology and Medicine,
University of London,
United Kingdom.

Nigel Gilbert
Social and Computer Sciences
Research Group,
Department of Sociology,
University of Surrey,
United Kingdom.

David Good
Department of Social and
Political Sciences,
University of Cambridge,
United Kingdom.

Paul Luff
Social and Computer Sciences
Research Group,
Department of Sociology,
University of Surrey,
United Kingdom.

Paul McIlvenny
Department of English,
University of Oulu,
Finland.

Michael Norman
Department of Computer Science,
University of Hull,
United Kingdom.

Pirrko Raudaskoski
Department of English,
University of Oulu,
Finland.

Hugh Robinson
Computing Department,
The Open University,
Milton Keynes,
United Kingdom.

Peter Thomas
Department of Computer Science,
University of Hull,
United Kingdom.

Robin Wooffitt
Social and Computer Sciences
Research Group,
Department of Sociology,
University of Surrey,
United Kingdom.

Table of Contents

Introduction

Paul Luff

How could the work done by sociologists studying the everyday conversations that people have with each other be relevant to designers of computer software? Can looking at a telephone conversation where Jenny tells Anne that Ida has got her new furniture, or the recording of a customer asking a newsagent for a packet of cigarettes, or Margaret Thatcher warning against the soft-centre of the Labour Party tell us anything about how to build more 'user-friendly' software? This book aims to show that, with some care, they can and that the work done by conversation analysts since the mid-sixties on people talking to each other is relevant to the way people 'interact' with computers. Conversation Analysis (CA) pays attention to the social context in which interactions take place, and it aims by rigorous and detailed examination of naturally-occurring data to show that there is an organised structure to those interactions. This is why it is attractive to designers of human-computer interactions.

CA is also an alternative to what may be called the cognitive science approach to artificial intelligence and human-computer interaction. This is the view that computer systems would be easier to use if they could infer the goals of the people using them. To do this the system has to second-guess its users; it has to discover what they are aiming to do. If they get in trouble, it also has to provide further facilities to make their task easier or help to clear up their misunderstandings. Several of the following chapters will describe problems associated with this 'cognitive science' approach and will show that an alternative approach with concerns similar to those of Conversation Analysis can be useful for building interactive artifacts.

In fact, in the chapters of this book there are examples of Conversation Analysis informing a wide range of activities, from analysing what a computer system is required to do, specifying how it should do it, designing its interaction with its users and, finally, evaluating it.

Before discussing its usefulness some introduction to the field of Conversation Analysis is necessary. In Chapter 1, Robin Wooffitt describes how CA emerged as a research discipline, and its main methodological concerns. He emphasises two aspects of CA: first, that it aims to show the recurring structures and patterns in the organisation of conversation and, second, that CA is concerned with interactions between people in their everyday behaviour. He illustrates these two points by looking at two recent studies in CA: Jefferson's analysis of the structure of lists in everyday conversation (Jefferson in press), and Drew's analysis of teasing (Drew 1987).

In Chapter 2, Hugh Robinson points out that this concern of CA for interaction and its social context may help human-computer interaction (HCI) overcome its lowly position at the margins of software engineering. He describes the present orientation of HCI as one which regards the interface between user and system as some sort of boundary, and the tasks that users have to perform as 'problems' or 'goals'. It is this orientation that has contributed to HCI's marginalisation. Robinson proposes an ethnographic approach, a "sociology of human-computer interaction", that concentrates on the social world of computer use. Analyses of mundane conversations, non-mundane conversations and 'studies of work' all have direct relevance to this new study.

This is the very idea that Michael Norman and Peter Thomas develop in Chapter 3. They suggest that the 'findings' of CA can offer practical assistance to the design of human-computer interactions. By examining a problem found in the design of a particular computer system they show the range of solutions that are possible. They go on to describe how previous work in CA informs the choice of one of these solutions and suggest that other findings of CA could inform other aspects of design. In general, they say, findings from CA are amenable to be formulated in terms of design guidelines.

Graham Button strongly argues against the idea that CA is a treasure-trove of routines, sequences and rules ready to be plundered for computational models of conversation. He warns, in Chapter 4, that applying the 'findings' of CA to human-computer interaction ignores the social aspect of the study, and that it was this social aspect that made CA attractive in the first place. Button illustrates this argument by showing how three well-known studies in CA have been misunderstood. He discusses the status of the rules of turn-taking, sequences as conversational resources, and the social occasion of the production of conversational routines.

In Chapter 5, Paul McIlvenny compares such arguments with similar ones about the Turing test (Turing 1950) and Artificial Intelligence (AI). In contrast to Button, he considers that the study of human interaction is essential to computer models of conversation. He points to some of the problems with current approaches to AI and HCI and considers how a 'partnership' between computers and Conversation Analysis could help. McIlvenny terms his proposed approach "embodied modelling" and illustrates it with examples of computer use analysed from a CA viewpoint.

The two succeeding chapters look at CA applied to one particular aspect of interaction: what happens when there is a breakdown or misunderstanding in communication? In Chapter 6, David Good examines what is termed the "repair system" of natural conversation, and in Chapter 7 Pirkko Raudaskoski shows how this can be applied to human-computer interaction. Good argues against models that rely on how a hearer infers the presumptions and assumptions behind a speaker's utterance while ignoring the context in which that utterance was spoken. Taking an example of such a model, Sperber and Wilson's 'Theory of Relevance' (Sperber and Wilson 1986), he compares a CA approach that does account for the external and interactional aspects of communication. He illustrates this argument with a conversation where the rationality of the participants cannot be assumed; one where a clinical psychologist talks to a thought-disordered schizophrenic. Even here there are structures to repair.

Raudaskoski investigates whether these structures could be appropriately applied to misunderstandings that occur in human-computer interaction. As both computer and system can misunderstand each other they both require devices to cope with repair. She describes a telephone message system that implements repair strategies based on the work of Schegloff (1981). Although her system can neither understand nor produce spoken utterances, by using a human intermediary Raudaskoski has been able to evaluate her repair strategies. Her approach can be seen as a way of analysing requirements for computer systems.

In Chapter 8, Anthony Finkelstein and Hugo Fuks look at another stage of building computer systems – the activity of specifying software. Specification is a process that is usually performed by a group of people who decide what a system should do and how it should do it. Therefore it involves these people in negotiation to come to a common understanding. Finkelstein and Fuks aim to understand this process and, later, support it with computer tools. As a first step along this path they intend to model specification using a formal logic of dialogues By means of this they can show how questions can be asked, assertions and challenges made, and issues resolved. What their model does not handle is the interactional aspect to specification. They turn to CA to model this.

The remaining chapters of this book show how CA can inform the design of interactive computer systems. In Chapter 9, David Frohlich and Paul Luff describe the Advice System. In many ways this is a conventional computer system where the user has to select items from menus and type characters into boxes. But, in the Advice System the user selects words, phrases and punctuation marks in order to construct utterances in a dialogue with the system. Frohlich and Luff describe how CA can be used to inform the design of this interaction. They contrast this approach with other dialogue control policies derived from work in linguistics, philosophy and psychology. They give details of how CA has been useful for providing resources for both system and user. In particular, they show how the interaction opens, how, like in Raudaskoski's system, repair of misunderstandings is provided for both system and user, how topics in the interaction are changed and how the interaction closes. Rather than attempting to model a conversation, they try to apply what Sacks (1984) called the 'technology of conversation', but the conversations to which the technology is applied are between a computer system and a user.

In Chapter 10, Alison Cawsey takes a similar approach to the design of a tutorial system that can explain how electronic circuits work. As well as providing resources for opening and closing the interaction, turn-taking and repair, the system also has specialised sequences to perform its purpose as a tutor. In contrast to other approaches taken in this volume, these sequences providing remediation and explanation are globally planned. Cawsey does, however, provide mechanisms to make these plans locally coherent to the user and to allow for local and unplanned deviations.

In the final chapter, Nigel Gilbert, Robin Wooffitt and Norman Fraser describe how CA could inform the design of systems that understand and generate spoken utterances. As a counter to Graham Button's earlier arguments they show, by using the example of adjacency-pairs, how CA can be used for human-computer interactions.

A notation that is fairly standard has developed so that spoken conversational data can be analysed. This is described in Button and Lee (1987) and summarised in some notes at the end of this volume.

These notes also include some less widely used notations for describing such things as gaze and gesture. As yet, there is no standard notation for describing human-computer conversations and authors have developed their own symbols for the details they want to describe.

As Frohlich and Luff show, CA is not the first body of knowledge to be plundered by AI and HCI. Theories from philosophy, techniques from linguistics and concepts from psychology have all been taken. There are obvious dangers with this activity. By not paying attention to the foundations underlying the original research, its findings may be inappropriately applied. What attracts designers of human-computer interactions to CA is its rigour, attention to detail and concern with social context and organisation. There are frequent warnings in the following chapters against what McIlvenny terms the "emasculation" of CA. Nevertheless, this book does contain attempts to describe appropriate applications of the 'technology of conversation'.

Acknowledgements

The original impetus for this book came from a Symposium held at the University of Surrey in September 1989. The editors would like to thank all those who attended for making it such a productive and enjoyable event. Special thanks go to Alison Mill-Ingen for tirelessly waiting on the whims of the participants and for her efforts in helping produce this volume. At the time of writing all the editors were members of the Social and Computer Sciences Research Group at the University of Surrey. We would like to thank the other members of our group for their assistance, patience and resources.

Chapter 1

On the Analysis of Interaction

An Introduction to Conversation Analysis

Robin Wooffitt

1.1 Introduction

In this chapter I will describe the programme of sociological research
which has come to be known as Conversation Analysis, or CA. In
particular, I will explain some of the objectives which underpin
empirical work and illustrate some general characteristics of ordinary
talk which have been revealed through conversation analytic
research.

In this chapter, I do not intend to provide a review of the available
literature which reports the results of conversation analytic studies.
This is because there is a burgeoning literature of CA work: a recent
bibliography, complied by John Heritage at the University of
California at Los Angeles, extends to twenty pages and several
hundred entries.[1] In a chapter of this length it would not be possible
to provide a comprehensive review. Besides which, there are already

---

[1] A published version of an earlier bibliography can be found in Heritage's 1985 paper.

overviews of the major 'findings', in addition to a growing number of edited collections of conversation analytic papers.[2]

As so much has already been written about CA, why is it necessary to have yet another introduction?

First, with the notable exception of a chapter in Levinson's *Pragmatics* (1983), most of the available introductions and overviews are written by sociologists for other sociologists. Most of these assume that the reader has at least some elementary knowledge of relevant sociological debates and issues. For example, some introductions to CA emphasize its intellectual roots in ethnomethodology (Lee 1987) or discuss more generally its relationship to other sociological, anthropological or philosophical approaches and traditions (Atkinson and Drew 1979: chapter 2; Heritage 1978, 1984). These issues will not be dealt with here. This chapter is included in a volume which addresses both sociologists and other researchers from a variety of disciplines, and I am assuming that a large proportion of the readership may have little knowledge of sociology, nor indeed any interest in wider sociological issues. Consequently, it seems unnecessary to describe in any great detail the broad theoretical background to the emergence of the analysis of conversation as a research project.

There is a second feature common to many of the reviews available in the literature: a tendency to focus on a limited number of particularly important findings and concepts. For example, it is easy enough to find a comprehensive discussion of the organisation of turn-taking, in particular, Sacks, Schegloff and Jefferson's (1974) 'Simplest Systematics' paper. This is true also of Schegloff and Sacks' (1973) discussion of the concept of adjacency pairs. As these aspects of conversational organisation have received considerable attention elsewhere (including in some later chapters of this volume) there is no need to rehearse them in detail here.

---

2   Useful collections of contemporary research papers can be found in Atkinson and Heritage 1984; Button, Drew and Heritage 1986; and Button and Lee 1987. Alternatively, Psathas 1979, Schenkein 1978 and Sudnow 1972, provide collections which contain some older papers. *Sociology*, 12, 1978, is a special edition devoted to the analysis of language use; while the papers in it are not purely conversation analytic, it is a useful introduction to ethnomethodologically informed examinations of language use. For an overview of major research findings, readers are referred to Levinson 1983, chapter 6; Heritage 1989 gives an up-to-date perspective on recent developments within CA. For a more general introduction to CA; readers should consult Heritage 1984, chapter 8. Alternatively, useful introductions can be found in Atkinson and Drew 1979, Heritage and Atkinson 1984, and Wootton 1989.

As I mentioned earlier, this chapter is written partly for computer scientists who may have had little previous exposure to sociological issues, let alone conversation analysis itself. It may also be read by sociologists who are interested in the field of human-computer interaction, but who have had little previous contact with CA. Consequently, the chapter will focus more on the intellectual and methodological concerns which are central to the conversation analytic investigation of natural language use than on the results or findings from such an endeavour.

In the following section of this chapter, I will provide a very general introduction to some of the insights which led Sacks and his colleagues to the detailed analysis of ordinary talk.[3] Wherever possible, Sacks' unique approach to the analysis of conversation will be illustrated by reference to empirical materials. Initially, by looking at some simple utterances, I will focus on the orderliness of everyday talk. In particular, I hope to show that even the most elementary turns exhibit a systematic design. In subsequent sections I will draw on data and analysis taken from two contemporary studies of conversational phenomena: listing (Jefferson in press) and teasing (Drew 1987). These two studies have been selected for close attention for three reasons. First, they provide a focus for discussion of two important features of conversation: the structural properties of recurrent and stable patterns which emerge from occasions of natural language use; and the interactional businesses which are mediated in conversational organisation.[4] Second, these studies deal with aspects of conversational behaviour which are easily recognizable. For example, it is an everyday occurrence to find oneself describing, say, a series of things we have done in a day, or intend to do; equally, we can all recall making playful jokes at someone else's expense, or being the butt of this kind of humour. Thus, I want to show how results from conversation analytic research can illuminate aspects of everyday behaviour with which readers will be able to identity.

Because it is a simple matter to recognise when someone is teasing, or producing a list, such as a list of attributes, it seems fair to assume that these forms of conversational behaviour are relatively

---

3   This is not meant to be a comprehensive academic account of the conditions in which CA emerged: excellent discussions of these issues can be found in Heritage (1984), and Schegloff (1989). It is included only to illustrate the kinds of concerns which motivated their enquiries and to show that there is a very clear connection to contemporary conversation analytic work.

4   Although I am making a distinction between these dimensions of conversational activity, this is purely for clarity of presentation, and it is not to be taken as a literal correspondence to a state of affairs in actual instances of conversational activity.

'gross': they are quite apparent in ordinary conversation and sophisticated analysis is not required to demonstrate their occurrence. In the analysis of these conversational events, however, both Jefferson and Drew reveal the operation of quite delicate but highly organised reasoning procedures. The third advantage of these two studies, then, lies in the way that they illustrate a primary contribution of CA research: its ability to reveal hitherto unanticipated levels of orderliness in the detail of verbal interaction.

1.2   Harvey Sacks: 'order at all points'

Conversation Analysis emerged in the early 1960s from the work of Harvey Sacks and his colleagues, Emanuel Schegloff and Gail Jefferson. The goal of this research tradition can be stated quite simply. CA sets out to detail the tacit, organised reasoning procedures which inform the production and recognition of naturally occurring talk. CA is a radical departure from previous forms of analysis in that the production of utterances, and the sense they obtain, is seen as an accomplishment, the achievement of which is inextricably tied to the circumstances in which they are produced. That is, words used in talk are not studied as semantic units, but as products or objects which are designed and used in respect of the interactions being negotiated through the talk: requests, proposals, accusations, complaints, and so on. The way in which utterances are designed is informed by speakers' communicative competences: the organised procedures, maxims, methods and resources which are available to them by virtue of their membership of a natural language speaking community. The analytic objective is to explicate the procedures on which participants rely to produce utterances, and by which they make sense of other people's talk: to describe the 'technology of conversation' (Sacks 1984, p.413).

A fundamental assumption informing CA is that ordinary talk is a highly organised, orderly phenomenon. The goal of analysis is to reveal the basis of this orderliness. It is important to note, however, that this analytic objective is not based on any theoretical speculation as to the 'nature' of conversation. Rather, insights about the character of conversational interaction are distilled from empirical investigation of specific materials.

Conversation Analysis began with a question. Sacks had been working on recordings of telephone conversations calls to the Los Angeles Suicide Prevention Center. He had observed that, in the majority of cases, if the Center's personnel gave their names at the beginning of the conversation, the callers would give their names in reply. Sacks came to notice, however, that in one call, the caller (B) seemed to be having trouble with the agent's name.

```
(1) Sacks Lecture 1, Fall 1964, p.1
A:            this is Mr. Smith, may I help you
B:            I can't hear you
A:            This is Mr Smith
B:            Smith
```

Sacks also observed that for the rest of the conversation the caller remained reluctant to disclose his identity. This was not a unique occurrence; the Center's personnel frequently experienced difficulties in getting callers to identify themselves. The issue Sacks began to explore was "where, in the course of the conversation could you tell that somebody would not give their name" (Lecture 1, Fall 1964, p.1). It was this problem, and this sequence, that led to Sacks' unique approach to the study of conversation. In a memoir of Sacks, Schegloff recalls that

> It was during a long talking walk during the late winter of 1964 that Sacks mentioned to me a "wild" possibility that had occurred to him. He had previously told me about a recurrent and much discussed practical problem faced by those who answered phone calls to the Suicide Prevention Center – the problem of getting the caller to give their name...On the one hand, Sacks noted, it appears that if the name is not forthcoming at the start it may prove problematic to get. On the other hand, overt requests for it may be resisted. Then he remarked: is it possible that the caller's declared problem in hearing is a methodical way of avoiding giving one's name in response to the other's having done so. *Could talk be organised at that level of detail? And in so designed a manner?*
>
> (Schegloff 1989b) [emphasis added]

With this question, Sacks raised the possibility of investigating utterances as items which speakers use to get things done in the course of their interactions with others. That is, an utterance as simple as "I can't hear you" might be analysed to reveal how it is being strategically employed to achieve a specific task in the course of the conversation. Sacks' subsequent analysis reveals that by doing 'not hearing', the caller is able to establish a sequential trajectory in the conversation in which it becomes inappropriate for the agent to request the caller's name. In this case, doing 'not hearing' may be one way of accomplishing 'not giving a name'.[5]

Sacks' subsequent detailed inspection of transcripts of recorded conversations began to highlight recurrent patterns in the ways in which words were used, and he began to fashion a distinctive analytic approach to the examination of empirical materials.

Sacks worked with the assumption that these objects, whether lengthy utterances, or even single words or small combinations of separate lexical items, were used methodically in mundane conversation. He did not treat an utterance as something that just happened to be said that way. Rather, he worked on the assumption that the things people said were methodically designed: as the product of the speaker's methods or procedures for using those objects. The goal of his analyses, then, was to describe these procedures: to explain how a speaker came to use these words, in this way, on this occasion.

It is important to strike a warning note here. Sacks' interest in describing the methodic reasoning procedures by which speakers came to use specific words, or combinations of words, in talk should not be taken to imply that he wanted to describe *psychological* reasoning processes. Neither does it imply that this form of analysis proposes that speakers *intentionally* use these words to achieve certain effects. The occasional use of an 'intentionalist language' (Heritage and Atkinson 1984, p.7) in no way implies that the analysis proposes the operation of corresponding events occurring consciously or unconsciously in people's heads. Sacks' work, and subsequent CA research, has focussed on talk in interaction as a domain of social activity that is inherently ordered, and not as a representation of mental processes or as a way of gaining insight to speakers' 'motivations' or 'intentions'. However, Sacks was aware that his mode of analysis could be taken to imply that he was engaged in an attempt to model or describe the psychological processes which underpinned competence in language use. He was at pains to be clear about this.

---

5   The transcripts of Sacks' first lectures have now been published in a special
        edition of *Human Studies*, Vol 12, 3-4 , December 1989.

> When people start to analyze social phenomena...then,
> if you have to make an elaborate analysis of it...you
> figure that they [speakers] couldn't have thought that
> fast.

> I want to suggest to you that you have to forget that
> completely. Don't worry about how fast they're
> thinking. First of all, don't worry about whether they're
> 'thinking'. Just come to terms with how it is that [the
> detail of talk] comes off. Because you'll find that they
> can do these things...Look to see how it is that persons
> go about producing what they do produce.
>
> (Sacks, Lecture 1, Fall 1964, p. 14)

In the following section we will explore further Sacks'
recommendation to "Look to see how it is that persons go about
producing what they produce". To give a focus to the discussion, we
will look at the way that utterances are designed to address inferential
concerns.

1.3   The inferential character of ordinary talk

To permit a clear focus on this aspect of everyday talk we will
consider some data drawn from recordings of courtroom interaction
(from Drew forthcoming). The exchange from which these are taken
cannot be termed an ordinary conversation. The turn-taking system
is very constrained, and the talk which occurs is done for the benefit
of a largely passive third party – the jury members. It is by virtue of
such unusual circumstances, however, that we have the opportunity
to examine turns which are not obscured in the 'messiness' of
everyday conversation.

In the following extracts the counsel ('C') for the defence is cross-
examining the prosecution's main witness ('W'), the victim of an
alleged rape. Note that both parties produce what might be termed
competing versions of the same incidents. The point I want to make
is that each version is designed to make available certain inferences to
the overhearing jury.

```
(2)
C:                    [referring to a club where the
                      defendant and the victim met]  it's
                      where girls and fellas meet isn't
                      it?
W:                    People go there.


(3)
C:                    And during the evening, didn't
                      Mr.O. [the defendant] come over to
                      sit with you?
W                     Sat at our table.
```

In (2) "where girls and fellas meet" is countered by "people go there", and in (3) "sat at our table" contrasts with "sit with you". These versions are not necessarily incompatible; they are not, in any logical sense, mutually exclusive. The significance of these utterances rests in the way that the speakers have designed them to describe events which present a certain set of inferable properties. From the inspection of these materials the overhearing jury can come to those conclusions each party to the cross-examination wishes them to arrive at.

For example, in extract (2), the counsel builds a question through a description of one specific feature of the club in which the defendant and the witness met on the night of the alleged attack. The counsel refers to the patrons of the club as "fellas" and "girls" rather than, say, "men or women" or "local people". Furthermore, he describes the club as place where males and females meet, rather than "go for a drink", "go dancing", and so on. Thus his characterisation carefully invokes the sense of young people out to make contact with members of the opposite sex; and from this the inference can be drawn that people go to the club with a view to meeting others for primarily sexual purposes. Building the question in this way thus provides for inferences which work to undermine aspects of the witness's account that are crucial if her version of events are to be believed; for example, that in no way could it be suggested that she was encouraging any sexual relations between herself and her alleged attacker. Her reply, "People go there", carefully reformulates the 'function' of the club to escape the inference that it is a place in which males and females come together for sexual purposes. This is achieved primarily through the way she refers to the patrons: whereas a sexual division is emphasised and exploited by the counsel, she provides a gender neutral classification.

In (3) the question "didn't he come over to sit with you" implies that the witness was sufficiently familiar with the defendant that they might sit together in a club. From this the jury members might reasonably infer that the witness was in fact friendly with the defendant and, possibly, aware of the nature of his interest in her. This information could be damaging to her testimony. By recasting the counsel's version of events, however, the witness makes it inferable that the defendant's behaviour was not prompted by any special relationship with her, but was due to familiarity with the group of people of which she was only one member. Thus, the counsel's description is constructed to implicate a friendship between the defendant and the witness. The witness's description is designed to reinforce further the implication that she was not in any way encouraging the man who was alleged to have attacked her.

It may appear from these examples that CA aims to produce no more than a rather gross kind of subjective interpretation of the materials being examined. For example, in the preceding data extracts, there may be other ways of interpreting why the speakers said those particular things on this particular occasion. On what basis, then, can conversation analysts claim any priority for their analyses? Does the reader have to take the analysts' interpretations on trust?

There are two relevant points. First, conversation analytic research papers invariably present the materials from which the analyses have been drawn. The 'public' character of the data ensures that the readers of a research report never have to take the analyst's interpretation on trust: they can inspect the relevant materials to see for themselves if the analyst's observations seem valid. Furthermore, knowing that an audience will be able to consult the data acts as a powerful constraint upon interpretative 'flights of fancy' and careless analysis.

Second, it is important to emphasize that the goal of Conversation Analysis is not to furnish an academic or 'outsider's' reading of some conversational sequence, but to describe the organised interpretations that *people themselves* employ in the moment-by-moment course of conversation. The following extract comes from an exchange between a mother and her son about a Parent Teachers Association meeting.

```
(4)
Mother:     Do you know who's going to that
            meeting?
Russ:       Who.
Mother:     I don't kno:w.
Russ:       Oh::. Prob'ly Missiz McOwen ('n
            detsa) en prob'ly Missiz Cadry and
            some of the teachers and the
            counselors.
```
                                        (from Schegloff 1988a)

In this extract, Mother's question "Do you know who's going to that meeting?" can be interpreted in two ways: as a genuine *request* for information about who is attending the meeting or as a *pre-announcement* of some news concerning the people who will be attending the meeting. In the examination of this exchange, the analyst can identify which of these interpretations Russ makes by looking at the next turn after Mother's question. He returns the floor to his mother with a question, thereby displaying that he treats her utterance as a pre-announcement. Mother's next turn displays that on this occasion Russ's inference was incorrect.

The kinds of interpretative and reasoning procedures that CA seeks to identify are thus displayed in the trajectory of language use which is organised on a turn-by-turn basis. It is for this reason that conversation analysts place great emphasis upon the examination of *sequences* of interaction, rather than the detailed analysis of utterances which have been extracted from the sequential context in which they occurred. The methodological import of this is stressed by Sacks et al.:

> while understandings of other turns' talk are displays to
> co-participants, they are available as well to professional
> analysts who are thereby afforded a proof criterion (and
> search procedure) for the analysis of what a turns' talk
> is occupied with. Since it is the parties' understandings
> of prior turns' talk that is relevant to their construction
> of next turns, it is *their* understandings that are wanted
> for analysis. The display of those understandings in the
> talk of subsequent turns afforded both a resource for the
> analysis of prior turns and a proof procedure for
> professional analysis of prior turns – resources that are
> intrinsic to the data themselves.
>   (Sacks, Schegloff and Jefferson 1978, p.45 [1974])
>   (original emphasis)

We can further illustrate this methodological approach to the analysis of naturally occurring materials in the following extract.

```
(5)  (Trip to Syracuse)

 1   A:    So tha:-:t
 2   B:        -k-hhh
 3   A:    Yihknow I really don't have a place
           tuh sta:y.
 4   B:    ·hhOh:::::.hhh
 5         (.2)
 6   B:    ·hhh So yih not g'nna go up this
           weeken?
 7         (.2)
 8   A:    Nu::h I don't think so.
 9   B:    How about the following weekend.
10         (.8)
11   A:    ·hh Dat's the vacation isn't it?
12   B:    ·hhhh Oh:. ·hh ALright so:- no
           hassle, (.)
13         s-o
14   A:       -Ye:h,
15   B:    Yihkno:w::
16   ():   ·hhh
17   B:    So we'll make it fer another ti:me
           then.
```

Earlier in this extract A has explained that he is unable to make a trip on a date which had been previously arranged. As an alternative, B proposes another date – "How about the following weekend." (line 9). After the pause, A refers to the revised proposal for the trip: "Dat's the vacation isn't it?". We may note, firstly, that in this utterance A has re-described the occasion which B had suggested as the revised date for the trip. He has substituted "next weekend" with "vacation".

When we describe, or refer to an object or state of affairs, there is a (potentially inexhaustible) range of words and combinations of words which may legitimately be used. For example, with regard to the description of location, or 'place' Schegloff has written:

> Were I now to formulate where my notes are, it would
> be correct to say that they are: right in front of me, next
> to the telephone, on the desk, in my office, in Room
> 213, in Lewisohn Hall, on campus, at school, at
> Columbia, in Morningside Heights, on the Upper West
> Side, in Manhattan, in New York, in the Northeast, on
> the Eastern Seaboard, in the United States, etc. Each of
> these terms could in some sense be correct...were its
> relevance provided for.
>
> (Schegloff 1982, p.97)

Even when speakers are describing the most routine and
commonplace events or states of affairs they have a wide range of
alternative words and combinations of words from which to choose.
Thus, speakers necessarily select which referential item or descriptive
utterance they wish to use on any occasion. Insofar as reference or
description involves a process of selection, any actual description can
be investigated to reveal the tacit reasoning which informed the
speaker's specific formulation in these circumstances.

With regard to the 'weekend/vacation' extract we can begin to
explore this issue by looking to see how the speakers themselves treat
this exchange. Immediately after the utterance "Dat's the vacation
isn't it?", B says "Oh:.'hh ALright so:- no hassle," and "So we'll make
it fer another ti:me then." That is, she treats A's utterance as
somehow indicating that he won't be able to make the trip on the date
B had suggested earlier. Clearly, this is not the only interpretation
which A's utterance could support. For example, B could have
interpreted A as mentioning that the following weekend was a
vacation as a way of clarifying that this is the weekend to which B was
referring.

B's analysis of A's prior turn can be inspected by A to discover if
the sense for which the utterance was designed was indeed the sense
which was adopted by the speaker. Insofar as A makes no attempt to
correct B – that is, demonstrate that the inferences she drew were on
this occasion incorrect ones – there appears to be evidence that his
utterance was indeed designed to inform B that he could not make
the trip.

How does "Dat's the vacation isn't it?" come to do this work? In
substituting "weekend" with "vacation", A draws attention to
features of that occasion which are glossed over or not emphasised by
"weekend". These are that this suggested date for the trip, being also a
vacation or national holiday, cannot be treated as any weekend. In

this sense highlighting these two days as a vacation not only makes relevant that fact, but also makes relevant for that moment of the conversation certain inferences from the word vacation. For example, people routinely have events arranged for holiday periods. That is, by using "vacation", A provides a set of materials from which B can infer that his selection of terms was designed to indicate why he would not be able to go on the trip at that time.

Thus, by re-describing the proposed occasion for the planned trip the speaker was able to achieve specific interactional tasks. He registered his inability to attend the trip on the date suggested by the co-participant. He did not have to state explicitly that he could not attend. The design of his utterance, and in particular, the selection of one particular item, accomplished this by permitting the recipient to analyse his utterance to locate its significance. The design of this utterance, then, was intimately related to the sequential context in which it was used: after a suggestion as to a possible date for a trip. Furthermore, as it does not perform an overt rejection, it constitutes an oblique but interactionally sensitive way of marking his unavailabiliy.

There is a further point in connection with this extract. I have suggested that the sense of the word 'vacation' is tied to the context in which it is used and the actions being performed with it. This illustrates a fundamental reflexive property of natural language resources. As Garfinkel and Sacks put it, whatever is said in talk provides further materials by which the sense of what is being said may be decided.

> ...the talk itself, in that it becomes a part of the self-same
> occasion of interaction, becomes another contingency of
> that interaction. It extends and elaborates indefinitely
> the circumstances it glosses and in this way it
> contributes to its own accountably sensible character.
> (Garfinkel and Sacks 1970, p.344-5)

The analytic observations suggest that what people say – the materials they use and the way in which they are used – may form the basis for co-interactants' inferential work. From an inspection of precisely these types of natural language materials co-participants can arrive at judgements and conclusions concerning the speaker's 'character', 'intentions', 'meaning', and so on.

To summarise, by focusing in detail upon the selection of specific words, and the design of short utterances, certain points have been made. First, the way in which something is said should not be regarded as 'simple or accidental'. Even the most elementary items may display systematic properties.[6] A second feature of everyday talk has been illustrated: that the procedures through which speakers assemble their utterances may be informed by interactional tasks which have been generated through the course of their interaction. That is, utterance design may reflect the speaker's tacit reasoning about the actions projected by that utterance. Furthermore, as we have seen, these interactional tasks may be inextricably tied to the context of their occurrence. For example, the use of the utterance "Dat's the vacation isn't it?" is sensitive to the prior utterance in which the co-participant proposed a date for the trip. Thus, turns in talk are sensitive to their sequential placement.

1.4   The structure of conversational organisation

So far I have examined some specific utterances to reveal some of the orderly properties of utterance design. However, CA deals primarily with regular patterns of conversational behaviour, and the object of analysis is to describe the systematic structural characteristics which underpin particular phenomena. In this section we will look at the practice of listing (Jefferson in press) to illustrate the character of structural properties of conversational interaction.

When in the course of ordinary conversation people produce lists, they are recurrently produced in three parts. For example:

```
(6)
Sydney:      While you've been talking to me I
             mended, two nightshirts,
             a pillow case?
             enna pair'v pants.


(7)
Roger:       That was a vicious school there- it
             was about
             forty percent Negro,
             bout twenny percent Japanese,
             the rest were rich Jews.
```

---

6   For example, there has been research on items which might initially appear to be relatively insignificant, such as "oh" (Heritage 1984, 1989); "mm hm" (Jefferson 1983) and "uh huh"(Schegloff 1982). In each case, the analysis revealed that the use of these items exhibited consistent patterns. Thus, even the most minor non-lexical noises may be highly ordered phenomena.

```
(8)
Maybelle:     I think if you
              exercise it
              an' work at it
              'n studied it
              you do become clairvoyant.
```

This phenomenon can also be observed in the way people repeat words in lists.

```
(9)
Carol:        Did the phone ring? I dialed twice
              en it
              rang' rang' rang

(10)
Maggie:       Working working working'
              you know how I do
```

The following extract is a story about a cavalry initiation rite. The first part of the list is itself constructed as a three part list, as is the second part.

```
(11)
Roger:        He was given
          1   three bottles a' champagne,
A         2   three horses,
          3   and three addresses of uh patronizing
              women y'know.
              And his object was tuh um
          1   ride a horse t'one address, share a
              bottle of champagne with'er, make love
              with 'er,
B         2   take the other horse t'y'know the next
              one
          3   and then the third one,
              And if he completed it within a certain
C             period it was three hours or something,
              was a full fledged cavalry officer.
```

Even the first item of the second part of the story is itself structured around three components.

```
              And his object was tuh um
1             ride a horse t'one address,
2             share a bottle of champagne with'er,
3             make love with 'er,
```

Three partedness is not confined to lists produced in ordinary conversation. Analysis has revealed that it is also common in political speeches.

```
(12)          (Inaugural speech as governor of
              Alabama, 1963.)
Wallace:      ...and I say
              segregation now
              (.2)
              segregation tomorrow
              (.2)
              and segregation for ever
              Audience applause
```
(Atkinson 1984, p.60)

```
(13)
Thatcher:     [referring to the Labour party] At
              a ti:me of growing danger (.7) for
              all
              who cherish and believe in freedom
              (.8) this party of the soft centre
              is
1             no shield
              (.2)
2             no refuge
              (.)
2             and no answer
              Audience Applause
```

(Heritage and Greatbatch 1986, p.126)

In the following extracts, speakers have produced two parts of a list, but either have exhausted the relevant items which could be used to extend the list, or cannot find an appropriate word with which to complete it. In each case they use an item such as "or something", "things like that", and so on, to complete the lists as a three part unit.

```
(14)
Heather:      And they had like a concession
              stand at a fair
              where you can buy
              coke
              and popcorn
              and that type of thing.
```

```
        (15)
        Sy:                Take up
                           m:Metacal er,
                           Carnation Slender
                           er something like that.


        (16)
        Rudd:              Oh they come from
                           Jamaica
                           en South Africa'n,
                           all over the place
```

By using what Jefferson terms 'generalized list completers', speakers seem to be displaying their tacit understanding that lists should have three parts. The use of a general item as the third component exhibits the speakers' orientation to list production as complete upon the provision of the third part.

It is not correct to say, however, that speakers are showing their understanding of some pre-defined 'rule' of list production which states that if it is not in three parts, it is not a 'proper' or 'correct' list. Speakers do not have to build lists in three parts; they may display varying degrees of awareness of the conventions which inform this conversational activity. Speakers may produce lists with more than three items.   However, in these cases it is noticeable that co-participants are likely to interrupt the list directly after the third item (Atkinson 1984, p.58). Consequently, although we may legitimately talk of the structural property of listing, these extracts indicate that there is a general constraint operating to structure list production. Thus, the structural organisation of listing is not to be understood as having the property of dictating or determining conversational activity: it is a structure which people orient to with varying degrees of awareness. In Jefferson's terms, "three partedness appears to have a 'programmatic relevance' for the construction of lists" (p. 66).

The programmatic relevance is a form of social organisation: it is a part of the shared common-sense knowledge which speakers bring to their interactions with others. Evidence for this can be found in the way that list production is monitored by participants as an interactional *resource*. In the following extracts the co-participants only begin to talk after the third item of a list.

```
(17)
Matt:              The good actors are all dyin out.
Tony:              They're all- they're all
                   dyin out -yeah.
Matt:                        -Tyrone Po:wuh. Clark
                   Gable, Gary Cooper,
Tony:              Now all of 'em are dyin.


(18)
Emma:              They go on en on en on -but the:hh
Nancy:                                       -Yeu::h
```

These extracts indicate that the co-participants have been monitoring the speaker's talk to find a recognizable 'Transition Relevance Place' (Sacks, Schegloff and Jefferson 1974). For example, in extract (17) the list of good but unfortunately dead actors could easily have been extended. It is not the case that there are only three names that legitimately fall into this category. Thus, Tony's decision to start talking at the end of the third item displays his analysis that this point is a possible transition relevance place. In extract (18), the place at which Nancy starts indicates that she has employed the same tacit knowledge as a resource in her monitoring of the list "on en on en on". Although there is a stretch of overlapping talk, this is not due to any failure to recognise the programmatic relevance of three partedness, but is a consequence of only one of the parties orienting to the transition relevance place of third items.

Evidence that this form of conversational organisation is a culturally available resource come from other domains of language use in which it is exploited by interactants. For example, both Atkinson (1984) and Heritage and Greatbatch (1986) suggest that devices such as the three part list may be resources in allowing the speakers in political conferences and meetings to orchestrate the responses of large crowds or audiences. Because in everyday conversation lists are complete upon the third item, public speakers use this knowledge to organise cues to generate the onset of clapping and cheering.

This chapter began with a brief discussion of Sacks' insight about the orderly and designed character of conversation. Jefferson's research on listing provides further examples of the fine-grained orderliness of everyday talk. Building on an observation from one of Sacks' lectures, she makes the point that words can be selected in "historically sensitive ways". That is, "selected by reference to prior or projected events" (Jefferson in press p.68). She goes on to provide examples where this phenomenon is revealed in the items people select for the third slot in the list. For example, in the following extract the final item "or so forth" continues an alliteration developed over the first two items.

```
(19)
Desk:          Is there anyone close to you
          1    friend
          2    or family
          3    or so forth
               that you could uh kind of be in
               contact with
```

This discussion of Jefferson's study is only a partial account of a complex analysis. However, it invites a discussion of a theme which I have touched upon only briefly so far, but which is central to conversation analytic research: the 'structural' properties of procedures and methods which inform conversational interaction. We can use listing behaviour to focus this point. Jefferson's research clearly indicates that lists are commonly constructed in three parts, and that people orient to the programmatic relevance of three partedness in list production. There is empirical evidence that here we have an example of a conversational structure.

It is indeed the case that conversation analysts talk about the structure(s) of conversational interaction,[7] but it is necessary to be clear about the way that this notion is used and what it means. This ground has been covered in the literature in many places before, but as it is a particularly significant aspect of CA research, some brief remarks are in order. The simplest way to illustrate these issues is to refer to the concept of the adjacency pair.

It is common to find conversational exchanges which occur as paired actions: greeting-greeting, request-acceptance/refusal, and so on. Even in his earliest lectures Sacks was beginning to examine the way that paired actions are systematically coordinated in conversation. He proposed the concept of the adjacency pair to account for the recurrent structural properties of the organisation of paired actions. The properties of the concept were originally described in Schegloff and Sacks (1973); Heritage (1984) provides the following formulation.

---

[7]   In their Introduction to their edited volume, Heritage and Atkinson (1984) make a point of explicitly drawing attention to their use of the word 'structures' in the title. Also, Heritage (1988a, p.130) cites, as a primary assumption informing CA, that interaction is structurally organized.

1) a sequence of two utterances which are

2) adjacent

3) produced by different speakers

4) ordered as a first part and second part

5) typed, so that a first part requires a particular second (or range of second parts)

(Heritage 1984, p. 246)

There are some important points which need to be stated clearly. First, the structural property of paired actions does not entail that these are necessarily produced as succeeding actions which occur next to each other. It is not a statement of empirical invariance. Neither is the concept used to capture some empirical generalisation, for example, that in 80% of cases second parts immediately follow first parts. Rather, the concept is important because it underlines the normative character of paired actions. That is, the production of a first part proposes that a relevant second part is expectable; a second part is made conditionally relevant by the production of a first part (Schegloff 1972). It is observable that, when a speaker fails to produce an appropriate second part, they may produce an utterance which accounts for this failure. Furthermore, by virtue of a common orientation to this relevance, speakers have the basis for inferences about the actions of co-participants. All these features may be illustrated in the following extract.

```
(20) SL 7   (This is taken from a corpus of
             calls to a flight information
             inquiry service.)
16    C:     are you able to tell me (.5)
17           er flight arrival times from
18           Zimbabwe oh no you can't i-
19           its at Gatwick
20           (.5)
21    A:     no what's the flight number
22           (1)
23    C:     urm
24           (.)
25    A:     what's the flight num-ber
26    C:                        -flight number
27           I don't know the flight number
28           it arrives Saturday morning
```

In line 21 the agent ('A') asks a question. According to the adjacency pair concept, this generates the expectation that an answer should follow. Clearly, the caller ('C') has some difficulty with the question insofar as there is a one second pause (although at this stage the basis of the difficulty is not apparent). The agent's subsequent turn exhibits her awareness of the norm that an answer is an appropriate second to a question: she repeats the question. However, this is not merely an echo of the initial formulation, for in the second version certain words and syllables are given greater stress. She has not rephrased the question, as she might if she perceived it to be ambiguous to the caller or unclear, rather she has reiterated it. Thus the professional analyst – and, more importantly, the caller – is presented with a turn which publicly displays the type of inference the agent drew from the caller's silence and these inferences are informed by her orientation to structural but normative features of the relationship between paired actions. The caller's subsequent utterance "I don't know the flight number" provides an account for why he could not answer the question. This displays his awareness of the expectation for appropriate second parts generated upon the provision of first parts. Indeed, it is interesting to note that the caller cuts short his original request and says "oh no you can't i- its at Gatwick". This exhibits his reasoning as to why the agent won't be able to give him an appropriate answer: he is calling the wrong airport. It also indicates the caller's inferential work which informed his sudden interruption of his own question.

Conversational structures, then, are normative, socially organised procedures. They are not 'hard wired' into cognitive processes in such a way that they determine or propel the turns that people produce in interaction. Nor do they exist independently of those occasions in which their relevance is oriented to by participants in conversation. Rather, they are instantiated in the local, turn-by-turn particulars of interaction. They are contingent upon, and realised through, people's orientation to their normative or programmatic character.

1.5 Social organisation and social interaction

The analysis of naturally occurring conversation undertaken in CA has begun to reveal some of the organised procedures through which people produce orderly conversation. In the previous section I have tried to illustrate some aspects of these procedures by looking at conversational listing and the concept of the adjacency pair. I want to emphasise, however, that CA also attends to the ways in which these methods and procedures are employed by speakers as vehicles through which they may accomplish discrete interactional tasks, locally occasioned in the particulars of the conversation. In this sense, the study of the methods by which speakers orchestrate conversational interaction is a distinctly *sociological* enterprise.

> In spite of its name [conversation analysis] is concerned with the understanding of talk-in-interaction more generally, and with interaction *per se* more generally still. However, it takes ordinary conversation to be the fundamental form of talk-in-interaction....and the primordial site of human sociality and social life.
>
> (Schegloff 1987, p.101)

In order to illustrate the sociological issues that CA addresses, I will rely on Drew's (1987) study of teasing. He begins by noting that a recurrent phenomenon is that a person who has been the object of a playful joke, or tease, will respond with a serious reply. This cannot be accounted for by claiming that the teased party does not realize that a tease is occurring: some indication that they recognise the humour of the occasion is displayed even as they produce a serious response. The following extract, for example, comes from a family dinner which is being video recorded. The tease "Do we have two forks 'cause we're on television?" is addressed by a daughter to her mother.

```
(21)
Dot:      Do we have two forks 'cause we're on
          television?
Mother:   -No we-
Angie:    -huh hh -huh  hh -h  (  )
Father:          -Yeahah  -h hah .hh=
Mother:                   uh huh  -huh huh
Angie:                            -heh heh heh
Father:                         -=Right yeh
          pro -bably the answer right (the -re)
Angie:        -eh hah hah
Mother:                                -.hhh
          You have pie You have pie:: tonight
```

In this extract Mother starts to respond to Dot's tease by saying "No we-"; this has the character of the beginning of a rebuttal, or a serious account for the unusual presence of two forks. At this point the laughter starts and Mother herself joins in. After Father's facetious remark that the teaser is probably correct, Mother completes the serious response she initiated earlier: "You have pie You have pie::

tonight" Thus, although she has laughed at the joke, she initially begins, and then completes, a serious or literal response to it.

This 'po-faced' character of the response to a tease is also evident in the following example.

```
(22)  (AL:83 002)   (The visitor has just come
                     into the house with Annette's
                     mother.)

Annette:    Hell -o:'
Visitor:        -He:llo::how are you:-:.
Annette:                          -Alright
            thank you?
Visitor:    I saw you Mum at the bu:s stop so I
            -(give her a li(h)ft)-
Annette:    -(and) you started ya- cking
Visitor:    No(hh)o I give her a lift back
```

The response to Annette's tease that her mother and the visitor started gossiping as soon as they came across each other is rebutted by the visitor's remark that she merely gave Annette's mother a lift in her car. The visitor is chuckling as she says this ("No(hh)o") and thereby exhibits her recognition of the playful element of Annette's remark.

In the first extract, the teased party starts to produce a serious response, laughs, and then goes on to provide a po-faced response. In the second, the laugh is built as a part of the serious counter. As a final illustration the next extract shows a po-faced receipt coming after the teased party's laughter.

```
(23)  (NB:II: 4: R: 14)   (Nancy is describing a
                           man she recently met.)

Nancy:      VERY personable VERY SWEET. .hhh
            VE:RY: (.) CONSIDERATE MY GOD ALL I
            HAD TO DO WAS LOOK AT A CIGARETTE
            AND HE WAS OUT OF THE CHAIR
            LIGHTING (h)IT YhhhOU KNO(h)OW=
Emma:         -I: K N O : W   I T  -
            =
Nancy         -.hehh.hh One of those  kind
            .hhhh=
Emma:         -Yes
            =
Nancy:        -A:nd so -    :but we were
```

```
Emma                      - THEY DO THAT BEFORE
                  AND A:FTER THEY DO:n't
Nancy:            HAH HAH.hhhh
Emma:             (Or he's)
Nancy:            N O:? e-MARTHAHAS known
                  Cli:ff,...((a good thirty years and
                  he's an absolute boy scout))
```

Emma teases Nancy that her new friend is the type of man who will pay attention to a woman only prior to his sexual conquest of her: "THEY DO THAT BEFORE AND A:FTER THEY DO:n't". Nancy laughs at this, but then goes on to produce a serious answer, citing a common friend who can vouch for Cliff's thoroughly decent character.

It might be argued that the reason why people produce po-faced responses is that they do not realize that they are being teased, and that they are treating the teases as serious remarks. However, there is evidence to suggest that this is not the case. The fact that people laugh shortly before or after or during the production of a po-faced receipt of a tease implies that they realize that they are the butt of a joke. Furthermore, the way in which teases are built indicates their non-serious character: they are designed to display that they are not to be taken as sincere proposals or serious descriptions. For example, teases may be built from words which are clearly exaggerations or over-done characterisations of the things to which they refer. So in extract (21) the word "television" is an overdone reference to the presence of the video recorder, and in (22) "yacking" is an extreme version of talking. Also, the use of formulaic expressions, such as the description, "THEY DO THAT BEFORE AND A:FTER THEY DO:n't" indicates levity rather than sincerity.

Drew identifies three common properties of teases. First, they are not topic initiators: they are not used by participants to begin a new topic, or dramatically refocus the emphasis of the current talk. Second, the prior turn to a teasing remark is invariably produced by the teased party; this is true not only in conversations where there are only two participants, but also in multi-party settings. Third, a tease exhibits a relationship to the immediately prior stretch of talk. That is, a tease does not randomly occur, but is a second to some prior utterance and, as a next turn, 'trades off' previous utterances.

Drew's examination of the following extract is reproduced at length because it focuses on the way in which a tease may be contingent upon the prior talk; this underlines the methodological significance of the analysis of sequences of turns. Furthermore, many of these observations illustrate an important feature of conversation analytic work that was discussed earlier: a sensitivity to, and examination of, the fine-grained design of utterances.

```
(24)    (Northridge: 2: JP/DP: 1)

Del:    What are you doing at ho.me.
        (1.7)
Paul:   Sitting down watching the tu: -be,
Del:                                -khnhhh::
        ih-huh .huh Watching n-hghn.h you-nghn
        (.4) watching dayti:me stories uh?
        (.)
Paul:   No I was just watching this: uh:m (.7)
        .h.khh you know one of them ga:me
        shows,
```

> Del's tease that Paul is watching daytime stories follows Paul's admission of laziness. It is an admission in response to an enquiry, "What are you doing at ho:me", which is already offence-relevant by Del calling and finding Paul at home in the middle of the afternoon and marking that by adding "at ho:me" (instead of just something like "what are you doing/are you busy"). In response to this Paul seems to be freely admitting the offence implied in his being at home (and not therefore at work, in the library, etc.), in depicting a kind of laziness. This is done by his including "Sitting down...": and then characterizing what he is doing as "watching the tu:be,", that is watching anything that happens to be on rather than some specific programme. Using the slang "tu:be" to refer to television completes his self-description as being slobby/lazy. And it's Paul's admission to being slobby which Del subsequently exploits in his teasing characterization of infantile, pulp, noninformative, noneducational television, "dayti:me stories".

> (Drew 1987, p.234-5)

Thus a recurrent pattern begins to emerge: in constructing a tease speakers' *exploit* the teased party's immediately prior turn(s). This invites examination of the utterances prior to teases to identify common characteristics which ensure an environment which is conducive to teasing.

Drew's analysis indicates that teases follow stretches of talk which are recognizably over-done or exaggerated. That is, the prior talk consists of extended, laboured or over-elaborate descriptions or remarks. In the following example Bill is describing in quite graphic terms some symptoms of a current illness. Arthur's tease exploits this lengthy description by sarcastically proposing that Bill's life expectancy may be drastically short.

```
(25)  (Campbell: 4: 5)

Bill:          ee I think it was food poisoning
               (last night)
               'cause I was
Arthur:        (     look     )
Bill:          I'm still gettin:g you know,hh .hh
               stomach pains I spewed last
               ni:ght,...chronic diarrhea as we-e-
               ll, just before I went to bed
               and...this morning (well) I've had
               this bad stomach.  So I guess the
               same's gonna happen tonight....I've
               been getting funny things in front
               of my eye:s actually. .hh A hi:t
               just slightly, Li:ght flashes.
                    .
                    .
                    .
Bill:          But uh, (.3) 'tsk (sti:ll.)
Arthur:        Well you probably got at least a
               week.
```

This pattern is also evident in previous data. For example, if we consider the trajectory of the conversation from which extract (23) was taken, we can see that Nancy extols the virtues of her new male friend at great length; it is only after this elaborate description that she is teased.

```
(26)

Nancy:  He's fifty two:,
Emma:   Mm -hm:, -
Nancy:     -.hhhh- mBut he:'s ju:st a rea:l: (.)
        dea:r,h(.4) ni:ce: (.2) gu:y.
        Ju -sta r:- r ea l: n- ice  gu:y
Emma:      -We:ll:- G O O ::d-
Nancy:  .hh -hh So we were really talking up -a storm=
Emma:      -.hhhhhhhh                    -.hhhh
Nancy:  =an:d.t having a r:eal good time had a few
        drinks an:d h-and so forth and he's a real:
        (.5) easygoing he was in: u-he was un (.) uh:m
        (.) ptch .hhhhhhhh (.4) CAPtain in the
        mari:nes.hh
```

```
Emma:    -Oo::: -
Nancy:   -A::nd-  reti:red e-a:nd now has worked for
         this:: he's got a real good job with a big air
         conditioning company:,h=
Emma:    =M -m: h m-
Nancy:     -A:nd  a- h, .hhh has been with them for
         about fifteen yea:rs.h a:nd ah,h So
         co:nsequently he's very? (.) he intelligent?
         and he's ah .hh NOT HA:NDSOME. .hh But he's
         ni:ce looki:ng
         -ih a::nd- ah just a rea:l real nice:=
Emma     -M m  hm -
Nancy:   =PERsonable, VERY personable VERY SWEET. .hhh
         VE:RY: (.) CONSIDERATE MY GOD ALL I HAD TO DO
         WAS LOOK AT A CIGARETTE AND HE WAS OUT OF THE
         CHAIR LIGHTING (h)IT YhhhOU KNO(h)OW=
Emma:      -I: K N O : W  I T  -
           =
Nancy      -.hehh.hh One of those  kind .hhhh=
Emma:      -Yes
           =
Nancy:     -A:nd so -     :but we were
Emma                  - THEY DO THAT BEFORE AND A:FTER
         THEY DO:n't
Nancy:   HAH HAH.hhhh
Emma:      (Or he's)
Nancy:   N O:? e-MARTHAHAS known Cli:ff,...((a good
         thirty years and he's an absolute boy scout))
```

In both these cases, the tease focuses on the exaggerated or laboured character of the prior talk. Furthermore, in both cases, the tease provides a non-serious gloss or upshot of the topic of the prior turn: in the previous example Arthur undermines the severity of Bill's illness, and in the last extract Emma subtly challenges Nancy's rather glowing appreciation of her friend. Thus, we can see one clear basis for the production of po-faced responses: they are a method by which a speaker may reassert the seriousness or accuracy of, or the warrant for the stretch of the talk on which the tease was targeted.

There is, however, another basis for the po-faced receipt of teases. The design of the tease ascribes a mildly deviant identity to the teased party, or proposes that the teased party's behaviour is marginally out of the ordinary. To return to example (21), "Do we have two forks 'cause we're on television?" implies that Mother is being pretentious or phoney by laying out two forks simply because they were being video recorded ("on television"). Also, in extract (24) "watching dayti:me stories" implies the teased party is merely vegetating in front of the some of the worst kind of mindless television. Finally, in extract (22) "(and) you started yacking" proposes the gossipy or frivolous character of the visitor's behaviour with the teaser's mother. In each case a 'tease implicated deviant identity' (Drew 1987, p.246) is ascribed by the tease.

Furthermore, the basis for the ascription of this deviant identity rests in the materials provided by the teased parties themselves in their immediately prior utterances. For example, the warrant for the tease "Well you probably got at least a week", is the previous speaker's extended complaint about his health. The tease implies that Bill is making more of his illness than is reasonable; in a mild way, this portrays Bill as overly worried, or even as a hypochondriac.

In po-faced or serious responses the speakers reassert the validity of the remarks they had made prior to the tease. Whether these responses re-establish the warrant for their behaviour, or reinforce the legitimacy of their complaints or praises, they actively counter the implication of a deviant identity established through the construction of the tease.

Sequential analysis of the environments in which teases occur, and the examination of the materials through which they are constructed, suggests that they are a form of humourous remark which regularly appears on occasions in which a prior speaker has been producing some overdone or exaggerated stretch of talk. The implication of the co-participant's scepticism, and the subtle ascription of a deviant quality to the teased party, serve to act as a form of social control for this apparently minor form of conversational transgression. And, as Drew points out, like any form of social control, it may be met with resistence: in this case, a serious or po-faced response.

1.6   The methodology of conversation analysis

It seems reasonable to assume that scientists who have had formal methodological training, such as those who work in the design and implementation of computer programs and interfaces, will inquire about the methodology that conversation analysts employ to do their research. Conversation analysts themselves have not devoted much attention to this issue. There are notable exceptions: Wootton (1989) presents a useful summary of some of the procedures employed in analysis; more generally, he provides a clear introduction to the objectives which inform CA. Heritage's (1988) discussion of the way that CA treats the accounts speakers produce in natural conversation also furnishes some interesting insights. Overall, however, there appears to be little written on the subject of how to analyse conversational materials in the manner exemplified by the studies reviewed here. A novice to this approach can consult introductions to CA and glean from them the concerns and analytic priorities which inform this type of research, but there is little to indicate how such analyses are actually carried out.

There is one obvious reason for this, and although it has been stated earlier, it is worth repeating. Conversation analysts try to describe the methods which *people themselves* use to make sense when they talk to each other. Analysis of empirical materials proceeds without theoretical speculation as to the nature of conversation. CA is a polar opposite to approaches which treat language use as a screen onto which can be plotted sociological and political assumptions about the participants' statuses and the relations between them. Nor do conversation analysts assume that the procedures which are displayed in naturally occurring talk have to answer to, and are thereby less significant than, underlying and determinant cognitive realities. The apparent lack of interest in articulating its own methods may reflect CA's rare concern to describe in detail the activities that people actually do and the methods by which these activities get done.

A related point is that there is no one way of 'doing' CA. Analysts develop their own particular interests, and clearly these will be reflected in the style of their work and their approach to data analysis. An attempt to distil a single 'method' from the various ways people proceed in analysis would be dangerous in that it might reify as one programme what is in fact a range of delicate skills.

There is also a danger that an attempt to formulate the methodology that informs CA fosters the impression that the process of analysis is simply a case of *application*: the researcher has the data in front of her, she 'applies' CA, and the results come flooding out. It is more accurate to say that analysts employ a range of intuitive skills in their empirical research. What Schenkein (1978b) has described as the 'analytic mentality' is more a cast of mind, or a way of looking at materials, than a prescriptive and static set of methodological instructions which analysts bring to bear when they confront their data. Consequently, these types of skills do not lend themselves to description in the way that one can describe, for example, the relevant considerations and procedures involved in the use of a particular statistical formula. This is not to claim that conversation analysts possess skills which are in any way mysterious.[8] It is simply to acknowledge that some of the skills of CA are tacit, in much the same way as are the skills of, say, riding a bicycle.

Having made these points, however, it is important also to emphasize that the development of a suitable analytic mentality is merely one dimension of CA.   Empirical work involves the application of many other systematic skills and practices.   For example, the preliminary stage of analysis involves the collection and detailed study of several cases of what, superficially at least, appear to be examples of the same conversational phenomena.   Rigorous and painstaking examination of such collections is essential if the analyst is to obtain insight in to the interactional events occurring in the data.

I have emphasised that CA attends to the organised interpretative and reasoning practices that inform people's actual contributions to conversation and which are displayed in the design of their turns in interaction.   By virtue of these unfolding public displays, the sequential trajectory of talk permits the analyst a foothold in the explication of these competences.   Consequently, another useful preliminary methodological strategy is to analyse a single conversation, or section of one, to track the various interpretative strategies which inform contributions to it.   Such an analytic strategy need not be driven by any interest in specific details of the materials being examined.   Moreover, as one of the primary insights from CA is that conversation is ordered at a fine-grained level of detail, no item or event should be discarded as unworthy of close analysis, regardless of its 'obvious' or intuitive insignificance.

The benefit of such an approach is that a close inspection of data which is unmotivated as to what might emerge from an analysis inevitably generates interesting observations.   Having isolated a phenomenon which gains the analyst's interest, or which appears to have significant consequences for the trajectory of the interaction, the

---

8   Outside CA it seems a commonly held idea that the novice analyst has to sit in with someone who knows what they're doing and simply get immersed in the process of analysis.   Indeed, there is some truth in this: CA is a rigorously empirical approach to analysis and there is much that can be gained by watching how experienced analysts begin to deal with data.   In some respects, this process is similar to the war-time practice by which women, new to factory work, were introduced to the tasks they had to do on the production line. Newcomers were sat next to someone who knew what they were doing, and were told to watch what their neighbour was doing and do the same. This sophisticated training programme was known as 'sitting next to Nellie'. From personal experience, there certainly is an element of this in acquiring a CA training. (With due apologies to the Nellie in question.)

analyst can consult larger corpora to see if the same phenomenon also occurs elsewhere. Once a collection of examples of broadly similar phenomena has been established, the analyst can examine the materials with a view to answering two (related) questions: what interactional business is being mediated in the examples? And what organisational strategies and procedures inform the ways in which speakers demonstrate their orientation to this business?

Having made a collection of the same or similar conversational phenomena, and having carefully described the outline of those data, it is often useful to examine in detail an extract in which some aspect of the pattern is absent. The study of such 'deviant' cases can often alert the analyst to dimensions of the phenomenon hitherto obscured.[9] For example, a study of listing in conversation might have produced countless occasions in which speakers stop listing when they have reached a third part. This does not inform us about the socially organised basis of listing. However, when a speaker stops after two items it can be observed that co-particpants actually volunteer a possible third item. Also, when speakers continue to a fourth or fifth item co-participants are likely to interrupt, usually as soon as it is apparent that the third part is not going to be the last item. Thus the study of two or four part lists can provide insights to the commonly held expectations which inform the construction of three part lists in conversation.

1.7 Conclusion

In writing this introduction I have had three goals. First, I have tried to outline the main analytic objectives which analysts pursue in their research and describe the methodological assumptions which inform analyses. Second, I have provided a flavour of the type of inferential work that is negotiated in conversation, and demonstrated the organised basis of this inferential work. Third, I have emphasised those aspects of Conversation Analysis which, I think, are most

---

[9] Perhaps the most notable example of this is in Schegloff's (1968) study of the openings to telephone conversations. Schegloff observed a pattern which was common to 499 examples from a corpus of 500 data. His detailed examination of the one 'deviant' case led to a reinvestigation of the other extracts, which in turn resulted in a revision of the analysis. Consequently, he was able to explicate the organisational basis which was common to both the 'deviant' example and the rest of the data.

significant for people who may have had little previous contact with or interest in CA, or sociology more generally. In this respect I have underlined the point that CA is essentially a sociological enterprise, rather than peculiar branch of linguistics or social psychology. Consequently, this has been a partisan account, and others who work in Conversation Analysis may have preferred different emphases. Interested readers can obtain a more rounded representation of CA by consulting the other introductory works mentioned in this chapter (see note 2). Furthermore, I have not touched on the extent to which the results from empirical studies can legitimately inform the design of human-computer interactions. This is a controversial area and in a chapter of this length there is no space to consider the arguments in sufficient detail; this issue is properly addressed in the subsequent chapters of this volume.

Acknowledgements

I would like to thank Nigel Gilbert, David Frohlich, Paul Luff, Paul Drew and Norman Fraser for their observations and advice during the preparation of this chapter.

Chapter 2

Towards a Sociology of Human-Computer Interaction

A Software Engineer's Perspective

Hugh Robinson

2.1 Introduction

This chapter is about two of the substantive areas of computer science — software engineering and human-computer interaction (HCI). It discusses how a sociology of HCI may both illuminate the nature of HCI and its relationship with software engineering and contribute to the development of HCI in particular, and of software engineering in general. In many senses, the chapter is a conscious re-working, from the perspective of a software engineer, of Woolgar's (1985) paper on a sociology of machines.

The chapter has the following structure. The first two sections discuss the nature of software engineering and HCI and, *inter alia*, make the case for a sociology of human-computer interaction. The next section examines what one possible sociology — that based on ethnomethodological ethnography — might reasonably be expected to do. The subsequent, and final, section concludes the chapter by discussing how progress is made in software engineering generally, and in HCI specifically, and the likely contribution that a sociology of human-computer interaction can make to such "progress".

2.2   The nature of software engineering

This section gives one account of software engineering: an account in terms of the accepted and public descriptions (and prescriptions) made by software engineers.   Here is a definition of software engineering from one of the standard texts on the subject.

> ... software engineering is concerned with software systems which are built by teams rather than individual programmers, uses engineering principles in the development of these systems, and is made up of both technical and non-technical aspects.
>
> (Sommerville 1989, p.3)

As the quotation illustrates, software engineering is conceived as being an engineering discipline, in much the same way as civil or mechanical engineering.   There is an overt concern with producing artefacts that are "tried and tested, up to full specification and on time". Considerable emphasis is placed on separating *what* is required of an artefact — its specification — from *how* that artefact may be produced — its implementation.   A major factor in achieving and utilising this separation of specification from implementation is an abstraction based on formal methods.   A specification is described in a formal language based, preferably, on discrete mathematics (see Ince 1988, for example). Similarly, the implementation is stated in another formal language — in some programming language.   Potentially, an implementation will be capable of being proved correct mathematically, insofar as it realises the specification.   There is an assumption that natural language is inadequate and inappropriate as the principal means for describing the specification of software artefacts.   Natural language is seen as ambiguous, vague and incapable of supporting the reasoning necessary to establish the correctness of a specification and its subsequent implementation (see Ince 1988 or Maddison and Stanczyk 1988, for example).   In contrast, a formal language, based on discrete mathematics, is seen as unambiguous, precise and fully capable of supporting the necessary reasoning. Furthermore, the abstraction that constitutes the specification emphasises the functionality of the desired artefact at the (deliberate) expense of suppressing the detail of its implementation: a good specification will be capable of being realised as several different implementations, each in different situations and contexts (see Robinson 1981, pp.189-190, for example). That is to say, the nature of an artefact is determined by *what* it does, rather than *how* it does it. As such, the specification is seen as a neutral and objective statement of requirements. In summary, there is a rhetoric of objective engineering practice based on mathematical science. This is aptly shown in the titles of some of the more polemical papers: Hoare's (1984) *Programming: sorcery or science* and Milner's (1986) *Is computing an experimental science?* are typical illustrations.

All this is not to say that the rhetoric *is* the reality. Importantly, the conscious emphasis on engineering as the practical and effective construction of software, of designing and creating enduring artefacts that take their place in the world's work, gives occasional rise to a disdain. This disdain is for theory and formality, generated by the daily practical experience of 'doing the job', of constructing and maintaining software systems. There is a sense in which situation and context are seen as being as important as abstraction; where the nature of an artefact is determined by *how* it does it, as well as *what* it does. Theory is critically examined and utilised where its efficacy is clear but there is a readiness to reject what are seen as the arcane and suspicious reaches of theory. Dependency theory, in database design, is an example. Working versions of normalisation up to third normal form are seen as practical and appropriate — theory is often said to merely embody good practice — but normalisation beyond third normal form is rejected as inappropriate — it is too 'theoretical' (see Robinson 1989, pp.64-103). Respected software engineering experts can publicly acknowledge such disdain — Parnas and Clements' (1985) paper being a case in point.[1]

Given this, what price sociology and software engineering? *First*, there is a firmly held belief that software engineers need to be aware of the social implications of their technology. Indeed, courses on social

---

[1]   It can also be noted that empirical studies of practice, using ethnomethodological ethnography, give (as might be expected) a different account of practice to that which might be imagined from the accepted and public descriptions of software engineering, as Walker (1989) shows.

implications are mandatory in the majority of degree courses in computing and in the syllabus of professional qualifications. *Second*, there is a recognition of the importance of the 'non-technical aspects', mentioned in the quotation from Sommerville, above. These non-technical aspects concern the business of working in a team, managing a software project and, importantly for this chapter, the business of user interface design. To be fair, these non-technical aspects are seen as somewhat peripheral to the main activities of software engineering. They are to concerned with the way in which human and social issues impact on the essentially technical business of software engineering or on the way in which the products of software engineering impact on the society within which they are embedded (cf. Woolgar's 1985, p.558: *In this view, 'social' has to do with the effects of artificial intelligence, but not with its genesis*). This notion of a barrier between the technical and non-technical is now explored in terms of one of its manifestations — the user interface.

2.3   The nature of HCI

The principal concerns of HCI are with the *user interface* and its appropriate design within the overall business of producing a software artefact. In terms of slogan, an implicit belief of HCI is that the medium is the message — the way in which a software system is presented to the user crucially determines the comprehension of the system by the user (e.g. Norman and Draper 1986 or Nickerson 1986). That is, in contrast with software engineering, the nature of an artefact is determined by *how* it does it, rather than by *what* it does. This tension between HCI and software engineering is suppressed in two principal ways: by the way in which the notion of *interface* defines and asserts a Cartesian dualism, and the manner in which HCI is seen to be about tasks.

HCI draws on several disciplines in an eclectic fashion, but one central discipline is that of cognitive psychology. Put (extremely) simplistically, cognitive psychology would claim that behaviour can be explained by reference to cognitive or mental states. That is to say, it is a variant of Cartesian dualism, in the sense described by Ryle (1963). Behaviour can be explained and understood by opening a window on men's souls or, at least, building a model of what might be seen through such a window.

The notion of *interface* is a variation on this theme of Cartesian dualism. The interface stands as the boundary between what is the work of HCI and what is the work of the software engineer. The 'true' nature of the system — *what* it does — is defined by the state of the software 'behind' the interface. A window may be opened on the soul of the machine because that soul has been specified as a neutral and objective abstraction whose functionality has been realised in the code of some programming language. *How* that functionality appears as behaviour is defined by the interface and, just as a specification may be realised by several different implementations, so the neutral and objective functionality of the 'internal' state may be realised by alternative interface designs. Although alternative interface designs may be different, this difference is more apparent than real: they reflect the same neutral and objective state of the software. The business of an HCI practitioner is to choose the manner in which that neutral and objective software state may appear to a user, with the clear understanding that, whatever manner is eventually chosen, this will not alter what is 'really' going on. The interface stands as a defining and sustaining boundary for the business of HCI, both conceptually and literally.

One effect of this notion of interface is the *marginalisation* of HCI work within the central disciplines of software engineering. HCI work is seen as being not 'real' software engineering and computer scientists working in the HCI area are seen as being engaged in peripheral activities. There is considerable anecdotal evidence that software engineers see specialised HCI work as, at best, largely irrelevant to the practical issues at hand or, at worse, the "last resort of the hand-wavers". HCI is 'soft', whereas software engineering is 'hard'. There is also evidence that HCI practitioners are not unaware of this marginalisation: a discussion at the end of a recent workshop complained of the current *conservative* view of the scope and possibilities of HCI (Preece and Robinson 1989).

Coupled with the notion of interface is the orientation to *tasks* as problems (or goals) and their effective rendition and solution (or attainment) through the interface. Task analysis can be seen as an attempt to gain the abstract and objective neutrality of the software system for the activities that the interface must support. A *task* is an abstraction of the user away from situation and context: it is the depiction of the user as a set functional objects capable of precise description, in much the same way as a specification of a software system. For example, Moran's (1981) command language grammar offers a framework in which a complete model of the interface is described, hierarchically, at the task, conceptual (that is, semantic), syntactic and lexical, and interactional levels of design. Other hierarchical task analysis methods exist that have the same intent of design abstraction — Card, Moran and Newell (1983), for example.

One effect of this orientation to tasks (as abstractions) is to discard the detail of situation and context. That is to say, HCI work is marginalised further by being divorced from the richness and detail of the (social) world within which software systems are embedded. Indeed, the very term *user* evokes a participant who brings little of relevance to the encounter; who is, in a sense, a Lockean blank sheet onto which the task may be inscribed.

In summary, the notion of interface and the orientation to tasks marginalises HCI from both its mechanistic and social concerns.

2.4 A sociology of interaction for software engineering

The burden of the previous sections is that there is a case for a sociology of human-computer interaction: a sociology that explicates and accounts for the interaction; that attends to its genesis, rather than to its effects. The arguments that such a sociology should be one based on ethnomethodological ethnography (Garfinkel 1967, Heritage 1984) have been well rehearsed elsewhere, by Suchman (1987) and others (see Cooper 1989, for example). In essence, such a sociology emphasises the situated and contingent nature of interaction with computers and construes software states and tasks as resources for reasoning about interaction, as opposed to being determinants of interaction.

What relevance does such a sociology have to the concerns of software engineering and HCI work within software engineering: to the production of artefacts that are "tried and tested, up to full specification and on time"? Or, to put matters at a more personal level, why should the author of this chapter, who lays claim to being a software engineer, be interested in ethnomethodology? Here are *some* answers.

First, the account given of the nature of HCI indicates an unsatisfactory state of affairs insofar as HCI work is marginalised within software engineering and placed outside any context and situation. Ethnomethodology offers a way of restoring context and situation to the descriptions and accounts of human-computer interaction; a way that re-appraises the relevance of the 'non-technical' issues of software engineering so that they do not stand divorced from the 'technical' issues. Indeed, it offers a re-appraisal of the very distinction between the 'non-technical' and the 'technical', in much the same way as Woolgar (1985, p.559) suggests that the distinction between the 'technical' aspects of science and the peripheral 'social' factors is transcended. This is not to say that software engineers would sit down and read Garfinkel with a sense of revelation and determination. However, Suchman's (1987) work, for example, has received sympathetic reviews and not inconsiderable publicity within the computing industry press. For instance, there is Durham's (1987) article on Suchman, entitled *Why computers are socially disadvantaged* in a weekly computing publication.

Second, the (apparent) atheoretical nature of ethnomethodology and the way in which ethnomethodological work involves a close attention to the fine grain of empirical detail is not out of sympathy with some of the concerns of software engineers for 'practical' theory. Again, the outcomes of Suchman's work are impressive from this point of view — 'hard' facts are produced (from 'soft' science?).

Third, the findings of one particular form of ethnomethodological work, that of Conversation Analysis, seem *prima facie* to be directly relevant to human-computer interaction. Work such as that of Sacks, Schegloff and Jefferson (1974) gives an account of the managed accomplishment of mundane conversation. This work emphasises the practical reasoning displayed in the organisation of opening conversation, turn-taking within conversation, the repair of breakdown within conversation and the closing of conversation. This practical reasoning can be thought of as a set of tacit, normative and reciprocal rules to which partners orient when doing conversation. Human-computer interaction can be conceived as a form of conversation with a computer. This is an idea that has a persistent potency; for example, one of the earliest texts on software engineering (Martin 1967[2]) stresses the importance of (what was then termed) the man-machine interface and, in addition, devotes a complete chapter to what are termed *conversations with a computer*. A suggestive line of direct relevance for ethnomethodology would be that of engineering human-computer

---

[2]   Martin's text actually pre-dates the widespread introduction of the term software engineering.

interaction so that it exhibits just this practical reasoning displayed in conversation. Conversations with computers would then exhibit the turn-taking, repair of breakdown, etc. of mundane conversation. Mundane conversation is assumed to exhibit the natural and 'user-friendly' quality that is a desired feature of human-computer interaction. Work by Frohlich and Luff (1989 and this volume) can be seen as working within this broad application of ethnomethodology[3].

These answers are not without their problems. The atheoretical nature of ethnomethodology raises the spectre of atheoretical data. An injunction (a theoretical one?) of ethnomethodology is to look at the mundane features of the social world as if they were anthropologically strange and to attend to the fine grain of this empirical detail. But just what is the data — what is the empirical detail? Human-computer interaction is sufficiently rich that the assertion that it is characterisable as dialogue or conversation is, at the very least, open to contention. For example, some initial work of Cooper (1989), based on a preliminary analysis of videotapes of interactions with Macintosh-based software systems (including HyperCard[4]), indicates that the spatial arrangement and organisation of the desktop, the deployment of the focus of attention and the aural response accompanying the (successful) opening and closing of files are important components of the interaction. In addition, the data suggests that the (computer) orchestrated insertion of discs is also a significant material practice. From this point of view, it may well be argued that what Heritage (1984, pp.293-304) has called the studies-of-work programme within ethnomethodology is at least as appropriate to a study of human-computer-interaction as is Conversation Analysis (see Lynch, Livingston and Garfinkel 1983 for an account of a 'study of work' in the natural sciences[5]). Heritage characterises the studies-of-work programme as *analysing the specific, concrete material practices which compose the moment-to-moment, day-by-day work of occupational life* (ibid., p.293). Such a programme, applied to human-computer interaction would, at the very least, empirically question whether conversation (or dialogue) was *the* autochthonous material of interaction practice in the sense, for example, that talk is *the* material of health visiting practice (see Robinson 1987).

---

3   See also Gilbert, Wooffitt and Fraser (this volume).
4   Macintosh and HyperCard are registered trademarks of Apple Computer Inc.
5   See also Walker (1989) for studies, in a similar vein, in computer science.

Furthermore, the application of Conversation Analysis is not without its own problems. The majority of the conversational structures[6] to be engineered into the interface are those derived from mundane conversation. Of course, many other conversation systems exist and several have been subjected to Conversation Analysis (Atkinson and Drew 1979, Dingwall 1980 and Robinson 1987 are examples). Whilst being dialects of mundane conversation, such systems exhibit significant differences in the organisation of talk, such as in the pre-allocation of turn-taking (Atkinson and Drew 1979) or in the orchestration of turn-taking (Dingwall 1980, Robinson 1987). It may well be just as appropriate to engineer structures from these conversation systems into the interface as those of mundane conversation. The interaction involved in a guided tutorial on HyperCard, for example, may have more features — such as the orchestration of turn-taking by the computer — in common with an orchestrated encounter than with mundane conversation. Indeed, more radically, there is a need to carry out conversation analysis on talk in a range of institutional settings — including those of business — in order to assess those particular structures which may be fruitfully deployed in any given interactional setting involving human and computer. In addition, the structures are not acontextual. That is to say, there is no guarantee that features found in mundane conversation, engineered into a human-computer interaction, will necessarily result in the same managed accomplishment observed in their original context.

In a sense, however, these problems are not worrying. They are evidence of the richness of a sociology of human-computer interaction and, more significantly, the sociology suggests they are largely empirical questions. That is to say, the question of whether or not human-computer interaction is a form of conversation is rendered as the question "when, and under what circumstances, does the interaction display the managed accomplishment characteristic of conversation?"

---

[6] There is a tendency, in Conversation Analysis, to emphasis openings, turn-taking, closings, etc. as almost syntactic structures rather than as the practical reasoni

that is evidence of managed accomplishment by members.

2.5 Making progress

One point of software engineering is to change the world by constructing artefacts that shape and affect the world. Software engineering is both practically concerned with the construction of these artefacts and practically concerned with the manner in which it organises and goes about this construction. The history of software engineering is, in many ways, the history of a pre-occupation with methods: from structured programming to data flow analysis to formal methods; from systematic file design to conceptual data modelling to object-oriented design. Software engineering looks to 'theory' that informs it how to go about this task in a 'better' fashion: more reliably, more effectively, more cheaply, more professionally, or whatever. It looks to how things are with a desire to make things how they might otherwise be. Yet this progress is also intimately connected with empirical claims. Conceptual data modelling, for example, can, and is, justified in terms of an internal logic of elegance and abstraction but it is also justified in terms of its practical achievements in constructing databases in a more effective manner. In no small part it is an empirical claim about how practice should be conducted. This much Milner (1986) recognises, behind the overt concerns for paralleling the methodological model of the natural sciences. Specifically, in the area of HCI, empirical claims are made about the nature of human-computer interaction and about the way in which human-computer interaction should be engineered.

A sociology of human-computer interaction, based on ethnomethodology, leaves everything as it is, so to speak (cf. Wittgenstein 1958, p.124). It produces accounts of how things are; it does not produce accounts of how things ought to be. Analysis of mundane conversation does not lead to a prescription for mundane interaction. Yet such a sociology has much to offer in the business of making 'progress'. It offers one way of assessing empirical claims in HCI about the nature of the interaction. Importantly, it offers ways which are suitably 'strange' in their results. For example, analysis of the Macintosh interface could reveal that its 'user-friendliness' stems from its very formality in comparison to older, less 'friendly' forms of interaction (see Atkinson 1982 for a useful discussion on formality). The accounts produced of interaction stand as a mirror by which to judge and assess progress. To complain that an account does not lead directly to a prescription is to complain that history does not lead directly to a prediction of the future.

But a sociology of human-computer interaction can do more than this. It can explicate the business of practice, of how practitioners go about doing HCI (or doing software engineering). In this sense, a studies-of-work programme has much to offer in our understanding of the mundane practice of HCI (and of software engineering) and of the nature of the 'progress' it achieves and the knowledge that it secures. At the very least, such studies would question the accounts given, in this chapter, of software engineering and HCI.

Acknowledgements

In constructing this chapter, the author is grateful for many helpful discussions with Kate Robinson and, similarly, with Geoff Cooper.

Chapter 3

The Very Idea

Informing HCI Design from Conversation Analysis

Michael Norman and Peter Thomas

3.1 Introduction

This chapter describes research which employs the perspective, methods and findings of Conversation Analysis within the research enterprise of Human-Computer Interaction (HCI). The research is centred on the notion that Conversation Analysis may be employed for the formulation of *design guidelines*.

Section 3.2 provides a thumbnail sketch of the prominent concerns of HCI research. It should be emphasised that we view 'human-computer interaction' from a perspective which emphasises the *totality* of methods available for interaction between human and machine. In this sense, this work is both distinct from, yet complements, work which attempts to employ conversation analytic findings in the design of speech and natural language interfaces (Frohlich and Luff; Gilbert et al.; Cawsey this volume). We would view natural language as only one, of many, ways in which human-computer interaction may take place. In proposing that

Conversation Analysis may inform the design of human-computer interaction, we are proposing its relevance to all modalities which the designer of systems may employ. The design of visual, auditory, and haptic interaction, in addition to interaction conducted through speech and natural language, provides an opportunity for the application of Conversation Analysis. Although we would not wish to challenge the importance of work in speech and natural language processing, we would see these first three interactional modes, since they represent quotidian methods of human-computer interaction, as more important and pressing areas of interest. Our concern, then, is with 'human-computer interaction' in the large.

Section 3.3 outlines the rationale of the research in terms of the characteristics of human-computer interaction, HCI research and Conversation Analysis. The way in which we interpret both the findings and methods of Conversation Analysis, and the way in which we view their applicability is discussed in respect to both the likely view of practitioners of Conversation Analysis, and the view of other contributors to this volume.

Section 3.4 provides a brief illustration of our approach, drawing upon previous work based on a corpus of video-recorded human-computer interactions, and explores one sequence of human-computer interaction in detail.

The final sections of the chapter reflect on the implications of this illustration, and address wider issues concerned with some prerequisites for the success of this enterprise, from the perspective of HCI.

3.2 Human-computer interaction

In the most general terms, HCI research concerns the possibility of enhanced system *usability*. Representing acceptability, usability is crucial in determining the commercial success of information technology.

Presently, the particular rôle of HCI research within the design cycle for information technology is problematic. In part this is attributable to the comparatively limited scope of our available knowledge – which in any activity that seeks to include the human component as part of its area of study is inevitably problematic – and in part to the way in which our knowledge is made available to designers and applied in system design.

In terms of the provision of this knowledge it is possible to trace the development of HCI as it has moved from a discipline which contributed to design *after* the construction of the artefact, via the development of various sets of guidelines to aid the designer (Shackel, Eason, Gardener and McKenzie 1988; Smith and Mosier 1984), through to the provision of software tools, techniques and methods (Farooq and Dominick 1988). The focus in HCI is on informing the designer about aspects of interaction through various characterizations of computer-based systems and the features of the interface.

The sources of this knowledge are diverse. Addressing the concerns of people, technology, and the relationship between them, HCI is essentially a multi-disciplinary activity. The character of HCI in this respect is problematic, however: whilst cross-disciplinary integration is desirable, it is clear that partial accounts from disciplines with inimical perspectives and incompatible methodologies blunt the effect of such collaboration.

As a consequence, the tendency in HCI has been toward finding pragmatic solutions. But to provide for the further development of HCI, there must be *principled* solutions to the problems of design. HCI must progress from the identification of applicable areas of study towards the development of principled approaches to the issues involved in the interaction between people and technology through a process of cross-disciplinary collaboration.

In pursuit of this goal it seems to us that Conversation Analysis has much to offer. Conversation Analysis provides a set of *findings* about interaction which may be related to interface design, and a *methodology* which will prove useful in the investigation of human-computer interaction. Conversation Analysis seems to us to offer the possibility of the provision of comprehensive and secure design information based on a coherent view of interaction, although representing an investigative paradigm quite different to those currently employed in HCI research.

3.3   Conversation analysis and human-computer interaction

The very idea of using Conversation Analysis in HCI design is motivated by several concerns and observations. Not the least of these is the often overlooked fact that *users* are *people*. The experiences, expectancies, skills, reasoning abilities and commonsense knowledge of users as people are brought, inevitably, to their interaction with computer systems. Work by Lucy Suchman (Suchman 1982, 1987) for example, would seem to provide confirmation of this intuitively reasonable notion. Suchman's investigation of the interaction between users and an intelligent help system demonstrates the problems which are occasioned when expectations about interaction tacitly held by users are contravened in the design, and as a consequence in the behaviour, of interactive systems. Similarly, the use of 'sense-making methods' or 'interpretive procedures' (Garfinkel 1967; Cicourel 1973) to comprehend the behaviour of systems, the most familiar being that discussed by Weizenbaum (1976), would seem to confirm the pervasiveness of everyday abilities and their presence in human-computer interaction. It is also the case that users may view interactive computer systems as *social actors* an unproblematic notion, since as Gilbert et al. (this volume) note, and as Turkle's *Second Self* (1984) reveals, such judgements are not contingent upon inherent properties of the entity involved, but reside with other social actors. To this extent at least, the notion that a sociologically-based discipline such as Conversation Analysis – both in its ethnographic and sequential guises (Button 1981) – is usable in connection with human-computer interaction, is rendered appealing.

There are also motivations which particularly concern the nature of technological development, and thus of HCI as a research enterprise. Rapid progress in the development of new interactional technology means that there are possibilities for users to engage in ever-more complex interaction with systems (Gaines and Shaw 1986a). This complexity, although providing users with *more* ways to interact, also means that designers who seek to employ this technology have increasingly *less* control over the ways in which it may be effectively used in the design of systems (Gaines and Shaw 1986b). HCI research must therefore turn to investigation of not only the properties of specific technologies and the effects of their combinations in any single system, but to the investigation of the relationship between those technologies and the pre-existing characteristics and abilities of users. One desideratum for guidance formulated under these auspices is that it should be *concerned with* technology but must be *independent of* technology, if it is not to be superseded by some next generation of interactional device. If this is to be achieved, such research, and the guidance which results, should address the nature of *interaction as a process independent of technology.*

In this light, it seems that both the kinds of phenomena with which Conversation Analysis deals, and the kinds of description which it provides of them, are amenable to formulation in terms of design guidelines. Whilst Conversation Analysis provides a perspective on interaction as a process, it additionally provides specific details about the recurrent sequencing of actions in interaction and descriptions of the machineries of which they are a reflex. Guidelines generated on the basis of Conversation Analysis offer the promise of advice *specific* enough to provide the designer with leverage into the design of particular interactional sequences, yet *general* enough to be applicable to current and emerging technologies.[1]

A view of Conversation Analysis as appropriate for the design of human-computer interaction is presented by other contributors to this volume (see Frohlich and Luff; Robinson; and Gilbert et al. this volume), and we will only briefly elaborate on the points presented there. Conversation Analysis and its findings (summarised and cited in Heritage 1985, 1988a) reveal interaction to be an accomplishment more in the nature of ensemble improvisation than an enactment of predetermined dialogue rôles. The kinds of descriptions generated by Conversation Analysis deal both with the nature of the social actor's understandings of interaction in terms of the details of the relationships between past, current and forthcoming actions, and with understandings in terms of the commonsense categories and reasoning required for participating in interaction. Conversation

---

[1] This is part of a larger argument concerning the efficacy of HCI research and the dissemination of its findings, which is addressed elsewhere. See Thomas (forthcoming).

Analysis formulates these understandings in such a way that we can view the systematic regularities which are observable in interaction as the result of commonly-held skills and methods for, and expectancies about, interaction.

This account of Conversation Analysis may not, of course, be found palatable by some of its practitioners. Although this point will be taken up again below, the attraction that Conversation Analysis holds for us, and our particular interest in its findings about interaction, is not engendered by its *rule-like* descriptions of interaction, but by its specification of normative formats which operate at the level of *expectations* about the relationships between actions in interaction.   Findings about, for example, the organisation of openings, closings, turn-taking, topic, repair and the rest of the conversation analytic canon are thus findings about the ways in which these activities are performed in expectable ways and in recognisable formats.   Thus for us, the enterprise of using Conversation Analysis in HCI design is decidedly *not* that of 'modelling' human abilities, generating computational representations of cognitive-interactional processes, attempting to provide computational artefacts with interactional abilities on a par with those of humans, manufacturing human-computer 'conversations', or attempting to, in Oldman and Drucker's (1985) terms, "reduce ethnomethods". It is rather to provide for the design of interaction in ways which are *in accordance with expectations* about interaction.

If it is the case that the perspectives and findings of Conversation Analysis may be available for use in HCI, it is also the case that human-computer interaction may be productively examined using the *methods* of Conversation Analysis. Whilst the purely inductive approach characteristic of Conversation Analysis may be untenable in a practical enterprise such as HCI, it is clear that an approach which combines both the parallel examination of collections of sequences, and investigation of the details of the internal structure of individual sequences, is applicable to the kinds of interaction which constitute what users experience *as* human-computer interaction. At the risk of overstatement, this is not to suggest that human-computer interaction is conversation: much human-computer interaction is, to all intents and purposes, *pro forma*. It is simply to say that there are occasions where the skills required for, and the expectations which are held about, interaction between humans will be relevant for interaction between human and machine. And it is *here* where the methods of Conversation Analysis are useful in locating the users' understandings of the details of interaction in ways which are, simply, unavailable to current approaches to design.

Explicitly, this means that we view conversation analytic methods, which are often lauded for their specificity in dealing with talk (or 'talk-in-interaction' or 'speech-exchange systems') as more generally applicable to the investigation of *actions* in interaction (see Bilmes 1988). This is, of course, not entirely unproblematic. Since, unlike conversation, the understandings of users in human-computer interaction concerning prior machine actions are not explicitly displayed in a 'current turn', we, as investigators, have restricted access to what users may have made of some system action, or to their understandings of the current state of the interaction. Of course, one approach to this lack of evidential resource would be to adopt the strategy of Suchman (1987) who employs the device of two-person protocols to locate users' understandings. This device, along with others, such as think-aloud protocols (Ericsson and Simon 1980), is not without its shortcomings. The issue of appropriate methodology in the investigation of human-computer interaction is one which we do not intend to address here, but we might briefly comment that the artefactual contribution of method to findings is an issue which must be seriously addressed. One possible route would be, as Lave (1988) discusses and demonstrates, the adoption of some form of multi-method investigative strategy.

Many of the objections which might be raised against the use of Conversation Analysis in this fashion are debated in other contributions to this volume and we will not rehearse them again here in any detail. We will however touch upon the most frequently and fervently expressed objection, voiced by Button (this volume), concerning what Pateman (1985) has called the "rule-normativity argument". Clearly there is, as Button notes, a disjunction between the nature of abilities for conversation as a 'technical achievement' – in terms of 'rules', 'machineries', 'routines', and 'structures' – and possible computational representations of 'rules', 'machineries', 'routines', and 'structures'. This disjunction centres upon a view of 'rules' as arising from human behaviour, rather than as pre-existing external constraints which govern behaviour. Any simple attempt to transliterate conversation analytic findings as 'rule-governed' behaviour into computational schemata is thus fundamentally misguided. Button's argument is not without force, yet it would seem, as we have made clear for our own work, that other contributors to this volume are *not* engaged in this sort of enterprise at all. Frohlich and Luff, for example, aim to use the 'technology of conversation' to *support* sequences of interaction in the provision of a 'technology for conversation',[2] trading on the fact that there are expectations about the ways in which repair is normatively accomplished rather than the fact that repair is a 'rule-governed' activity, the rules of which may be abstracted and used to generate conversational behaviour (see also Finkelstein and Fuks, this volume).

In this light, we see the outstanding problem not as a *theoretical* one, concerning the discrepancies between the ethnomethodological account of 'rule-governed behaviour' and computational 'rules', concerning the misuse of terms such as 'sequence' 'routine' or 'resources', and thus concerning the relevance of conversation analysis, and its methods, findings and perspective to human-computer interaction. The problem is rather a *practical* one, concerned with the provision of a framework to map the findings of Conversation Analysis to the concerns of design in practically effective ways.

3.4   Informing HCI design from Conversation Analysis: an example

We have so far argued that Conversation Analysis is relevant to HCI design, and, since HCI deals with the entire range of interactional possibilities, Conversation Analysis is potentially relevant to a range

---

2   The notion that the Advice System described by Frohlich and Luff is engaged in *conversation* is problematic, however. As Wilson (1989) notes, 'conversation' may be seen as one speech-event amongst many, and it thus may not be clear that findings about 'casual' conversation are applicable to human-computer interaction. The 'conversational metaphor' has, of course, a long history in HCI (see, for example, Foley and Wallace 1974; Gaines and Shaw 1984; Nickerson 1976, 1981; Orr 1968; and on this topic, Robinson; McIlvenny, this volume).

of concerns in HCI design. We will now provide a simple example of the way in which we have attempted to employ the methods and findings of Conversation Analysis in relation to HCI design in a practical fashion. The discussion here is abstracted from work we have carried out based upon a corpus of videotaped data which shows users interacting with a variety of interactive systems in unconstrained settings and performing commonplace, naturally-occurring tasks (Norman and Thomas 1989; Norman and Thomas in press; Thomas forthcoming; Thomas and Norman 1989). In examining the video-recordings our interest was initially drawn to instances where users experienced problems in interaction, and where the progress of the user in the performance of the current task was noticeably impeded. These were often concerned with the performance of what were clearly only envisaged as simple 'housekeeping' tasks such as the opening or closing of files. The instance we cite here is representative of a larger collection of similar sequences.

This concerned a user's problems with a standard file selection box. The options offered in such a dialogue box are the possibility of cancelling the interaction, opening the file that is selected, and browsing through various levels of the file structure. The user found the dialogue box problematic in that the object that was to be selected seemed not to exist in the file system. This was the case since it was an inappropriate type of file object (in fact an application rather than a HyperCard[3] stack). The recording shows the user repeatedly selecting, browsing, and de-selecting the dialogue box in search of the appropriate object. In the normal course of events, this dialogue box would not be problematic, and it is in general terms an efficient and pragmatic mechanism for the specific transaction of selecting a file. However the difficulty was not one of knowing *how* to use this particular dialogue box: it is in fact far more obvious – that the general purpose nature of the dialogue box leads one to expect that *any* file is selectable through it. This is not the case: the user has fallen foul of that old *bête noir* – hidden modes. The user is in the wrong context to select the file. Although it is not indicated anywhere, the file search space is constrained by the current context, and the operation of the dialogue box is context sensitive.

---

3   HyperCard is a registered trademark of Apple Computer Inc.

There are a variety of observations which we might wish to make about this, and a collection of other, similar, sequences. These concern the ways in which, and the reasons why, non-responsiveness may be construed by the user as purposeful, the similarity between users' and conversationalists' attempts to pursue responses and its implications for the ways in which interaction may be designed, and the ways in which the users' expectations regarding turn-taking are relevant to such sequences. However, we will restrict ourselves here to some simple observations regarding the ways in which such a sequence may be construed in terms of HCI design and ways in which it may contribute to an understanding of the wider issues in design.

Returning to our example, there are of course any number of pragmatic solutions to this type of problem which might be adopted and which possess varying degrees of merit. What is important here for the user is that this is a case where *a repeated sequence of actions receives no response*. The sequence should leave us in no doubt that there was some interaction which was to be completed and that some response was required. The difficulty, at least on one view, seems to have come about because in developing easy to use interactional methods we have *separated the selection and action components of a task as discrete elements* and thereby removed the requirement that designers need see them as *related actions*. The possibility has come about that users may interact with systems by simply undertaking a never-ending sequence of selections, without any consequent action being performed. The problem arises because, in the separation of selection and action, the designer is not obliged to take account of *the prior actions of the user* as a determinant of the provision of adequate responses.

If we were to attempt to give the designer guidance on the basis of the findings of Conversation Analysis it would be, simply, to *provide a response*: in conversation, a variety of types of actions, such as summonses for example, create a strong expectation that an appropriate response should be immediately forthcoming. This has the corollary that when responses or accounts for their absence do not occur it is not simply that they are *missing*, but that *inferences* are generated regarding the absence of a response. Although this requires considerably more elaboration than we are able to provide here, the concern of Conversation Analysis with interaction as a matter of the relationship between previous, current and forthcoming actions as crucial to the developing sense of that interaction, is thus useful in examining human-computer interaction.

However, in asserting that some response must be provided, we are not simply saying that the design should provide 'feedback' – an often heard and particularly vague piece of design guidance. Conversation Analysis can provide us with the notion that the next action (or sequence of actions) may in fact be (or amount to) a *repair* of the user's previous action, which is initiated, by the system, in next turn (see Frohlich and Luff, this volume). The findings of Conversation Analysis also provide us with a view of the normative ways in which repairs are constructed, of particular features of repair such as the use of 'graded' other-repair initiators (Schegloff et al. 1977), and of alternative ways of accomplishing repair (Jefferson 1984). In general terms, then, it is possible to sensitise the designer to matters of interactional process, such as the nature of conditional relevance (Schegloff and Sacks 1973), the distinction between interactional and physical presence (Schegloff 1968), between interactional recipiency and availability (Heath 1982), and their contributions to the investigation of problematic interaction and the redesign of systems. In specific terms, it is possible to provide design guidance for, in this example, the ways in which repairs may be effected, as a component of providing appropriate responses.

3.5 The applicability of Conversation Analysis to HCI

Having provided a simple example to demonstrate the applicability of conversation analytic methods and findings to human-computer interaction, we now return to more general issues concerning the nature of that applicability.

The earlier concerns of interface design with simple command line systems – in terms of memorability, consistency, and completeness – have led on to the deeper concerns related to the nature of human-computer interaction. However, whether these are concerns with the strategies users employ, the decomposition of tasks, or the handling of the superstructure of systems, they are all matters of *interactional process* rather than features of technology. This provides the common ground between Conversation Analysis and HCI, which lies in their joint concern with the nature of *practical solutions to interactional problems.*

Nevertheless, the HCI researcher's work is directed toward the concerns of the use of technology. The arena in which that work is conducted is bounded by considerations of three elements: *user, task* and *system.* The results of research, if they are to inform HCI design, have to take this into account. Indeed, one reason why HCI issues have not been readily taken up by software engineers and others concerned with the design and implementation of computer based artefacts is the lack of applicability of this work (see Robinson this volume). At one end of the scale the results of studies are so precise about the circumstances in which they are valid that they have no general applicability; at the other are results which are so general they cannot be applied without considerable interpretation and (unwelcome) additional effort by the designer. In order to inform HCI design the guidance should ideally be explicit, and in a form accessible and comprehensible to the designer (Maguire 1982; Gould and Lewis 1985).

Prospectively, the use of insights from Conversation Analysis avoids one of the difficulties. The claim would be for the *universality* of its findings, and therefore the lack of any need to differentiate *classes of user.* Consequently, all that is required from Conversation Analysis is a statement for the designer of the findings, which can then be applied directly to concerns of HCI design, because it will apply to all users.

Certainly, there is considerable benefit in providing new insights into the scope of user requirements, albeit in a fragmentary way, and giving a new focus for design. However, it is reasonable for the designer to accept that providing responses is a crucial issue in designing the interaction with the user, and then to ask what it particularly relates to – *how does it apply?* It is not possible to answer that question without relating it to system features that the designer employs. In this respect the insights from Conversation Analysis that are currently accessible are, as presently formulated, no better than previous HCI guidelines. They still require considerable interpretation, and it is this which is the principal issue in making sense of the very idea that Conversation Analysis can inform HCI design.

3.6   Guidelines for the designer

The advantage that Conversation Analysis has to offer is the wide ranging nature of material, and the possibility that a single discipline can provide leverage into HCI issues across the board.   Moreover, this knowledge can be formulated in terms of structures to be employed in interactional sequences between the system and the user.   The guidance offered to the HCI designer, in contrast to that from other sources, is both *principled* and does not prescribe the *substantive* content of the interaction.

In the example above, the designer's difficulties can be traced back to an over-emphasis on the provision of general purpose interactional objects, and the consequent separation in the design of selection and action.   However, if we take the notion of *closings* for example, the situation is not so clear.   It is not obvious that a 'closing' is an appropriate description for any interactional sequence except the obvious case of logging off.   Similarly, the notion of closing does not seem to be immediately applicable to interface objects such as windows, icons, or files.   Nevertheless, based on (a gross simplification of) the findings of Conversation Analysis with regard to the way in which conversations are brought to a close through the introduction of previously-unmentioned topics (Schegloff and Sacks 1973; Button 1987), advice to the designer might take the form that *during the completion of a sequence of interaction, provide the possibility that users may perform unrelated new actions during the closing sequence* (see Frohlich and Luff, this volume for a similar formulation).   Advice of this kind is unlikely to have been considered or available to the designer from other sources.   It is appealing in its simplicity and potentially of benefit to the user.   However, whist it may appear so, the not unreasonable questions from the designer arise: *How do I make sense of this finding, where does it apply, and is it worth taking into account?*

In the case of closings the answers to these questions may not be easily derived.   Firstly, it is not evident that 'closing' as an activity is of any consequence in human-computer interaction: there is nothing inherently problematic in present systems in this respect, nor any immediately evident constraint arising from other design considerations which would lead us to believe that it would be problematic. Secondly, even if closing *is* found to be relevant, it may well prove to be applicable to any number of interactional objects and features that the designer employs, and the potential effect of using the findings of Conversation Analysis to redesign these objects and features may vary, from negligible improvement to considerable enhancement in the quality of interaction.

If we are to provide answers to such questions it seems to us that it is necessary to proceed in three ways. Firstly, the relationship between *specific findings from Conversation Analysis* and the *concerns of HCI* needs to be evaluated. This requires detailed empirical studies of human-computer interaction in a variety of settings. Secondly, the effect of *implementing an interactional structure* in relation to the *different interactional objects* in the system, such as windows or icons for example, should be assessed, involving a re-examination of the interaction between user and redesigned system. Thirdly, and finally, the *change* may be assessed in relation to *user performance* and *design effort* through some form of cost/benefit analysis. Then, and only then, would it be reasonable to suggest to the designer that the guidance proposed is of value.

It is the undertaking of these steps which amounts to providing a principled approach to informing HCI design from Conversation Analysis. This process itself depends on the provision of an adequate framework which describes human-computer interaction, and presently that is far from complete. The potential insights and benefits of Conversation Analysis will remain as inapplicable and inaccessible as other forms of guidance that have been put forward to the designer if such a framework is not provided.

3.7 Conclusion

The issue, then, is not whether Conversation Analysis can inform HCI design. On the contrary, insights from Conversation Analysis are one of the keys to improved human-computer interaction. The work that has to be carried out is not to further the concerns of Conversation Analysis (although we would not envisage a merely inquiline relationship between HCI and Conversation Analysis): it is to provide, through empirical evaluation, knowledge about the application of insights from Conversation Analysis. The key to accomplishing this is an adequate depiction of human-computer interaction, and that is where our future work must lie in order to make possible an interpretation of Conversation Analysis in the designer's terms. To undertake anything less would be to misjudge the problem and the issues - the very idea!

Chapter 4

Going Up a Blind Alley

Conflating Conversation Analysis and Computational Modelling

Graham Button

4.1 Introduction

The arguments presented in this chapter are at odds with the prevailing sentiment that runs through this collection over two issues: first, the desirability of developing computational models of conversational phenomena, and second, the supportive rôle given to Conversation Analysis in the development of such models.[1] The arguments are not, however, levelled at some of the pragmatic aspects that are involved in this. For example, I do not want to suggest that a computational model of conversation cannot reproduce something that might appear to be a routine or a set piece of conversation – a simulacrum of conversation.[2]

---

[1] Many of the chapters reference Conversation Analysis by mentioning Levinson (1983). There are, however, a number of edited collections of Conversation Analysis and a number of special journal editions that have been dominated by conversation analytic articles which furnish more insight into the field than a review can: Sudnow (1972), Schenkien (1978), Atkinson and Heritage (1984), Psathas (1979), Zimmerman (1980), Atkinson and Heritage (1984), van Dijk (1985), Button, Drew and Heritage (1986), Button and Lee (1987), Maynard (1987), Maynard (1988), Boden and Zimmerman (forthcoming), Psathas (forthcoming), and Drew and Heritage (forthcoming). For more recent reviews of developments in conversation analysis see Heritage (1985), Heritage (1988), and Button (1989).

[2] I am indebted to Wes Sharrock for this formulation.

Plainly, some of the authors in this volume are convinced they have done this; for instance, Frohlich and Luff, Cawsey, and Raudaskoski.

I also do not want to suggest that people in the field of human-computer interaction will not be able to find, in Conversation Analysis, descriptions of interactional artefacts that might be useful in designing 'interactive' software. The arguments presented in this chapter are not an attempt to restrict the range of creative resources that software designers might turn to for inspiration. If, as Norman and Thomas (this volume) suggest, they find the observation that conversation is organised into turns useful in formulating design protocols then who could or who would want to gainsay them? (As long as their pragmatic, design or engineering concerns are not then thought of as sociologically adequate descriptions of human action).

However, lurking behind the general sentiment is an idea that I do want to take issue with: the idea that it is possible to develop computer systems that can **converse** with humans.[3] An extravagant formulation of this idea is summed up in the title of Reichman's book "Getting Computers To Talk Like You And Me", (Reichman 1985). However, although the idea is less extravagantly stated within the pages of this volume, it is, nevertheless, both implicitly and explicitly endorsed on a number of occasions. In particular, it is implicitly endorsed in the attempts to develop descriptively adequate models of conversation for use in computer systems, and explicitly endorsed when it is argued that by providing a simulacrum of conversation one has naturally occurring conversation between computers and humans. The irony is that the work in Conversation Analysis that is appealed to would suggest that this ambition leads up a blind alley.

---

3   There are some telling arguments against computational models of cognition which draw upon the work of Wittgenstein and which either overtly, or implicitly, address this issue. See, Malcolm (1971), Hunter (1973), Cooper (1975), Coulter (1983, 1989 and forthcoming), and Shanker (1987). Coulter (forthcoming) in particular addresses the idea of 'conversing' with a machine and other supportive arguments can be found in Coulter (1983). This present chapter will, however, take a somewhat different tack, for its arguments are not so much rooted in a philosophical tradition but draw off the empirical inspection of conversation. I hope they provide an empirical compliment to the philosophical arguments that question the appropriateness of computational models of mind and language, and by extrapolation or overt reference, a computational model of 'conversing'.

The reason for this resides in the nature of the rules that are formulated to account for aspects of the organisation of conversation.[4] Models of conversation which are developed for computer systems have to provide for conversation and language as rule-governed in the sense in which playing chess or calculating might be described as rule-governed. By formulating some rules of chess and some rules for calculating, and building those into computer systems as programming rules or sets of instructions, it has been possible to play chess with computers and to use them to do very complex calculations. In order to conceive of developing systems that could converse with humans it would also be necessary to conceive of conversation as organised by a set of rules that have the same status as the rules that are programmed into computers to play chess or to do calculations.

The attraction of Conversation Analysis for people who want to develop rules of conversational organisation that can be used to program computers is two-fold. First, Conversation Analysis might seem to provide a ready-made package of conversational rules that they can use or adapt for their purposes. Second, their models may be authorised by appealing to Conversation Analysis.

However, turning to Conversation Analysis in order to utilise its 'findings' to develop a computational model of conversation is to treat the question of whether a machine can be made to converse with a human as an engineering problem. It is not. It is not just a matter of taking the rules that Conversation Analysis has formulated and then writing those up as a set of instructions that operate a computer. It is important to understand that the formulation of rules involved in the organisation of conversation that have been provided by Conversation Analysis are not of the same order as the formulation of rules required to program computer systems.

---

[4]   In their review and criticism of arguments against a computational approach to conversation, Gilbert, Wooffitt and Fraser (this volume), take one argument to be the possibility that computers and people use rules in different ways. The argument that computers actually use or follow rules is a strange one, and it is not made in ethnomethodology or Conversation Analysis. I suspect that it is Gilbert et al.'s way of expressing the matter. Hunter (1973) throws some light on the abundant confusions that thinking that computers follow rules involves. In any case, the arguments over the status of rules in conversation that are offered in this chapter object to the conflation of computational and conversation analytic interests, are different to the one they address.

Gilbert, Wooffitt and Fraser (this volume) suggest that this is a flawed argument: "The idea that the findings of Conversation Analysis are not susceptible to computer implementation depends on a rather simple-minded notion of what a computer model can do." I think that argument is the wrong way round. Rather, the idea that Conversation Analysis lends itself to computer modelling depends upon a simple-minded notion of what conversation is and of what order of description of human action Conversation Analysis provides. Gutting Conversation Analysis of its sociological import and merely offering up what is considered to be a 'finding' in Conversation Analysis leads to a misinterpretation not only of what Conversation Analysis provides by the way of appropriate descriptions of action-in-interaction but also of the very ways in which conversation as action-in-interaction works.

In order to show this I shall first take some studies in Conversation Analysis that formulate their descriptions of action and interaction in terms of rules. These studies will reflect the various aspects of Conversation Analysis that have attracted the attention of researchers who wish to develop computational models of conversation: turn-taking, sequences, and routines. I shall then move to discussing the status of the rules that Conversation Analysis formulates for these areas of conversational organisation and their relationship to computational models of conversation.

4.2   Conversation and rules

4.2.1   Turn-taking

One of the most referenced studies in Conversation Analysis, Sacks, Schegloff and Jefferson's (1974) "A Simplest Systematics For The Organisation Of Turn-Taking In Ordinary Conversation", might appear to support the view that the structure of conversation is organised by a system of constraining, even determining rules. Sacks et al. refer to the model they generate as comprising two components and a set of rules. One component is a turn-constructional component which refers to the building blocks from which talk in a turn is constructed. The other component is the turn-allocation component which refers to techniques that allocate a next turn to a next speaker. The set of rules is that which governs turn construction and provides for the allocation of a next turn to one conversationalist with the minimisation of gap and overlap. It is:

(1) For any turn, at the initial transition-relevance place of an initial turn constructional unit:

(a) If the turn-so-far is so constructed as to involve the use of a 'current speaker selects next' technique, then the party so selected has the right and is obliged to take next turn to speak; no others have such rights or obligations, and transfer occurs at that place.

(b) If the turn-so-far is so constructed as not to involve the use of a 'current speaker selects next' technique, then self-selection for next speakership may, but need not, be instituted; first starter acquires rights to a turn, transfer occurs at that place.

(c) If the turn-so-far is so constructed as not to involve the use of a 'current speaker selects next' technique, then current speaker may, but need not, continue, unless another self-selects.

(2) If, at the initial transition-relevance place of an initial turn-construction unit, neither 1a nor 1b has operated, and, following the provision of 1c, current speaker has continued, then the rule set a-c reapplies at the next transition-relevance place, and recursively at each next transition-relevance place, until transfer is effected.

(Sacks, Schegloff and Jefferson 1974, p.704)

This model might be viewed as an example of the codifiable rules of conversational organisation posited by some computational linguists. For example, Gazdar and Mellish (1987) talk of rules that provide for when and how turn-taking should happen. Certainly, Searle (1986), although not a computational linguist, has taken Sacks et al. to be formulating a set of causally recursive rules for replicating turn-taking in conversation.

4.2.2   Sequencing

An examination of Sacks' early work on sequencing might reinforce the idea that Conversation Analysis attempts to formulate conversational structure in terms of rules, and that conversational structure is amenable to formulations of rules. Sacks speaks of sequencing rules thus: "The first thing we need is some rules of sequencing, and then some objects that will be handled by the rules of sequencing." (Sacks 1965). Later, in a series of lectures in Spring 1966, he provides some activities as objects to be handled by rules, for instance, questions and answers, and some 'tying rules' that work on those objects. He formulates what he then called "first speaker rules" which provide for the recognisability of second utterances. For example, answers are recognisable via their production as seconds to questions. Sacks: "The second members are not recognisable, the first are. The second are only recognisable given the fact you recognise the first and are therefore looking for the second." (Sacks 1966a). Sacks might be heard to be suggesting that there are rules that provide for second utterances and that classes of activities are organised together via rules, so that producing one activity provides, via the first speaker rule, for the next activity.

Conversation Analysis has specified a whole range of conversational sequences and, from its subsequent and numerous explications of their organisation,[5] it might be understood to be providing rules that link utterances together in such a way that in hand are rules that people follow to generate sequences of talk. It might then be a relatively simple matter to represent these rules as algorithms. Something akin to this is provided in Gilbert, Wooffitt and Fraser (this volume).

The description of ordered sequences of talk implicates organisations that provide for the activities that are produced in the turns that people take. Thus, having a turn at talk, the adjacency pair mechanism (Schegloff and Sacks 1973) provides for what might go into that turn as an answer if the turn before asked a question. The turn-taking system does not, in itself, provide for the content of turns. The turn-taking system provides for the organisation of taking turns at talk, and the local sequential ordering of activities provides for the talk that goes into those turns. In this respect Conversation Analysis might look like a treasure chest for those who think that is possible to uncover and formulate the

---

5   See note 1 for a range of appropriate studies.

rules behind conversation in order to build computational models of conversation. Not only has it formulated a model of turn-taking partly in terms of a rule set, but it also provides numerous descriptions of organisations external to, but that work with, the turn-taking organisation to link utterances coherently together into intelligible sequences of conversation. These organisations have been or can be formulated in terms of rules.

4.2.3 Conversational routines

Other work in Conversation Analysis, although it does not formulate its descriptions in terms of rules, might, nevertheless, seem to hold out the possibility of going even further because it displays that pairs of utterances can be linked into 'routines' of conversation. For example, Schegloff's (1986) description of conversational openings richly details the component parts that can be used to make up a conversational opening. He describes a number of core opening sequences which are organised in terms of pairs of utterances: (a) the summons/answer sequence which organises the opening and confirms the openness of a channel of communication; (b) the identification (and/or recognition) sequence which organises a sensitivity to the interlocutors who are involved in the conversation; (c) the greeting sequence which provides, amongst other things, for mutual participation; (d) the "how are you" sequence which provides for the early introduction of some matters that have a joint priority over others. Schegloff writes:

> Each of these sequences is ordinarily composed of
> conventional parts with determinate and differential
> sequential consequences. It is by the deployment of these
> in the unfolding series of turns organised by these
> sequences that 'normal' openings get constituted.
>
> (Schegloff 1986, p.118)

An opening may then be thought of as a 'routine' of talk that is built by linking together sequences of activities. Seeming 'routines' of talk have been studied at other places in conversation. For example, closings might also be understood to be a 'routine' of talk for they are repeatedly built up from specifiable and differentiable component parts (Schegloff and Sacks 1973; Button 1987; Button forthcoming a). Schegloff even notes the interest of the seemingly formulaic character of a section of talk as a 'routine', "in 'artificial intelligence' studies on the production and processing of natural language use" (Schegloff 1986, p.113).

One place where conversational 'routines' are often produced is at junctures that are used for the overall management of conversation. These junctures may be used to initiate new topics or to initiate closings (Button forthcoming b). They are constituted by sequences of conversation that organise a juncture in a topic-in-progress by offering its possible completion. These sequences are: (1) 'formulating the conversation' (Heritage and Watson 1980) and having the formulation agreed to; (2) drawing an aphoristic conclusion (Schegloff and Sacks 1973) and having that agreed to; (3) offering an assessment and having that agreed to in a second assessment (Pomerantz 1975); and (4) concluding arrangements (Schegloff and Sacks 1973). At the junctures in a topic-in-progress that these sequences can organise, other sequences of talk, designed to initiate topic, may be invoked. Three sequences, each made up of different and optionally used components, have been described (Button and Casey 1984, 1985). The three sequences are: 'topic initial elicitor sequences', 'itemised-news enquiry sequences' and 'news announcement sequences'. In the spirit of some of the other chapters in this volume, a schematic representation can be given of the 'routines' that are run through to start a topic.[6]

At the organisation of closing junctures in a topic-in-progress by either (1), (2), (3) or (4) above then:

(1) If topic is mutually generated:

	Topic Initial Elicitor	Itemised News Enquiry	News Announcement
1st Turn	topic initial elicitor	itemised news enquiry	news announcement
2nd Turn	possible topic	elaborated response	topicaliser
3rd Turn	topicaliser	on topic talk	on topic talk
4th Turn	on topic talk		

---

[6]   See Button and Casey (1984, 1985) for detailed descriptions of the workings of the sequences provided in this schematic.

2) If topic initiation is declined:

	Topic Initial Elicitor	Itemised News Enquiry	News Announcement
1st Turn	topic initial elicitor	itemised news enquiry	news announcement
2nd Turn	decline	minimal response	minimal response
Next Turn	< possible closing moves >		

3) If topic initiation is pursued:

	Topic Initial Elicitor	Itemised News Enquiry	News Announcement
1st Turn	topic initial elicitor	itemised news enquiry	news announcement
2nd Turn	decline	minimal response	minimal response
3rd Turn	i) recycle decline or ii) itemised news enquiry	news announcement	itemised news enquiry
4th Turn	on topic talk	on topic talk	on topic talk

It has also been found that at the junctures at which a new topic may be initiated, closings may also be methodically entered into (Button forthcoming b). Closings, as mentioned above, are comprised of repeatedly used components and have a seemingly routine formulaic character similar to openings. Thus the schematic possibilities outlined for topic initiation at the junctures indicated above, could also be outlined for closings. Consequently, it might appear that we can start to provide for some very complicated organisational developments in terms of sets of conversational 'routines'. Conceiving of the organisations as 'formulas' or 'routines' might suggest the possibility that they could be codified. Large swathes of conversation, even whole conversations, might then be understood to be generated by rules. This understanding of 'routines' of conversation can be found in this volume; Frohlich and Luff's system utilises the idea of conversational openings and closings as 'routines' of talk that are generated by what they call "interactional rules".

In all of its studies, of which the above gross areas of investigation represent only a small proportion of its interest in talk-in-interaction, Conversation Analysis aims to provide the precise, rigorous technical specification of conversational machineries. It might appear that the technology of Conversation Analysis provides support and succour for machine technology, as its descriptions of some conversational organisations in terms of rules may be seen, by some, to be transformable into rules, or sets of instructions with which to program computer systems and thereby facilitate human-machine conversation.

If we pursued that line of argument I propose that we would be going up a blind alley. Appealing to Conversation Analysis to furnish a computational model of conversation from rather elementary observations may produce a simulacrum of conversation but it neither means that the model employed is an adequate description of conversational activity nor that machines have been given the capability of conversing with humans. The possible success of building a simulacrum of conversation, and the seeming rôle that Conversation Analysis may play in this, beckons the unwary up a blind alley. The reason for this is that Conversation Analysis has quite clearly demonstrated that conversational action-in-interaction is **not** rule governed in the sense that it would have to be in order to have machines converse with humans in the same way in which they can be used to play chess or do mathematical calculations. The fact that 'routines' can be built should not be taken as offering anything more than a simulacrum of conversation. To think that appeals to Conversation Analysis can authorise computational 'routines' to be conversation is to misunderstand both how conversation works and the status of rules in conversation analytic descriptions of conversational organisation.

4.3   The status of rules in the description of human action

It is sometimes forgotten that the interest that Conversation Analysis has in talk is not so much in talk as a linguistic phenomena but in **action-in-interaction**. Schegloff and Sacks (1973) made this very clear, very early on. They provided for the origins of Conversation Analysis in the attempt to develop empirical, rigorous and formal accounts of social action. The fact that the social actions examined are actions accomplished in conversation means that the organisation of conversation has to be invoked in the description of those actions. Thus, to say that aspects of that organisation are governed by rules is to directly involve ourselves in the issue over the extent to which human action can be said to be rule-governed and over the status of the rules that are said to govern social action.[7]

If we wish to produce programs that would facilitate human-computer conversation then it is quite clear that the rules that are said to govern human action, such as action accomplished in conversation, must be of a certain order: they must be equivalent to the sets of instructions, or what are called rules, that are used in computer systems. The question then becomes what status do the rules programmed into computers have? Block (1980) sums up a predominate view when he suggests that they are determining systems, and, incidentally, that we can understand human reasoning in a similar way.

> A ... computer is a device one knows is rule-governed, for the rules are inserted by us as part of the program. In the .... computer, some operations are accomplished 'automatically' by hard-wired circuitry, and via the application of any represented rules. Sometimes a rule causally controls reasoning 'automatically', in the way the machine language command 'ADD 1' causes the representation in a register to change, by the operation of hard-wired circuitry, and not by any process involving reasoning.
>
> (Block 1980, p.5)

In such accounts rules are state-switching commands and seemingly we can formulate the rules that govern language as algorithms. On this understanding, rules are 'internal representations' and human action such as that done in and as language is the product of a mental machinery of rules. Human beings have internalised the rules which generate language. People do not need to know these internal mental rules under whose auspices their language construction is determined. The understanding of rules that this entails is **causal**. X is done **because**

---

7   In this respect, to say that computational linguistics has a role to play in examining conversation is also make a more dubious argument that computational linguistics has a role to play in the sociological study of action.

of the rule. The rule stands behind the action, it accounts for its production, and structures the form the action takes. So, if the rules involved in conversation are to be usable for developing programs that would allow computers to converse with human beings, they have to be conceived of as part of a determining mental machinery.

Is this how rules are conceived of in Conversation Analysis or does Conversation Analysis display a different understanding of rules and thus a different understanding of how conversation is organised?

I have mentioned a number of examinations in Conversation Analysis that formulate their descriptions in terms of rules, or could be seen to be describing formulaic 'routines' of conversation. I want to return to these and explore the status of the rules and the idea of routines that figure in the descriptions to see if they square with a computational understanding of rules.

4.3.1   Turn-taking: an orientation to rules

Schegloff's discussion with Searle about the formulation of the rules in "A Simplest Systematics For The Organization Of Turn-Taking For Conversation" (hereafter referred to as the Simplest Systematics paper) makes it quite clear that the rules involved in turn construction, next turn allocation and speaker transfer are not causal (Schegloff forthcoming). His argument is that Searle (1986) has misunderstood the description of the rule set formulated in the Simplest Systematics paper as a description of causally recursive rules. The mistake is made, in part, because that is how Searle understands the relationship between rules and human action and the status of rules. Searle's understanding is equivalent to the idea that rules are an interior mental machinery. A feature of this general argument is that it is unnecessary to know the rules under whose auspices one is said to perform, in the same way as it is unnecessary to know the laws of gravity that determine my behaviour of falling to the ground when I trip over. In this respect the rules that analysts might posit have very little to do with how participants might orient to rules in the production of their activities.

Schegloff stresses that the rules that were formulated in the Simplest Systematics paper are not as Searle construes them to be. Rather, they are rules that **in their conduct people display an orientation to**. That is, the relevance of the rules for a person's conduct is displayed and preserved **in** their actual conduct. There is a distinction then between rules that people can be shown to orient to, and rules that are said to be an interior mental machinery. On the latter understanding, rules stand behind action, on the former, rules are embedded within the action.

This is an important distinction for the description of conversational organisation. Searle's understanding of rules as causal mechanisms leads him to misunderstand Sacks et al.'s description of speaker transfer. Schegloff quotes Searle as saying that the rules mean that "whoever starts talking gets to keep on talking". They would only **get** to keep on talking if the rules determined the action. Schegloff however points out that they do not **get** to keep on talking but that **they end up keeping on talking**. Schegloff's understanding here is that keeping on talking is an **achievement** that is done through an orientation to the rules, rather than it being a given product of the rules. In this respect, it seems quite clear that the rule set that is posited in the Simplest Systematics paper does not lie behind the actions of constructing a turn, allocating a turn, and co-ordinating speaker transfer and thereby causing those things to happen. We do not **get** a turn **because** of the rules. Rather, the way in which a turn is taken displays an orientation to the rule. A rule is followed as part of accomplishing the action. The sense of rule here, is then,part of the logical grammar of the action. There is not an internalised rule that causes the action. The rule does not **precede** the action. Rather, the rule is discoverable **in** the action.

In many respects this argument takes us back to one of the early arguments of ethnomethodology that (despite the fact that it has either been overlooked or forgotten in the debates surrounding language use and rules[8]) is very pertinent to the whole issue. Garfinkel writes:

> ...a leading policy (of ethnomethodology) is to refuse serious consideration to the prevailing proposal that...rational properties of practical activities be assessed, recognised, categorized, described by using a rule or a standard obtained outside actual settings within which such properties are recognized, used, produced, and talked about by settings' members.
>
> (Garfinkel 1967, p.3)

---

[8] A notable exception is Coulter's (1983) examination of rules and human conduct in his book *Rethinking Cognitive Theory*, where he draws off ethnomethodology and Wittgenstein in an erudite attack upon the view that language is the product of a mental machinery of rules.

Garfinkel's argument here is that formulating rules of conduct outside of occasions of actual conduct ignores the circumstances of rule use. It ignores the fact that there are judgemental and interpretive practices involved in using rules. Garfinkel distinguishes between the analytic prescription of human conduct through the analytic imputation of rules, and the study of rule use in actual occasions and contexts of action.

Schegloff's discussion of the rule set that was formulated in the Simplest Systematics paper emphasises this issue. The rules are those that, in the construction of their activities, participants display an orientation to. Thus, the rules are not analytic prescriptions formulated outside of actual occasions of conduct for how to take turns. In terms of the Simplest Systematics paper it is **rule use** involved in the accomplishment of some social action in interaction that is being studied; Sacks et al. are not attempting to formulate a set of abstract rules for how to get or take a turn. Having a turn is the achievement of the situated use of rules, not the determined product of a set of prescribed rules that have been analytically formulated without reference to the situated occasions of their use.

Further, speaker transfer is organised around **possible** transition relevance places and although the rules are applied at particular places, the rules themselves do **not** provide for those places. Neither are those places constituted by following other sets of rules. Rather, whilst possible completion places are structurally ordered and oriented to places in a turn, that order and orientation is a contextually on-going accomplishment: "...possible completion is something projected continuously (and potentially shifting) by the developing course and structure of the talk." (Schegloff forthcoming). The fact that these structurally organised places are **possible** transition relevance places means that it is a contextually decidable matter whether or not actual transition takes place. Thus, because the rules do not, so to speak, determine their own application (using the rules is not determined by the rules themselves), there have to be other features involved in the application of the rules. This is the orientation to possible transition places, and in the Simplest Systematics paper there is no description of these places being formulated in terms of rules for their production. Possible transition places are the contextual achievement of the unfolding structuring of the turn in progress. Possible completion places are not, then, provided for in advance by codifiable rules, they are situatedly achieved in and for a particular turn.

If we turn to two of the chapters in this volume that have appealed to Conversation Analysis in the development of computational models of conversation, we can observe the results of the confusion over the status of rules in conversation and the status of rules in computer programming. Frohlich and Luff, and Gilbert, Wooffitt and Fraser make strong claims. Although tentatively couched, both chapters claim to be able to provide for conversation between humans and computers that is of a similar order to conversation between humans because their systems are based upon the organisational details of conversation as revealed by Conversation Analysis. For instance, Frohlich and Luff want to see how "... the technology of conversation can be used to reproduce the details of actual, naturally occurring conversations between people and computers."

It might be suggested, however, that both papers have failed to develop a computational model of turn-taking that actually does provide for the **details** of the organisation of turn-taking as it is organised in conversation. Instead, they have provided a computational model that is capable of furnishing a set piece in response to a question. One reason for thinking that this is a replication of turn-taking in conversation is a failure to understand the relationship between the organisation of turn-taking and the organisation of the activities that go into turns. For instance, Gilbert, Wooffitt and Fraser seem to think that organisations that provide for next activities organise turn-taking. However, asking a question constrains what a next action should be but it does not in itself provide for speaker transfer (Sacks, Schegloff and Jefferson 1974). In this respect, it might well be possible to build a simulacrum of conversation that provides for a response from a computer when a human 'asks it a question' – both chapters report on success in this direction. However, what goes on when this happens may be accounted for in different ways to the way in which turn-taking in conversation is organised. For example, it can be accounted for through the parsing of grammatical units so that upon the grammatical completion of a question the instruction is to furnish a set response. The fact that there appears to be a next turn that is taken is not, however, the result of applying the technology of conversation to machines because this is not how the transfer of speakership is organised in conversation.

The systems reported on in the two chapters have been developed despite a misunderstanding of the way in which Conversation Analysis has revealed aspects of the organisation of conversation. This might tell us something about the different activities that go on when people operate computers, even if they 'speak' to them, and when they converse with one another. The fact that there is a difference, even though the system might work for the purposes it was designed for, is not a problem. If the systems work for all practical purposes then does it matter that operating a machine is different from humans conversing with one another? I would suggest that it does not. However, it does seem to matter for Frohlich and Luff because they rebut what they say is my criticism by claiming that they "have done it", by which I presume they mean they have provided a system through which humans and computers can converse in a way that preserves the details of human conversation. They have done no such thing. Their computational model of turn-taking for conversation does not provide for the primordial organisation of conversation, the organisation of speaker transfer, as it is accomplished in and for conversation. Conversation Analysis displays that the organisation of turn-taking is not codifiable and cannot be reduced to an algorithm. The transfer of speakership in conversation is not organised in the way in which the systems described provide for a computer to give an answer when asked a question. To think that a computer providing a set piece in response to a question is a first step to having computers and humans converse, that Conversation Analysis authorises the model used, and that this may thus promise further gains is to hover in the mouth of a blind alley.

The Simplest Systematics paper is, in part, a description of the situated **use** of rules. It is a description of conversational practices or usage, something that Schegloff points out: "I am willing to adopt for now an alternative term, such as 'practice' or 'usage'". (Schegloff forthcoming). In these terms it would be wrong to see that Conversation Analysis is providing codifiable instructions in terms of an abstractly formulated set of rules that stand outside of actual practices and determine those practices. Conversation Analysis has not discovered the rules that lie behind and generate conversation. It just does not understand the relationship between rules and human conduct in this way.

The Simplest Systematics paper is, amongst many other things, a telling testimony to Garfinkel's distinction between analysts' rules (formulated for analysts' purposes) and members' rules (formulated for members' purposes). It also seems to sympathetically resonate with a number of the philosophical formulations concerning rules made by Wittgenstein.

Wittgenstein (1953) makes the distinction between a process being in accordance with a rule, and a process involving a rule. For a process to involve a rule we have to know the rule that is involved.[9] If our action was in accordance with a rule, it does not mean that we knew or followed the rule when performing it. Therefore to say that an action involves a rule is to say that the rule is in some ways 'known'. But 'knowing a rule' does not mean that people have to be able to formulate the rule. One way of showing that a rule is 'known' is through an **empirical** inspection of peoples' activities. If it can be shown that an activity involved a rule because we can show that participants **oriented** to the rule in the process, we can say they 'knew' the rule. The Simplest Systematics paper is describing the rules to which people display an orientation in their actions or, in other words, the rules of which, by their actions, they display their knowledge.

Wittgenstein (1953) also makes the point that rules do not determine their own application. The Simplest Systematics paper is a study of the situated application of rules. As we have seen the rule set does not specify a possible transition relevance place. Thus, applying the rule set involves situated interpretive and judgemental practices which are not formulated by the rules. Further, Wittgenstein points out that it is not possible to definitively detail the situations in which a rule may be relevant in advance of encountering those situations. In that respect rule use is a contextual matter; for example, people finding some rules relevant for some contexts. The Simplest Systematics paper empirically shows just how detailed an issue context might be, and how contextual details form a resource for the accomplishment of conversational activities. The description of the continual interactional achievement of possible transition relevance places is a fine grained specification of context. The relevance of the application of the rule set is dependent upon the achievement of possible transition relevance as a contextual site for their application.

I have not made this very brief (and perhaps too brief) play between some of Wittgenstein's remarks about rules and Conversation Analysis

---

[9]   See Waismann (1965), Warnock (1971), and Backer & Hacker (1984 , 1985).

formulations, for its own sake. It has to do with the fact that others have
had occasion to invoke Wittgenstein in their considerations of the
relationship between human thinking and machine computation. For
instance, Malcolm (1971), Hunter (1973), Cooper (1975), Coulter (1983,
1989 and forthcoming), and Shanker (1987) have strenuously sought to
refute a computational model of mind, in part by invoking some of
Wittgenstein's arguments on mind and language. I do not have enough
time to elaborate those arguments but I am suggesting that the studies of
action-in-interaction conducted by Conversation Analysis, at least in
terms of its study of the turn-taking system for conversation, is an
empirical complement to the general thrust of these philosophical
arguments. Conversation analysis displays: that the rules involved in
the organisation of turn-taking for conversation are not part of a mental
machinery of rules that stand outside of actual occasions of activity; that
they are not algorithms; that they are not sets of instructions; that they
are not programs of human thought; that they are not the cause of
human action. Rules are oriented to features of action; they are
contextual, situated practices of use. Wittgenstein posited an autonomy
of grammar – we do not have to postulate the existence of prior acts of
consciousness to address the meaning of words. Conversation Analysis
posits the autonomy of action – we do not have to postulate mechanisms
that stand outside of the action to address the structure of that action.
Neither grammar nor action is the product of an internal mental
machinery. Machineries there may be, but they are machineries of
practice, machineries of use that are an integral part of the action. For
Wittgenstein and Conversation Analysis, language is social praxis.[10]

4.3.2   Sequencing: rules as resources

We can return to Sacks' remarks about tying rules. Both of the chapters
by Frohlich and Luff, and Gilbert, Wooffitt and Fraser set a great deal by
the idea that adjacency pairs (Schegloff and Sacks 1973) provide for the
relationship between actions that constitute first and second parts of a
pair type. One reason for this is that it seems to provide for the
generation of strings of consecutive actions. For example, Gilbert,

---

[10]   See Coulter forthcoming (b) for an investigation of the logic of language that
stresses the connection between Wittgenstein and ethnomethodology over this
issue of social praxis.

Wooffitt and Fraser propose some grammar rules for adjacency pairs. However, formulating the relationship in terms of what amounts to a generative rule, misunderstands the relationship between pairs of activities such as questions and answers as described in conversation analytic studies. It also misunderstands the status of the rules that may be involved here, such as Sacks' formulation of tying rules exemplified by 'first speaker rules'.[11] We can get at this through Sacks' description of 'second speaker rules' which follows his description of 'first speaker rules'.

With second speaker rules we have a recognisable second that provides for the recognition of a first. "...second speaker rules tie some second utterance to something which may not have been produced as an intended first utterance for some pair." (Sacks 1966b). Thus we have the organisation of a sequence, a pair of utterances, through the situated use of a rule. If the rule **determined** human conduct we could not have an intelligible second unless there had been a first. We could not have the response without the cause. If we formulated a rule that upon the production of a question the next utterance should be an answer, we could not have the case where a second transforms a prior utterance into a first, and thereby achieves its coherence with the first. Thus, if a first speaker rule were a determining rule, Sacks' formulation of a second speaker's rule would be a contradiction. This is because, if a question provides for an answer, we could not have the case of an answer without a question.

It should be clear from Sacks' discussion of first speaker and second speaker rules that he is not describing generative rules; rules for generating next actions. Rather, he is explicating devices or resources that a person can use to make sense of their actions, and thus achieve ordered interaction. Sacks' explication of the coherence between utterances in terms of tying rules is then an explication of **conversationalists' resources** through which they achieve their ordered conduct. The rule that may be used with relation to questions and

---

[11]   Indeed Schegloff and Sacks (1973) do not formulate the relationship between the activities of asking a question and giving an answer in terms of codifiable rules. Their explication of adjacency pairs is not an explication of rules for generating correct responses. Coulter (1983) makes an interesting argument that sequential structures such as adjacency pairs are *a priori* structures and their explication in Conversation Analysis is then often akin to the explications of *a priori* knowledge found in linguistic and ordinary language philosophy.

answers is not reducible to a simple codification of human conduct. The claims to be providing systems that facilitate human-machine conversation is undermined if the rules that people might use as resources to make sense of their activities are reduced to specifications of how to do those actions.

4.3.3   Conversational routines: the social occasion of their production

In his discussion of the rules formulated in the Simplest Systematics paper, Schegloff (forthcoming) emphasises the idea of 'achievement' involved in the co-ordination of speaker transfer. The importance of what is involved in the idea of 'achievement' for understanding how conversation works can be seen by returning to the idea of conversational 'routines'. In his consideration of opening sequences in conversation, Schegloff juxtaposes a view of openings as a ritual or formula gone through in which little is seen to happen, with his analysis of the organisational work done in them. Part of this organisational work is the provision of what Schegloff describes as an 'anchor position' for the introduction of 'first topic'. However, getting to the 'anchor position' is not just a matter of working through the 'routine'. Rather, it is one of co-ordinating, through collaborative action, the development of the core sequences that can make up an opening. The organisational work that each core sequence achieves with respect to opening a channel of communication, identifying, ratifying mutual participation and prioritising current states can involve the possibility of getting to first topic before the anchor position.

> 'Routine' openings in which 'nothing happens' need,
> therefore, to be understood as achievements arrived at out
> of a welter of possibilities for pre-emptive moves or claims,
> rather than a mechanical or automatic playing out of pre-
> scripted routines.
>
> (Schegloff 1986, p.117)

If we were to try to provide a set of rules that combine sequences of talk into 'routines' we would miss the details of the organisation of the talk as an accomplishment. In order to illustrate what is involved here we can return to the schematic devised in the above discussion of topic initiation.

One of the sequences that was represented in the schematic is designed to pursue a topic in the event of a curtailing response to a topic initiating move. The sequence is routinely used, and it appears again and again in a similar format. However, to describe the sequence as a 'routine' of talk would miss the very interactional negotiations that such sequences of conversation are designed to achieve. Such sequences are not set routines for getting a topic initiated, rather they are an interactional negotiation, the outcome of which is the organisation of *how* a topic will be initiated. Let us take one instance by way of illustration.

In the examination of topic nomination (Button and Casey 1985) it was described how 'news announcements' that 'headline the news' may be 'topicalised' in a next turn by a response that provides for the person headlining the news to elaborate the news. However, whilst this is regularly the outcome, it is possible that, on occasions, instead of elaborating on the news, the news announcer might curtail talk on the news they themselves announced. They may do this by only minimally responding to the topicaliser. In that eventuality the recipient of the news announcement may pursue the topic by making an 'itemised news enquiry' about the announced news, right after the curtailing minimal response. On such occasions the original news announcer may then talk to the news enquiry and thus elaborate upon the original news announcement that they had just attempted to curtail. Routinely, this is a way in which a topic can be initiated.[12]

---

12   The following extract is an example. Jenny in lines 1-3 announces the news that Ida has got her furniture and that she went to see it. Ann, in line 4, topicalises the news by providing for Jenny to elaborate it. However, Jenny minimally responds and curtails talk on the news. It is only when Ann makes a specific or itemised enquiry that Jenny elaborates.

[Rahman:13:1:5MH(13):4-5] Simplified transcript

```
1   Jenny:    I went round lahs' night cuz Ida'd got
2             huhr fuhr::niture so she'd rung me up ti
3                say
                     [
4   Ann:             Oh hahs she.
5   Jenny:    Mm  ::
                   [
6   Ann:          Dz it look ni:ce.
7   Jenny:    hhhh Well its beautiful fuhrnitchuh.  But...
```

However, although this is routinely done, this sequence of talk is not just a 'routine' that is mechanically followed or gone through to get a topic going in the advent of a curtailed response. This can be seen by noticing that the sequence changes the 'form' of the telling. In the course of the sequences, the news telling is changed from a 'volunteering' to 'an answering'.[13] That is, developing on the news following a topicalising response is to **volunteer** the telling, whereas to develop on the news following an itemised news enquiry is to tell the news as **elicited**. These sequences may thus organise **how** headlined news is to be elaborated. By withholding an elaboration of announced news in the next turn to a topicalising response, a news announcer may make a move to change the status of their telling.

Such an activity can be sensitive to contextual relevances. For instance, in the example presented in note 12 the news that was eventually delivered was detrimental about a mutual friend of the co-participants. This can be a sensitive matter, the news can backfire on the teller and they can be heard as being malicious. This telling the news may be organised so as to have the co-participant elicit it. The co-participant is then an accomplice in its telling and the possibility of attributing questionable motives to the news announcer may accordingly be minimised.

A description of sequences which may organise the initiation of a new topic is not an analytic occasion for the specification of the rules for topic organisation. Instead, the way in which the topic is initiated can be seen to be a methodically contextual issue. It builds in a contextual sensitivity to social matters, such as issues of friendship, possible sanctions, the relevant identity of the participants, and a whole lot more. In other words, designing a sequence in this way displays that for this occasion the interactants are orienting to these matters as consequential to their interaction.

The same order of issues is oriented to in openings and closings for conversation. In openings, for example, the "how are you" sequence provides for participants to bring each other up to date with any consequential news **between them** (Schegloff 1986). Conversationalists can design their closings in order to leave one another in particular kinds of ways that attest to or constitute the occasioned character of **their** 'relationship' to one another (Button forthcoming). Openings and

---

13   See Pomerantz (1980) in this connection.

closings are not gone through to just mechanically 'open' or to 'close' a conversation but are used to open or close it in a way that allows participants to build into their talk the situated details of their contingent social circumstances. To provide 'interaction rules' (Frohlich and Luff this volume) for the mechanical opening and closing of conversation that do not provide for, or even recognise that openings and closings are designed to allow complex negotiations about the management of a single conversation, is to not understand the nature of the interaction that is accomplished in such sections or 'routines' of talk. In terms of research in Conversation Analysis it would seem that conversation is just not organised as a 'routine', in the formulaic sense of that term. We should be very careful, then, in glossing over sections of talk such as openings or closings as set pieces.

4.4   Conclusion

Gilbert, Wooffitt and Fraser (this volume) would no doubt view the arguments in this chapter as at best a sceptical, and at worst a hostile reaction to "the idea of applying CA findings to the design of computer systems and more generally, (to) developing computational models of conversational phenomena...". I will stress a point made in the introduction. The arguments are not a hostile reaction to software designers who find Conversation Analysis to be an inspiration. Neither are the arguments in any way an attempt to deny that it is possible to construct a simulacrum of conversation.

   If there is any scepticism or hostility it is directed at the ambitions and claims that are tied to the development of a computational model of conversation. Arguing that humans and machines could converse is not just an unfortunate way of conceptualising what humans do or could do when they operate a computer, even if they talk to it, but a thorough misunderstanding of the empirical organisation of conversation. The irony is that Conversation Analysis, which has done so much to reveal how detailed that organisation is, is used to authorise computational models of conversation that misrepresent the details of how conversation works. To claim that a computational model of conversation is an adequate description of action-in-interaction is to ignore the very details of conversation that such a model would have to reproduce. To also claim that a simulacrum of conversation is a naturally occurring conversation between computers and humans is to not understand the implications that conversation analytic treatments of conversation as 'social praxis' have for descriptions of conversational organisation.

Chapter 5

Communicative Action and Computers

Re-embodying Conversation Analysis?

Paul McIlvenny

5.1 Introduction

I have heard a story that a well known author is paranoid about doubles or dopplegangers and, like most authors who draw on their own experience, they are to be found in some of his stories. He has a fear that people are imitating him in some other place – maybe at the same time, maybe not. Of course this is odd, but in his case understandable. Because of his fame as an author, somebody has made it his business to imitate him at various functions and occasions. He is being portrayed publicly as someone he is not. And yet this 'other' has succeeded in fooling acquaintances in practical engagement that he is the real author. He has done practical things, made speeches and more importantly conversed with people in their company. He has had to improvise in encounters and circumstances beyond control or anticipation. In addition, speaking to people who are physically present is the prime locus of the public self and the most personal, intimate thing. You are on display in many ways that are not discursively available. The physical and social circumstances of face-to-face interaction are rich and transparent resources indeed. In a way, the real author is embodied in this other person, but unfortunately has no recollection, only stories and surprises in the newspapers and from friends, that he has been somewhere else – the actual 'I was there and I did it' feeling is missing.

The story is not simply about an impersonation, but that someone is *being you* and doing things as you, i.e. that there could be two selves in time-space as part of one whole, and you are not the only 'you'.[1] The fear expressed by the author is similar to the compulsive interest and rhetoric around the idea of the machine *being us*. The heated arguments over differences between human and machine are based on the inherent humanness of intelligent or social conduct. In terms of the story, the debate could focus on the issue: could a machine imitate someone in conversation?[2] Well, make it simpler, could it embody anyone, or *be an other* rather than just an object or artefact?

Mention must be made of the popular, though not original, formulation of Turing's famous operational 'machine intelligence' test (Turing 1950) that uses 'conversation' as the crucial factor in determining intelligence. A machine and a human play an imitation game in which they must convince a human interrogator that 'it' is human within a limited period of time. The interrogator can address any questions to the unseen participants through the exchange of typewritten messages. However, besides the philosophical objections, the test in this form is restrictive. It explicitly denies those features that are discussed in this chapter in the process of narrowing the determination of intelligence within operational limits. Conduct is disembodied, activity-less, and without the rich circumstances of co-presence, though to pass the test still requires skillful management of contingent topic.

The story and the Turing test illustrate a number of important points relevant to this chapter. They both have in common conversation as an important and complex activity much bound up with the self and intelligence. The story shows some important features of practical activity that are the focus of investigation in this chapter. The Turing test avoids them. For example: the rich

---

1   A parable called "Borges and I" by Jorge Luis Borges - on doubles and selfhood - ends with the line, "I do not know which one of us has written this page".

2   The tables can be turned by asking the question: can a person be a machine's double? This line is more realistic, though still problematic, and is being used in a variant form when simulating and testing designs before full implementation.

circumstances of co-presence; improvisation; physical corporeal embodiment in the practical world. However, this chapter will move away from fanciful doubles and science fiction, and lie pragmatically between them and the Turing test. Against the idea of communication as the abstract interchange of symbols between individual cognitive processors – a methodological individualism – and the AI enterprise which sees situated circumstance and contingency as a hindrance or problem – something to be dealt with and overcome by an abstract intelligence; the key goal is to develop *a theory of practice and a practice of improvisation*. Bound up with this forward looking direction are three particular critiques: the 'interchange' model – the alternative is **interactivity**; 'out of the moment' planning – the alternative is **situated action**; and the Rationalist ideas behind models of action – the alternative is **embodied modelling**.

A fundamental tenet of this chapter is that looking at the dynamics of human interaction is essential for computer modelling and design, but this does not necessarily imply developing a mechanistic double or copy. The possibility, acceptance, and appropriateness of such an enterprise is not by any means guaranteed. The important point in looking at human interaction is to locate the crucial and essential local interactive processes or methods involved in the constitution of shared meaning, of achieving intersubjectivity, between actors in the practical circumstances of action and activity, rather than merely replicating a spoken 'conversation' language. Unavoidably, the vocabulary of human studies will be used to describe human-machine interaction or machine-machine interaction. It remains to be seen how far the notion of repair or intersubjectivity will be applicable, or that the interactions will be studied with the same fascination as those of human conduct.

What about this notion in the subtitle of **re-embodying Conversation Analysis**? It is not meant in the sense of biological matter, nor having the form of a human body, nor a brain-machine placed inside a human body (as in the techno-film "Robocop"), nor a brain placed in another body (as in the comedy film "The Man with Two Brains").[3] The title is meant to suggest the following idea. Conversation Analysis investigates embodied conduct. Research in empirical investigations of communicative action disembody and

---

3   The mention in the story about multiple selves can be taken up with respect to the possible multiple embodiment and multi-presence of machines. A machine is a physical device, but will it have a sense of individual self and embodiment connected to location in space-time? For instance, will it talk all the time, to many people at once?

objectify phenomena – bracket it, talk about it, and understand it. So, can the analyses be used to help constitute or realise a talking, conversing machine? How can the objects be made real again? At the present time, this has to be done the hard way – the experimenter or designer has to play God or evolution's game. Taking the metaphor maybe a little too far, what about the alternative title question: Embalming CA? Will CA be statically preserved or emasculated? This is a danger that is raised again in the conclusion.

The chapter is basically divided into two halves. The first half contains a general discussion drawing out the notion of re-embodiment by contrast with other possibilities. Two main directions are outlined: the pragmatic use of the findings and methods of CA in the design and evaluation of intelligible systems; and the theoretical and practical task of embodied modelling of social action, activity and structure, through which a fruitful synthesis of cognitive studies and social studies into an empirically grounded theory of situated cognition and activity may emerge. In order to further these two approaches, the second half describes two parallel empirical investigations that use ethnomethodology and CA in a study concerned with the nature and importance of interactivity and situated dialogue. A metaphor of social relations – of partners, courtship, partnership and divorce – runs through parts of the chapter.

5.2 Background partners?

The main aim of this section is to introduce the broad topic of the chapter: the notion that computers and conversation could be mutually informing. Has there been a convergence on phenomena, methods, tools in the fields supporting research into computers and conversation? How could the thought come to be considered and what useful questions or issues need to be dealt with? It is imperative that the questions are appropriate to the enterprise of finding answers, so a little exploration of the partners' background and status is required to draw out some of the issues at this preliminary stage.

5.2.1   Computers and conversation (the partners)

The **notion of computer** – automata; machine; the mindless, emotionless tool; hard reasoning and intensely logical. It has radically altered our societies and our talk about ourselves – the human condition. Woolgar (1987, p.325) hits the nail when he states, "discussions about technology embody fundamental preconceptions about the character of mankind." See Turkle (1982), who discusses many questions about adult and child perceptions of the computer in modern life. Also, Gregory (1984) in his book, "Mind in Science", deals with the complex relationship between our understanding of the physical world and the development of science and technology.[4]

The **phenomenon of conversation** – a routine and complex accomplishment carried through by almost all members of society with great skill and transparent ease. Not only speech but also the signs of the deaf community. Note, there is a contrast between the everyday general use of 'conversation', i.e. 'conversational activity' versus the speech event 'conversation' which can be characterised as talk-in-interaction maintaining equal speaker rights (Wilson 1989).[5]

A first answer to the suggestion of mixing computers and conversation is that of science fiction: to reproduce what people do that has been entertained in imaginative ways – the talking machine from early science fiction to Hal in the film '2001' – but usually with anthropomorphic blinkers. It hardly seems likely that the two can be integrated sensibly in their ordinary sense, so what is it about them that is appropriately investigated? We need to look deeper into their particular characteristics and features that lend force to the argument for cross-fertilisation.

5.2.2   Background: artefacts and CA

5.2.2.1   Recent Research AI and HCI

The focus in this section is on the development of the primitive 'interactive artefact'. First, a little clarification: I am dealing with a subfield of HCI and AI that might be called 'pragmatic AI'. Because of its utilitarian aims it has to consider the dynamic interface between the computer and user as a priority.

The last 25 years have seen the rise of the notion of the 'intelligent' computer and a computational theory of mind.

---

4   Note the re-emergence of animism with a mechanistic flavour in future artefactual environments. For example, computer-generated virtual environments in which to act, where the 'world' will work in the world's own image. That is, inanimate objects anciently thought to be animated by an immaterial force will be animated by a mechanical god or prime mover.

5   The term 'conversation analysis' is sometimes complained about because it is ambiguous between CA and the study of conversation in general, including other approaches. I will use capitals to refer to the specific discipline and lower case to refer to the general investigation of the phenomena.

Suchman (1987, chapter 2) has coined the useful term "**interactive artefact**" that focuses attention on interaction, mutual intelligibility and the artifactual nature of machines, rather than on mind and representation. As computers can be designed to produce products, or fragments of behaviour, that are human-like and can be reactive, the question arises: can the behaviour of a reactive artefact in the environment of human action be meaningful with respect to the actions of people – i.e. as social action? Suchman argues that because the computer artefact is reactive, language-using and opaque to the user, these are good reasons to consider it 'purposeful' in everyday vocabulary.

It is useful to compare this notion with Giddens (1987, pp.100-1) on the cultural object or artefact. He argues that cultural objects, like texts and electronic media, have the following characteristics:

(1) Distanciation of 'producer' from 'consumer'.

(2) Consumer becomes more important than the producer in the interpretative process.

(3) a) Durable medium of transmission across contexts.

b) A means of storage.

c) A means of retrieval.

The characteristics are similar for the interactive artefact, however, a stranger sort of distance occurs. The artefact, in a sense, manages meaning in the absence of the 'producer'. Meaning escapes the design horizons in processes of user-machine interaction as the user attempts to interpret the artefact's responses. It is difficult to talk about the designer/author, the user and the machine in appropriate ways. New hermeneutic accounts have to be debated because of the dilemma created by considering the machine as a social object or subject. It does have the qualities of a text in that the designer plays an important part as author, and there is a distance between designer and user. But yet, the interactive artefact is not like a static text; it is dynamic and reactive. It must stand on its own, with no help from the absent designer, in moments of user engagement, i.e. the artefact becomes a 'participant' in managing meaningful conduct. However, it must be remembered that the user sustains and grounds the appearance of a second person interface. An alternative, human-centred[6] way of putting it is that the artefact must react in appropriate

---

6   Notice that there are always two perspectives when accounting for the human-machine relationship: machine-centred where the focus is on the computer system to manage; or human-centred where the focus is on human interpretation.

ways for the user, so that the user finds it intelligible in terms of the project underway.

Note the gradual progression towards recovering the referential qualities of talk in designing AI computer artefacts. The interactive artefact, as can be seen in the design of instructional systems that can be contrasted with textual materials, is reclaiming in small simple steps what the written language has lost by suspending reference and divorcing itself from the modalities of everyday experience.[7]

Before summarising and discussing the investigation of conversation, a hint of its relevance to computers can be found in the rapid and sometimes unreflective importation of metaphors from the domain of human activity. For example, the 'interaction' or 'dialogue' metaphor is common. Books with titles like "The Articulate Computer" (McTear 1987) and "Getting Computers to Talk like You and Me" (Reichman 1985) are examples. The 'dialogue partner' perspective versus the tool, the system, and the media perspectives on the use of computers is discussed in Kammersgaard (1985). Also, metaphors of person have been used to give perspectives on interfaces, e.g. 'direct manipulation'. A reaction against the restricted metaphor can be found in Goranzon et al. (1988). They reinvest the concept of dialogue with the richness that has been lost by its appropriation as computer jargon.[8]

5.2.2.1   Investigation of conversation

The investigation of conversation as conversation was largely absent from academic disciplines until the second half of this century. The discipline one would have expected to have taken it under its wing, Linguistics, has largely avoided the issue, claiming disorder and unruliness. The importance and complex social order of conversation was discovered by an empirical discipline known as Conversation Analysis that grew out of a quirky sociological enterprise called ethnomethodology. At first, no particular priority was assigned to conversation as its subject matter. Unfortunately, the rise of ethnomethodology and other 'interpretative' approaches has had little effect on computational theories of human intelligence and behaviour, though this may change quite radically in the future.

---

[7]   In the sense of: "Meaning and reference are ordinarily closely combined in talk, not because talk is in any way primarily oriented towards description, but because it is carried on and organised within practical contexts of action." (Giddens 1987, p.04)

[8]   It is difficult to arbitrate prescriptively or normatively. Is the use of intentional vocabulary and the borrowing of everyday human social vocabulary satisfactory and to be accepted?

It is important to note that the field is fragmented in several ways, not least because of the peculiar nature of ethnomethodology, in that a failsafe method or approach is difficult to define in general because it emerges from the specifics of each activity. Also, there are many approaches that can come under the rubric of 'investigations of everyday social life' and these tend to be grouped together, e.g. Coulter (1979), Goffman (1981). See Heritage (1984a) for a discussion of Garfinkel's contributions, and Sharrock and Anderson (1986) for a similar broad brushstroke.

It is important to note that two strains of ethnomethodology are present in Garfinkel and continue on today (Giddens 1976, p.52). On the one hand, authors like Cicourel (1973) and McHugh (1973) maintain a reflexive perspective, and the recent work by Garfinkel's contemporaries examines particular instances with this in mind. On the other hand, a refinement of naturalistic description without foundational and philosophical argument is definitely in evidence – "the possibility of achieving a naturalistic observational discipline that could deal with the details of social action(s) rigorously, empirically, and formally." (Schegloff and Sacks 1973). So one of the issues discussed in this chapter is maybe better phrased in two parts: how is CA useful to HCI? and how is ethnomethodology useful to HCI? For example, the work of Frohlich and Luff (see this volume), Gilbert et al. (this volume) compared with the work of Cooper (1989).

One thing that is obviously outside of the scope of CA is that it cannot address the 'going on' of conduct, or social causality. It only deals with the description of regularities by a competent observer – treating conduct as a constituted social object and drawing on the experience and knowledgeability of a competent member to circumscribe some of its accountable features. CA shows more interest in the organisation *per se* than in the contexts of application. This is not a fault as such, just that CA sticks close to phenomena and at this stage it must be carefully described and plotted.

Thus, there are subtly distinct approaches that must be kept in mind when considering possible directions. There is a need to widen the scope of techniques and methods to an interdisciplinary level, but keeping the empirical and critical backbone of CA and ethnomethodology.

5.2.3   A marriage?

Why might CA be relevant to HCI and *vice versa*? I will now discuss the practicalities of this pragmatic marriage.

The relevance of CA can be found, first, wherever the second person metaphor is present in HCI, i.e. in the development of reactive machines that are amenable to a vision of talking computers in 'dialogue' with their users – the social subject rather than object. Second, it can be found in the practical and traditional approach in which engineering certain features of human conversation may enhance the human-computer interface, for example, Nickerson (1977) and the notion of 'graceful interaction' coined by Hayes and Reddy (1983). The issue of conversational computers versus appropriate interfaces has been debated for a while. Both sides have good and misleading points. The prime metaphor and model we have is our own conversation. This is so for many reasons: it is extremely difficult to think of a radical alternative; people have to use artefacts; we have a more intimate experiential understanding of our own as opposed to other creatures' behaviour; and, as CA and other investigations have shown, it is undoubtably a rich, valuable and dynamic phenomenon that works in unobvious ways. However, CA studies meaningful social action in naturally organised, ordinary activities. So can CA be used in HCI given the primary interest in the above phenomena? Are the principles mutually compatible, or must radical synthesis emerge? Both are rigorous in their own way: CA is empirical, non-conceptual, and holds to the principle of demonstrable evidence in the data; AI/HCI has formal notions of computational decidability, and implementation criteria. Are the tools and methods relevant? CA uses data recording, impressionistic rendering and empirical analysis; AI/HCI uses formalism, reactive behaviour, and programs conceptualised as computation over representation. One thing is for sure, there are non-intuitive consequences and dynamics in HCI so investigation must be empirical.

5.2.4   Time to reconsider

So far the discussion has been narrowing down on two particular research paradigms and comparing features of both. It is now time to briefly expand the issues dealt with in the chapter.

The focus on **conversation** by HCI/AI is indicative of the movement towards the social; in particular communicative interaction and intersubjectivity, i.e. the problem of understanding others and achieving a shared reality and social order.[9] The methods

---

[9]   The notion of 'social' needs to be loosened when describing the conduct and activity of machines and creatures. As with intelligence it will be the subject of intense debate. Woolgar(1985, p.557) notes, "that one of the more important options is to view the AI phenomenon as an occasion for reassessing the

of study, findings and metaphors are the crucial facets for partnership. With **computers** it is the technology, metaphors and models that come with automata/machines that are of corresponding importance. With careful attention to the attendant dangers and limitations, they may give rise to sophisticated and informative paradigms leading to other perspectives on understanding the complexity of human conduct. Much has been learnt in hindsight, by careful criticism, after the rapid and excessive adoption of the computational metaphor in studies of intelligence, cognition and the brain.

5.2.5   Conclusion

It is an interesting time for paradigm clashes and syntheses. Computers and conversation are highly charged notions by which many combinations of relevance are possible. Research should not be restricted to just considering the machine as 'technology for conversation'. Now some alternative futures for the partners will be considered.

5.3   Some possible directions: courtship

The previous section clarified the general issues which arise when considering computers and conversation. Now, some of the fruitful directions that can be explored will be outlined and two particular directions will be highlighted and discussed. I will not undertake the hazardous task of cataloguing or listing the possibilities, just discuss some that are clearly emerging.

5.3.1   Conversations for computers?

Are ideas about conversation useful for investigating people and computers? Two interesting areas where a social action perspective is being taken, almost by necessity, are computer-supported cooperative work (CSCW) and computer-mediated communication (CMC). No stance is taken on the 'intelligent' machine as the relationship of the machine to the users is one of tool or medium. CSCW is the 'humanistic' study of group activity using computer technology in order to enhance collaboration within the 'hi-tech' workplace. (See Sorgaard (1988), Stefik et al. (1987)). CMC is the study of those communication technologies that could come under the CSCW

central axiom of sociology that there is something distinctively 'social' about heading, but deal specifically with communication, e.g. the work by Bowers and Churcher reported in Young (1988).

Given the metaphor of human-computer dialogue, an alternative is to use the methods and findings of traditional investigations of conversation or discourse to design artefacts. This is a valid way of proceeding in HCI, but it sides with the pre-design and global control that is characteristic of highly structured institutional contexts. It remains to be seen if this approach has a niche in artefact development. See for example, Cawsey (1989a and this volume), who borrows from the Birmingham discourse school and takes a computer-centred approach.

5.3.2   Computers for conversation?

Are computers useful for doing research into human conversation? Consider this question in terms of metaphors, technology and models. The least useful of these ideas seems to be the 'metaphor'. The notion of cognition as a symbolic computation process is taken as the guiding principle and metaphor for the interdisciplinary field of cognitive science. But, a preoccupation with 'in the head' engenders a mentalist and individual perspective. Usually, the metaphor moves from the social domain to the description of internal processes, e.g. there is a tendency to borrow folk language and social vocabulary to describe the 'insides' of machines and people, e.g. 'society of minds', a search, or a list, etc.

Computer technology is at its most useful in artefacts and tools. However, the relevance to the human sciences is expressed simply in Suchman (1987, p.189): "Just as the project of building intelligent artefacts has been enlisted in the service of a theory of mind, the attempt to build interactive artefacts, taken seriously, could contribute much to an account of situated human action and shared understanding." This chapter whole-heartedly agrees and attempts to contribute to the development of an account.

What about computer modelling techniques? The main approach is 'disembodied modelling'. Its particular characteristics include some of the following: formal description of process; pre-constituted inputs and outputs; symbolic computation over representations; no real practical consequence or situation; heavily interpreted and assisted process – the human interpretation crutch; unlimited time-space. Examples include most of the traditional work in cognitive science and AI. The former is faithful to 'psychological reality' and the latter

---

human behaviour".

to a 'do it anyway' approach. Of course, this work is useful and productive but it has its blind spot. It is methodologically individualistic and lacks external constraint, which consequently leads to over-representation and reification.

In summary, technology and models are quite appropriate for challenging current ideas about human conduct, and extending conversation analysis in new ways.

5.3.3   Re-embodying CA?

The directions discussed above all have prospects and some are in full swing, but I have left two particular directions for further detail because they seem to offer a different perspective, more in tune with the 'doing' than the description of conduct.

One direction centres on the question: can CA findings be re-embodied in the sense of engineering interactive artefacts or building embodied machines? That is, can it be made living in a phenomenal domain as opposed to being pinned down and discursively objectified by analysts. If so, the implicit consequence is that the re-embodied will also be open to analysis, although the application of CA methods is contingent on an everyday accountable social reality. This could be a useful testing ground for CA and ethnomethodological ideas at a basic level.   An exploration of 'ethno' methods for machines, and emergent machine-specific 'ethno' methods.   It is also a test of ideas. This raises the difficult question of what is being embodied and how. Is it only the observable behaviour that is similar to human or is there some claim for 'experiential reality', i.e. the documentary method of interpretation?   I hear the cry of "Turing test" and "Behaviourism" raised once again.   Another tricky question is: does this mean that human behaviour is codifiable, formalisable or programmable?   I think this question needs to be avoided, because it falls into the trap of talking within the terms of rationalist models. Over-rationalisation may be replaced by a sort of methodological situationism that focuses on 'interaction with' rather than 'representation of'. Just what this means is one topic of the rest of this chapter, but it also requires future investigation.

The argument runs as follows. Artefacts and embodied machines are present and thus potentially dynamically active in the world and with others. Rather than use 'out of the moment' resources, why not find ways of 'going on', using the world and others as a positive place to be and act in and with (not a problematic, in-the-way world – like the retort by a salesperson, "if only we could get these people out of the way then we'd get a lot more done."). Then, plans can be studied as resources that guide action (Suchman 1987). The machine – artefactual or embodied – can involve gears, programs or whatever is designed on the basis of traditional rationalist or mentalist perspectives, but it will not 'go-on' very smoothly; in particular, the interaction can be 'interchange', but it will be primitive. The important point is that no approach can avoid the 'ongoing' and 'doing now' of situated conduct and nor is it desirable to do so.[10]

What sources suggest, motivate or can be drawn upon in forming the alternative notion of modelling by participatory and situated doing? There has to be a general recognition of the importance of philosophers like Heidegger, Wittgenstein, Dewey and Rorty, who all criticize the rationalist tradition and attempt to form an alternative. Their interpretative ideas are integral to the work of Winograd (1986), Suchman (1987), Hall (1987), Mallery et al. (1987) and Fraser (forthcoming). But, much catching up is yet to be done to harness contemporary philosophers like Gadamer and Habermas, and theorists like Maturana and Varelam (1980) and Giddens (1984).

5.3.3.1   Interactive artefacts

Before beginning this section proper, it is crucial to note that simulation or coding of human behaviour is not a goal of this research. Human conduct and conversation is one very useful source for the creative design of artefacts that may have similar characteristics; also, users may draw upon interactional resources in order to interpret and use the system.

The **first** approach, using conversation for computers, involves the pragmatic use of the findings and methods involved in the investigation of communicative interaction, like CA, in the design and evaluation of intelligible computer systems. This includes the suggestive thoughts of Schegloff (1980) and Wynn (1980), McTear (1985) on repair design suggestions; Gilbert (1988) and Frohlich and Luff (1989 and this volume) on explanation and dialogue management; and Raudaskoski (1989 and this volume) on repair implementation; and Gilbert et al. (this volume) on speech dialogue systems.

One of the first people to discuss the application of the conversational metaphor for HCI was Nickerson (1977). He gave a list of features of conversation that may be useful for design: bidirectionality; mixed initiative; sense of presence; non-verbal communication; intolerance for silence. The list, including many

---

10   Compare this with the phenomenological spatial description of the human condition as tottering inescapably forward in moments of Being and presence.

other items, is now ripe for re-evaluation given the rapidly developing new technology and conversational research in the last ten years. For example, consider the item, 'rules for transfer of control', which is representative of the signal view of turn-taking in contrast to the local opportunity management of CA, (see Wilson et al. 1984).

The findings and methods of CA are applicable to the human-computer environment in a number of different ways. In outline, the import of CA includes: using findings to search for similarities and differences in HCI compared to human interaction; and using findings to generate machine behaviour or predict user behaviour. The application of CA methods was successfully demonstrated in Suchman (1987) for prescriptive evaluation rather than description, with a focus on the asymmetry between human user and machine. An interesting property is that, though analysts have no access to machine 'experience', they do have access to the 'insides' or machinery of the computer as well as observable behaviour. This is a potential extra resource in addition to the observable participant displays of interpretation used by CA analysts of human conduct.[11]

Laurel (1986) works on the idea of artefact design as mimesis, i.e. artistic representation or imitation. However, Laurel only considers first person virtual worlds, i.e. artificial computer-generated environments in which a user can directly create and act as if immediately and experientially involved in that world. Examples are direct manipulation interfaces, data gloves, eye phones, etc. In addition, why not consider the ability to act in a second person interface – a virtual world including others? Dangers arise in second person interfaces in two ways. Users are denied access to the direct experience of *doing* with all the attendant riches of circumstance, constraint, and routine because the intermediary 'does'. Also, the user does not have a lively experience of *'doing' communication* with the mimetic intermediary or agent. In the human-machine environment, there is a live, present, interested, active human user. Why not use this person? Why not use these resources? The routine improvisation and mutual coordination of situated dialogue has been ignored, leading to gross conceptual and 'out of the moment' approaches, where dialogue is moulded as something in which to take part in discrete moments and to prepare for, as best as possible, in isolation. The roles of dialogue participants – producer and recipient

---

[11]   The analyst's human experience as a member of society is essential for illuminating frames of social meaning. In contrast to the machine and the human condition, this is not available as a resource for investigating creature interaction and behaviour.

– are taken in strict alternation. In sum, the argument is for interactivity in situated dialogue.

Channelling and sustaining the metaphor or mimesis is a priority goal. The asymmetry between user and computer means that user channelling techniques and alternative resources for the system will have to be developed recursively and contingently, with a distinction between particular cases of breakdown and general troubles with a system. The goal is to avoid or manage for contingency whilst recognising the essential human grounding and interpretative powers. It is essential to channel the user given the machine's restricted and asymmetric access to resources of situated action (Suchman 1987). The asymmetry is not only between human and machine interpretative powers, but also in what can be accepted by the machine and what can be produced, e.g. the system's responses can be quite complex linguistically, but the user has only a restricted language. With regard to difficulties, they can range from particular unavoidable breakdowns emerging from the routine for this person at this time, to repeated troubles that occur among the general user population because of bad or inappropriate design. The first category is implicitly a part of the nature of artefacts and cannot be accommodated by current machine-centred design methods. The second can be pinpointed and maybe resolved in the cycles of evaluation and redesign, e.g. by changing the system organisation or explicitly doing channelling work to avoid the problem *in situ*.

In the long term, understanding and decreasing the asymmetry between human and machine by incorporating interactivity, presence, local adaption, and repair will be a major development. Much can be gained from studying the:

- Micro-dynamics of intra-turn action: mutual coordination of moments of presence.

- Dynamics of inter-turn activity: constitution of a specific activity

- Macro-dynamics of activity: routine engagements over time and space.

In the investigations described later, I am only immediately concerned with the micro-dynamics, and bracket the structural and routine orders that partially constitute the potential to act.

5.3.3.2   Sociology of embodied machines

The second approach, using computers for conversation, has the theoretical and practical task of embodied modelling of social action, activity and structure, through which a fruitful synthesis of cognitive studies and social studies into an empirically grounded theory of situated cognition and activity may emerge (see Lave (1988) for a good practical account of developments in situated cognition). This involves a re-evaluation of the boundaries between mentalism and interactionism, social and cognitive, individual and public, etc. A comparison with other lines may help define by contrast.

- An early source is Power (1979) in which two robot agents have to cooperate in order to open a door by means of verbal communication.

- Multiple agent models of HCI, e.g. Storrs (1988).

- Disembodied modelling of human, creature or system organisation – e.g. social organisation, creature communities or parallel-distributed systems like workstation groupware, e.g. Doran (1988).

- Sociology of rational agents, with rational architectures, e.g. Kiss (1987, 1988).

In this chapter, the possible exploration of the metaphors of 'dialogue' and 'conversation' in relation to situated and embodied (cognitive) machinery is outlined. Key research has been carried out by Agre (1988) in reference to solitary activity with ideas about AI machinery and the dynamics of everyday human activity. Preliminary, but narrow, questions about dialogue – linguistic communication – between rational agents have been discussed in a recent workshop reported in (Galliers 1988). The suggestion that "for any agent, human or machine, operating in the ever-changing, and unpredictable real world, the inherent flexibility and expressiveness of linguistic communication is essential." (p. 11 of discussion reports) is also taken up in this chapter, though issues of intersubjectivity and collaboration may not always beg linguistic resources.

Research into a sociology of machines/artefacts will unfold by investigating the dynamics of situated and embodied machinery in interaction with its environment and 'others'. But, what sort of embodiment is envisaged? There are possibilities for real or virtual/mimetic environments. What constraints will embodiment have on the machine? By looking at human corporeality some ideas can be gained. For example, the time-space constraints: a constraint on human and machine activity given by the nature of embodiment and the physical contexts in which activity occurs, e.g. strict limitations on capabilities of movement and perception; time as a scarce resource; multi-task engagement limitation; movement in space is also in time; singular occupation of physical space (Hagerstrand 1975).

Dynamics and machinery are now discussed. The crucial notion is of dynamics – emergent patterns of activity or action in interaction. By investigating and giving it prominence, the aim is to go against accounts that put primacy on social structure, i.e. creating the 'judgmental dope' (Garfinkel 1967) and, also, those that emphasize the symbol processing individual – the 'cognitive dope' (Heritage 1984a) which leads to intense reification. They are not kicked out the door; the important constraints of social structure and cognitive machinery are recognised. The goal is just to add some new dimensions. So what about this notion of machinery? It is introduced in Agre (1988) to emphasize a formally specified device that is physical. Also, the machinery has an architecture. I am not concerned at present whether it should it be connectionist, knowledge-based, etc. Either way, we should motivate the search for reasonable and simple architectures by sticking close to the description of interaction dynamics that machineries participate in, and by comparing them to human conduct (Agre 1988). Simple machinery motivated by embodied modelling is a fundamental principle. Ideas on architecture should also filter from below as well, e.g. from brain science (Malloch forthcoming).

Plan-based accounts in AI and cognitive science attempt the problematic and unrealistic conceptual task of intent-action-event ascription and have been critiqued in Suchman (1986, 1987) and Agre and Chapman (1988). But alternatives are not quick to appear. This is maybe partly because of the mind-wrenching task of overcoming rationalist and everyday ways of thinking about action, and partly because the interpretative and hermeneutic traditions on which the criticism is based espouse a doctrine that is not easily reconciled with a methodology based on computers. Oldman and Drucker (1985) argue against the possibility – they claim deep problems with the incompatible notions of 'generation' of language and language as a 'toolkit'. Woolgar (1987) considers the arguments against cognitivism and concludes that there is a serious danger "that anticognitivism will merely reproduce the assumption of codifiability that characterizes the cognitivist position." (p. 323). Later, Woolgar notes parenthetically that codified means "formalised, reduced to a series of rules such as instructions or to an algorithm." (p. 325). He seems to equate explanation with codifiability. Also, he does not consider budding alternatives to rule-based systems that move away from the computational metaphor. Nor the prospect of exploring machineries for embodied action by drawing on dynamics and experiential 'interpretative' accounts of human conduct, e.g. phenomenology, ethnomethodology, hermeneutics. Button's arguments in this volume seem to stake out the same 'blind' alley in only arguing against the traditional rationalist assumptions of AI wrapped up in the notion of a 'talking machine'.

Will embodied modelling yield codified explanations? What could it explain? It is not trying to explain solely in social or cognitive terms, but seeks to explore the emergence of primitive behaviours from interactions between embodied machines – no claim is made for a reproduction of human social conduct, though insights may be forthcoming. So, the embodied machine need not embody a codification of social behaviour. In fact, much has to be explained in interpretative terms – for example, the approach just gives a handle on grasping some understanding of the possible rôle of machineries in the dynamics of interaction and the complex reproduction of structure, but need not codify or represent these processes in order to participate in them. Much like the human subject who does not have total knowledgeability and does not need to. Note, the modelling technique cannot explain many social phenomena – it is not a model of structural change. The key issue is what knowledge is required in order for structure to emerge and be sustained, and this may include some practical social theorising by the actors involved. This is similar to the empirical question of when planning and anticipation should be forsaken for an embodied response.

Recent research has begun to study solitary embodied activity (See Agre 1988). However, I am particularly interested in the questions of communicative action and intersubjectivity in practical collaborative activity. In AI terms the question becomes: how can rational agents communicate their plans and intentions to each other in 'dialogue'? A serious alternative formulation can be found by drawing on ideas from sociology. Embodied machines, creatures or humans will interact at many levels – in terms of human conduct we call this collaboration and cooperation. With embodied machines local interaction between 'others' and 'selves' and also between 'selves' and the environment does not have to be over-rationalised, reified or encoded. An embodied machine will have to deal with contingency – you cannot control the world or others. Actions continually escape control because of the routine contingent circumstances, unacknowledged conditions and unintended consequences of action.

So, the key aim of this model is to explore the notion of 'improvisation' rather than planning and generation. The concept of 'thrownness' – the routine reflexive monitoring and rationalisation in the inescapable time-space flow of routine, ongoing conduct – is useful here.

To conclude, a major goal of this approach is to explore ideas current in social theory about the duality of structure. Giddens (1984, p.375) construes "structure as the medium and outcome of the conduct it recursively organises; the structural properties of social systems do not exist outside of action but are chronically implicated in its production and reproduction." His theory turns around the duality of social subject and object, e.g. ideas about knowledgability on the one hand, and structural constraint and reproduction on the other, e.g. "Human social activities... are not brought into being by social actors but continually recreated by them via the very means whereby they express themselves as actors. In and through their activities agents reproduce the conditions that make those activities possible." (Giddens 1984, p.2). By acknowledging the roles of machinery, structure and situation, investigations of this duality seem feasible, if only to clarify the decisive line between human and machine in social terms.

5.3.4   Conclusion

An important difference between these two directions – the interactive artefact and the embodied machine – can be seen if an interactive artefact is placed with another. What happens? Nothing or garbled un-sense. Artefacts are designed for human consumption and rely on a pre-understanding by the user – e.g. the social context and the user's experience with machines and the particular machine – and channelling by instruction and dialogue design, whereas in embodied modelling, a 'social' machine is distinctly without this resource.

This section has drawn out two particular approaches that play with different ideas about computers and conversation. An investigation was conducted to clarify and develop some aspects relevant to these two prospects. The main aim of the investigation is to clarify the notion of interactivity in communicative interaction and to pin down and describe the dynamics of embodied human communicative action that may inform the design of artefact or machine. The best way to do this is to look at activities that are publicly 'out there' rather than those like reading or writing: particularly to look at activities that are situated, embodied, 'ongoing' and 'flowing', and so do not allow the planning, conceptual or mentalist models to take hold. More extensive discussion of the notion of re-embodiment and these two approaches can be found in McIlvenny (1989).

5.4 Empirical investigation of situated dialogue

So what steps forward can be taken? This section outlines two parallel empirical investigations that take a look at human interaction and dialogue. They are reported in full in McIlvenny (forthcoming). In summary, the investigations focus on situated, participatory and embodied communicative activity, particularly, the micro-dynamics of inter- and intra-turn action.

The investigations draw on ethnomethodological and Conversation Analytic perspectives. They are primarily concerned with the nature and importance of interactivity and its relevance to computational models of communicative action and human-computer communication. The slant of the investigations grew out of a dissatisfaction with conceptual and mentalist models. For example, a key paper in computational linguistics on discourse and dialogue by Grosz and Sidner (1986) is a step forward in acknowledging the shared nature of discourse, but it stays within the traditional conceptual framework of purposeful action and is sadly lacking in mechanisms by which structure could emerge in the dialogue process. Basically, it is not of much use to embodied modelling or artefact design where contingency rules, and improvisation and practical achievement are essential.

The idea is that empirically grounded and architecturally sound theories will emerge, rather than the conceptual models of structure characteristic of discourse analysis and computational models of dialogue, if embodied and situated activity is investigated in different ways. It must be made clear that the emphasis on human dialogue has pushed investigations 'into the head' ignoring the dynamics of interaction and the circumstances of conduct, e.g. the inescapable body constraints and time-space of situated conduct. This is because of the almost magical notion of abstract dialogic transfer from head to head that is a part of the 'conduit' metaphor. In contrast, opening outwards has its own problems: interactivity within the turn opens up Pandora's Box, for allowing action within the construction of a turn product means that all sorts of problems and resources become available. Actual implementation is not dealt with because, at this early stage of development, a perspective on situated communicative interaction is sought that will later inform design. Simply, insights are to be found in the analysis of data, and in this case from human conduct data. As CA has shown it is best to start with particular cases, and with observation and with description.

In the next section some important concepts are introduced and the background to the investigations described. In the results section, some data examples are discussed and analysed, though mainly with respect to the design of interactive artefacts.

5.4.1   Introduction

5.4.1.1   Interactivity and dynamics

Ideas about interactivity are usually implicit within a theory or way of talking, because the meaning of the word is so obvious, yet diffuse and multiplicitous. It depends on the activity in question: reading a book, walking down a street, using a computer, talking to someone; a physical or social phenomenon. Typically, with a computer system this means participating in the computational process. For example, with an interchange dialogue system, a user can interrupt the unit of, say, 'explanation' at explicit points. The explanation is not given as a monolithic rhetorical whole, but in sections according to some pre-design and user prompting. However, and this is the crucial point, the *participatory dialogue itself is not interactive* for the sections are not open for negotiation or interruption.

Here are the important concepts that have emerged from the investigations and data analysis. First, the *participation* of participants must be organised in some fashion. Mutual and simultaneous actions must be coordinated; they are not random events in a meaningless world. An *opportunity* for action is socially or physically organised and constrained. In opportunities there are *possibilities* which can also be socially or physically constrained. Action in interaction has a describable *grain size*: patterns of enabling opportunity for action. *Significance* is the potential effect on the whole interaction, i.e. the dynamics of activity.[12] What is important in interesting – i.e. contingent and practical – interaction is that all these must be organised locally and mutually within the emerging dynamics. For example, interruption has to be achieved, coordinated, managed and 'pulled off' collaboratively. Even disagreement,

---

12   Note that opportunity, possibility and significance come to hand *post hoc* or in breakdown and rationalisation. They are analytic terms. Normally and routinely, a space of possibility and opportunity in practical action or 'going on' is not apparent.

nonsense and chaos have to be coordinated and make sense. Very important are the *dynamics* or orders and patterns of activity in interaction with 'the world' and 'others', either machine or human. The notion of *constraint* and *resource* should also be introduced. There are physical and social constraints on action from time-space restraints and normative sanctions. However, it is important to see constraint and resource as part of the same bundle; figure and ground, where you do not get one without the other. Finally, an *interactional event* is an event endogenous (with cognitive and perceptual asides) to the interaction that is used as a resource by the participants, e.g. internal pace or rhythm constituted through the interaction.

Understanding constraint and resource can help a lot in explaining certain dynamics. For example, take the physical writing pen versus the computer-mouse technology. It is common for users, working in a multiple window space and coordinating the current visual workspace with the placement of current activity, to type into the wrong window. Why does 'mis-windowing' occur? A simple explanation is that the actual physical writing process is a constraint on the activity of writing on a particular sheet, because the sheet and pen must be in contact. This is also a resource for the coordination of the writing activity with the next action's placement. It is not easy to write on the wrong sheet given that the bodily actions of writing are so closely connected with the decision to write on a particular page. However, the removal of the constraint, through using a keyboard that distances the writing process from the graphic medium, means that it becomes easy to misplace a set of keystrokes. The mouse now serves as the middle man between the graphic medium and the activity. Reichman (1986) tries to explain the misplacement of actions by users in window systems through the metaphor of conversational embedding of context spaces. She is confused between conversational resources and action resources.

The dangers of not considering interactivity are illustrated in the following two examples. First, imagine trying to shake hands with someone when only discrete moments of opportunity are possible, i.e. by both following the instructions: face each other, close eyes and decide on next static hand position, move and open eyes; try and coordinate handshaking thus. (This simulates the sudden appearance of hands characteristic of singular opportunities for action.) Second, suppose the designers of cars came up with a push button steering system. Choices could be made about which direction to move, in order to ease the driver's lot, but the choices could be made only every few seconds. Luckily, design does not stray too far from functionality in the real world! Similar ideas applied to interactive video technology can be found in Brand (1988) and Laurel (1986).

5.4.2 Methods

The empirical investigation and analysis centred on the dialogue process and dynamics in a synchronous, computer-mediated modality called a 'keyboard phone'. Participants could communicate with each other in different rooms by typing at the terminal. They had the opportunity to type at any time in their respective windows, to see the other's type instantaneously, and to overlap responses – call this an 'open' floor or space. The computer-mediated modality was the only means for the participants to communicate and complete the task cooperatively. An investigation of co-present collaboration and the local, contingent coordination of concurrency and reciprocity in the flow of conduct was carried out.

The experiment ran as follows. Subjects were instructed that they were taking part in an experiment involving one of several communication modalities and that they would be asked to complete a task cooperatively with the other participant(s). The aim of the task was for the participants to plan a route through a city using a copy of a published "city map". One participant is given a map which has some destinations that must be visited and some routes already marked that must be followed. This participant is instructed to find a route that visits all the destinations and follows all the routes, and to guide the other to do the same. Participants have to find a mutually satisfactory solution cooperatively. The problem for the participants is that the maps differ from each other because they are not from the same publication. The participants have to achieve mutual orientation through the maps and, by the end have the same route-plan for all practical purposes. The task is not a naturally occurring one, but it draws upon the everyday methods of human actors – it should be easy to accomplish and requires no special training – and involves the participants in completing what is essentially a visual task through a modality with no visual contact. Subjects were left alone until a certain time had passed by and the experiment terminated. The layout of the experiment for the participants is shown in the appendix.

In addition, small experiments with co-present, telephone and keyboard interchange modalities were conducted. For co-presence, the parties were in face-to-face contact and could look at each other's maps. For the speech telephone, the parties could only speak to each other. For the keyboard interchange, the parties were linked by a computer-mediated restricted 'flip-flop' modality that allowed only a strict alternation of turns, in which turn allocation was under the current speaker's control.

5.4.2.1   Justification

In terms of *interactive artefact design*, I am not so much interested in borrowing wholesale from human interaction, but in understanding dynamics and processes in order to develop an appropriate 'flow of presence' within the constraints of HCI. For the *sociology of machines* approach, the motivation for the investigation is to understand the dynamics in order to posit machinery and interesting experiments. However, the relevance of the investigations to embodied modelling will take second place in the remainder of the chapter.

What are the benefits of an experiment using a restricted computer-mediated modality? Firstly, one can compare the results with computational work based on modalities and task dialogues, like that of Grosz and Sidner (1986). Secondly, because the modality is generally available and is used by some of the computer community. Thirdly, it is an interesting modality with peculiar emergent dynamics and characteristics of its own. Finally, the disruptions caused by the lack of resources or the strange circumstances reveal some of the routine features of interactivity. The disturbances and breakdowns to the normal flow require a local mutual transformation in order to achieve 'sense'. In parallel, an investigation of co-present collaboration was developed. The motive was to draw upon two contrasting communicative activities and to look at the highly developed dynamics.

The investigation developed as a sort of uncontrolled experimentation. No specific objectives were proposed so as to retain several promising lines. Different types of modality data were collected and as much as possible of the events recorded in order to extract or 'find' interesting material in the analysis-transcription cycles.

A technique called protocol generation in constructive interaction is possible in these restricted modalities (Miyake 1986; Suchman 1987). Basically, two co-participants are used on each side of the modality. Both pairs of co-participants used in the full experiments could carry out the task on their own, but they had to coordinate and demonstrate the sense of their actions to each other in collaborating on courses of action. This situation is not normal, but it is not untypical as people sometimes do this in real situations.

Video and audio recording technologies were used in order to get at observable events and make them available for detailed examination and review. A complex setup involving two cameras, two video recorders, a split-screen mixer, and a micro-second screen-clock timer was used. This resulted in a recording of the two co-participant pairs plus the co-screen display that both pairs had simultaneous access to. A perspective on the co-present interaction of co-participants emerged by transcribing a variety of details found in a strip of conduct. The method of transcription was under continuous and increasingly detailed development in order to be faithful to what was accountably 'real' for the co-participants and participants. Predominantly, the impressionistic CA transcription notation is used (Jefferson 1989). See the Notes on Transcription Conventions (p.261) for the notation, and the last part of this section for the arguments.

To conclude, the investigations were carried out in order to develop perspectives on situated communicative action, particularly, the nature of process, dynamics and presence in situated dialogue. In brief, the topics dealt with in the investigation include:

(1)   Dialogue process – achieving, negotiating and maintaining mutual intelligibility. With the additional notions of kairos – appropriate time – and reciprocity – interpretative relevance of successive actions to each other (see Erickson 1982). Fox (1987) clarifies some of the CA work by introducing the notion of 'interactional reconstruction'. She argues that contingent interpretation must be recognised and accommodated in discourse modelling by cognitive science.

(2) Communicative dynamics – patterns of interaction and participation. With notions of local management, temporality, and complementarity – the interpretative relevance of concurrent or simultaneous actions to each other (see Erickson 1982). There is a vertical and horizontal perspective to the interaction of two co-present participants in an encounter, of which reciprocity and complementarity are examples.

(3) Presence and co-presence – conjoint and reflexive monitoring of an encounter, with notions of fore-/background and simultaneity.

(4) Interactive creation and management of a 'communicative space' in which mutual intelligibility and a shared reality can be achieved.

5.4.3   Results

5.4.3.1   Data

Several types of experiments were conducted and recordings made, but only two types will be presented in this chapter, (1-1)KP, (2-2)KP.[13] The remainder of this section will attempt to illustrate some of the preceding arguments and prepare the ground for the analysis of the complex examples. The five examples given in the appendix will be used to illustrate some of the decisions made in designing and transcribing the experiment, e.g. how did such a complex transcription record evolve and for what purpose?

Example 1 This example shows the visual appearance of a screen display at a particular·instant in the course of the communicative activity. Both pairs of co-participants could see this visual display screen at the same time and in the same form. It is just a record or residue of events that occurred during the course of cooperating through the modality. There is a simple temporal history recoverable in this example: events higher up in the windows occurred before those below them. However, it is not quite true that the display is a sediment of events, as there are some events missing, e.g. a repair initiator by D in response to line J2 is not recorded at this later moment in time because it was almost immediately erased. Reconstruction by the analyst of what actually happened, the sequential organisation of 'turns', could be attempted by drawing on the findings of previous analyses and commonsense. A story could be constructed, much in the vein of Garfinkel's 'et cetera' clause experiments that demonstrated the indefiniteness of accounting procedures. Problems will occur because of lost lines, e.g. adjacently relevant lines are missing before D1 because of D's policy of double spacing 'turns' or responses. It is interesting to note that the co-participants face a similar, though practical, problem when they sometimes refer back to the display to reconstruct a past event that becomes important once again. However, the display is more

---

13   Referencing conventions:
(?-?) - number of participants across modality, e.g. (2-1) would be two co-participants communicating with a solitary participant.
KP – 'keyboard phone' modality.
C(KP) – focus on the co-present co-participants in KP.
Transcription figures are as follows. For (2-2)KP: 39 minutes out of 110 minutes + 52 minutes of (1-1)KP and (2-1)KP. For (2-2)C(KP): 91 minutes transcribed out of 300 minutes.

meaningful to the participants *in situ* because they have been a part of the process of constructing meaning of which the display is but a residue. This illustrates the often forgotten fact that remembering is not necessarily a mental process, but an interaction between a person and the world. Recall and memory is as much 'out there' as 'in the head'. In this case, the display is essential to the participants' remembering of what happened.

Example 2 How about a simple rendering in traditional script form? Basically, this example is an abstract sequential record, i.e. the turns are in discrete sequence time and they are labelled linearly down the page. In addition there is some attention to temporal overlap by recording the clock time when an overlap of two responses occurs. Unfortunately, this form of transcription misrepresents the participants' 'reality' because they are not in co-presence, like in conversation. Mutual monitoring is not a routine accomplishment in this case, and transmission and reception are distanced owing to a lack of resources. This means that alternative interpretation strips cannot be represented in this rendering. Here are some examples. Some turns are never noticed. For example, line 5, "Ang?", is never noticed by the other party. Some turns are not noticed until later. Line 2, "Ang", is not received until after the response to the prior in line 1. Lines 10 and 15 are not received until the end of the recipient's current turn. Other turns are quickly erased. Line 2 does not exist exactly in the same way as the others. It was typed and almost immediately deleted by D. Or they are edited, for example, line 3, "east" replaces "right".

Example 3 So, a rendering that allows alternative interpretative strips to be recovered is needed, and this is done by incorporating temporal flow; see example 3 in the appendix. The analyst can now isolate monitoring, reception and transmission.

However, this example is too simple. It is quite sequential. What happens when overlaps occur? Why do particular observable dynamics or behaviours occur? How do the participants interpret the other's conduct? What processes of monitored production are involved in constructing a response? These are questions that have no easy answers if normal observation is relied on because the resources available for the analyst are so restricted by the modality. Of course, theorising could take over at this point, but a different and more acceptable way out is adopted in the next example.[14]

---

14   The protocol generation technique, described earlier and motivated in example 4, is implicit in the analyses of examples 1 and 2. Some of the analyses could not have been made without this method.

Example 4   An advantage can be gained by using a restricted modality. The modality allows dyadic co-participant collaboration without too much distortion.   This is not available in normal conversation because constructing an experiment with a dyad acting conjointly as if a person in a conversation, in order to display the collaborative and observable work done by the dyad in achieving conversation with another, is not possible.   In a very loose sense, the method adopted can be compared to having access to the thoughts of a single participant.   Let no more be said of this analogy, before reification sets in.   In the example, the process of constructing a response is now available as a resource for the analyst.   This explains why the fragment "Reg" appeared in the communicative space.   The collaborative work done to construct the response is demonstrated in the talk of the co-participants.   And, because recipient design and monitoring is prevalent, G noticed the other's response in overlap and attended to it, thus leaving a half-constructed response.

Example 5   This example shows the full complexity of the transcription notation adopted in the investigation.

5.4.3.2 Analysis

Example 4   The 'keyboard phone' is an 'open' modality, so participation is feasible at any time.   Thus, it has to be socially organised within the physical constraints and emergent dynamics of the modality.   This means that concurrent activity, instead of the alternation of speaker and listener, and the significance given to interactional events, like temporal duration, can be studied.   An example of overlap and recipient monitoring can be found in example 4, e.g. the incomplete turn-construction "Reg".   Also, example 5 illustrates some recipient monitoring and orientation to a noticeable absence, e.g. the "go on!" response by D after a silence in activity after the incomplete turn-construction, "Our starting point is", by the other pair becomes interpretable as a lapse.

The physical characteristics of **transience** and **permanence** of a medium are important in this case. Speech and sign are transient, though they can be recorded and reviewed, whereas writing is generally permanent and creates a distance between producer and recipient.   The keyboard phone modality lies awkwardly between these two because participants can address turns as 'nows' or return to them or find them later as 'priors'.   That is, a turn can be produced as a complete unit to be received in a future time, or it can be constructed in monitored presence as a turn in progress.   It serves as both constraint and resource.   This is important for interactive artefacts where the physical characteristics can be creatively designed and may lead to new or difficult dynamics.

Can it be employed in building a CMC that incorporates permanence and transience as a differential resource? For example, a graphic slab that allows graphic expression with a continuum of permanence-transience. Participants could write or draw in two dimensions and they could control in some local, mutually agreeable way the degree of permanence of the drawing. Mutual monitoring of graphic expression with conversational characteristics would then be a possibility. Because of the participant controlled degree of permanence, characteristics of writing and talk, like divergence in collaboration, can be achieved.

The phenomenon of '**double dialogue**' emerges as an interesting dynamic in this modality because of its properties and the social resources methodically deployed in achieving sense. Basically, a two threaded dialogue is achieved as follows. Normally, participants in speech conversation achieve an accountable sequential adjacency through the operation of a 'turn-taking system' by which one person speaks at a time. Sequential adjacency is still important in the keyboard phone. However, participants do not need to monitor transient events and so more than one person can 'speak' at the same time. Either participant can produce a response while the other is doing the same, because the responses can be 'read a little later'. Topics can intertwine in a way that is not possible in spoken or signed dialogue.[15] The example in Figure 5.1 will illustrate. Two topical threads, (a) and (b), are maintained simultaneously. The numbering is incremental by turn within each thread and time progresses from left to right.

Simple examples occur in the data because of the type of task the participants are engaged in, but conversational uses of the modality have been observed in which extended 'double dialogues' are maintained. The coordinated movement into and out of, and the maintenance of 'double dialogue' is discussed and illustrated more fully in McIlvenny (forthcoming).

Example 5 This example illustrates several interesting phenomena: pursuit of mutual orientation and intelligibility in a disagreement sequence; complementarity in same-speaker and cross-speaker action; gesture and speech coordination and recipient design; and participant design. Some of the following ideas on intra-turn

---

[15] Besides the unorthodox and comical dramas like the Theatre of the Absurd plays by Pinter or Ionesco that can have similar structures read into them.

coordination types will be illustrated (the bracketted comments show the restricted view in the typical 'interchange' model) :

(1) Self-coordination and repair (as opposed to 'here is what you have been waiting for' planned action and revision); example 5a.

(2) Recipient design in concurrency – repair, accommodation and redirection (as opposed to a 'take it or leave it' product); example 5b.

(3) Mutual management of opportunities for participation (as opposed to 'wait until I say' interchange); example 5b.

The basis for some of the analyses is derived from Schegloff (1984), Erickson and Schultz (1982), Goodwin (1981), and Goodwin and Goodwin (1987).

```
A: 1aaaaa          3aaaaa 4aaaaaaa 2bbbb 6aaaaaa
B:      2aaaaaaaaaaa       1bbbbbb  5aaaaa        7aaaaa
        !                  !                      !
        one thread (a).    thread (b) begins      thread (b) is
                           here.                  dropped here.
```

Figure 5.1

Example 5a, e.g. [M5: 1'36"-1'40"] The focus is on the utterance, "is the a- a one th one three oh three", by R, which illustrates some dynamics of self coordination in concurrent action. Just prior to the utterance, R had still not succeeded in achieving agreement with J by claiming, "yeah it is yes", with a pointing gesture to the screen coordinated with the last "yes". R responds to the uneasy silence, a potential disagreement, with a turn holding "ah", reaffirms, and then begins a repeat of the line on the screen. A hanging right-hand point and the gesture to the screen are both withdrawn at this important transition. This is in preparation for R to look away from the screen to check for evidence on the map surface and identify the referent, given J's potential disagreement. Because of this, J cuts short the reading aloud of the line at the beginning of the noun phrase. The noun phrase is restarted after orientation to the map, but then it is postponed for a moment for identification by gesture to be coordinated with the attempted re-reading of the noun phrase. The reading aloud is not itself evidence for identification, so it has to be coordinated with a demonstration of the source of evidence on the map surface. The evidence now found and displayed, R returns gaze to the screen, closely followed by J. So, in this example, a participant coordinates several complementary actions, but contingency leads to repair of turn construction. It is important to note that in any multi-modal system, the mere fact that complementary actions with durations arc possible and monitored, means that self-coordination will be problematic because of internal contingency, although it will be manageable. In addition, why bother planning and then executing an action when doing an action will uncover contingencies *in situ*?

Example 5b, e.g. [M5:.1'42"-1'48"] This example is concerned with recipient design in cross-speaker concurrency, and gesture overlap and competition. It is a good example of third turn repair and re-explanation – R finds that J's actions display a misinterpretation and so R attempts to repair this in third turn. J begins a turn, after R's prompts to respond affirmatively, with "no it's not". This is coordinated with a shift of gaze to the map and the beginnings of a pointing gesture to display evidence for disagreement on the map surface. However, R simultaneously begins a pointing gesture towards the screen. This could be because of the second noticeable absence of expected agreement or action after R's "Yes. (pause) Yes." and short gesture to the screen. The competitive overlap is resolved by R dropping out and monitoring J's action, but still holding the pointing gesture to the screen. In this case, speakerhood is a practical issue, so concurrent gesture is a local problem to be resolved. Immediately after, latching onto J's disagreement, R responds verbally and gesturally with a repair of the misunderstanding. The held pointing gesture is now read back into the flow of conduct, post hitch, by reading the screen text into the talk once again. It is withdrawn after the reading is complete. However, during the reading a second complementary display of evidence on the map surface is managed concurrently with the talk. So, in this example, the coordination of gesture in talk is subject to participant contingencies. It has to be repaired and accommodated on occasions of concurrent action and recipient monitoring.

The differences between speech and gesture boundaries can be seen in this example. In [M5: 1'50"-55"] mutual agreement is achieved and displayed finally, after all the work done by R in repairing J's misunderstanding. R is closely monitoring for evidence of trouble or agreement. J withdraws a pointing gesture, looks to the keyboard and screen, hesitating, and then agrees with "yeah". During this, R gestures to the screen with "yes". A clue to the progression towards agreement is found just after J hesitates and looks to the keyboard, e.g. the retraction of both the map pointing gesture and the just prior gesture to the screen, plus the overlapped "so say" by R . So, gesture and speech can overlap unlike the normative organisation of speech itself, even though gesture is associated with speakerhood. This is because gesture can be hung or delayed in progress and remain latent.

5.4.4   Conclusion and discussion

A user of a good system should feel that direct, continuous engagement is possible. This phenomenon is very like the way films and video give the appearance of continuous movement, by exploiting the propensity of the human vision system to fill in the gaps and 'see' movement. Up to a certain point, a series of still visual frames shown in quick succession will appear as a jumpy series of images. However, at the crucial rate, a perceptual 'illusion' of coherent movement appears, provided the images are sufficiently cohesive in sequence.

Will an illusion of interactivity be possible in engineering dialogue systems, drawing upon the illusion found in visual display technology? That is: will the user perceive not a series of discrete opportunities or at worst a sequence of system controlled and rare opportunities, but a continuum for-all-practical-purposes? And will this be so even though the space of opportunities and possibilities is engineered and not socially constrained? For example, in designing a future telephone dialogue system that will have the appearance of an 'open floor' of participation, will the users feel that the system is responsive to their interactive demands?

5.5   Conclusions

So what is possible? Well, the next cycles of design need to draw upon investigations like the above and engineer situated dialogue: **process, dynamics and presence**. The investigations motivate the exploration of intra-turn micro-dynamics: resources for routine coordination, rather than explicit verbal interchange. In essence, this means breaking up the monolithic turn, and taking local management and reciprocal contingency below the turn in HCI. Some of the issues which need study are:

- What frameworks for participation should be available in HCI? For example, when can the machine or user act? Is it possible for resources for the local interactive achievement of opportunity, possibility and significance to be engineered at the interface?   The problem will be to investigate the compromise necessary due to the difference in the machine's access to resources and the peculiar properties of machine artefact dynamics.

- Situated circumstances and events, e.g. time, pace, sequential order, transience, duration, etc. that are used to constitute significance of action or coordinate action, e.g. duration can be used projectively to coordinate simultaneity or conjoint action.

- Try to engineer not only local turn opportunities or transition relevance places (TRP), as in the work of Frohlich and Luff (1989), but also next relevance places (NRP), i.e. places where a relevant next is contingent on intra-turn backchannels or concurrent action.   Thus, explanation or advice can not only be interactive within the discourse or rhetorical unit but also *within the dialogue itself*.

- There is much research to be done on the relations between dialogue events, resources, and interactional/ conversational work done *in situ*. Because of the distinctive constraints and dynamics of interactive artefacts, new resources may emerge or special interactional work be required which will require creative design, e.g. specific confirmational work in 'open' floor telephony dialogue systems because of the temporal significance of irregular delays for the user. Levinson (1983) explains that a basic CA methodology is to recursively find structures and organisation by feeding analyses back into data analysis. An analogous method in interactive artefact design is to develop the system incrementally according to the practical contingencies of human-machine dynamics. It may be possible to engineer the dynamics of local specialisation and selection so as to allow adaption and transformation. However, any attempt in this direction will have to confront the problem of order and explain the stability of routine conduct.

A profitable line of development will emerge, partly from the pressure of analysing odd environments of technology-supported human activity and partly from the application of technology itself. This will be of immense benefit for the analysis of HCI and CMC, as well as human talk, and a beginning has been made for the data collection reported in this chapter. CA itself is indebted to the invention of the audio recorder and then the video recorder for its deeply empirical methodology. Now, the computer may advance the state of empirical work in a number of ways using multi-channel digital interactive video with computer graphics and analysis. First, traditional means of collecting data can be complemented by computer real-time trapping of events – monitoring of machine processes integral to the system operation in HCI and CMC – and signal processing technologies. Second, transcribing could be aided by combining visual and aural notation in synchrony with the video image, thus moving data recording closer together. Finally, the analysis itself could be complemented by statistical, database and selective printing facilities as well as the trickier aids to the process of analysis itself. However, the search for accountable details in conduct must remain a guiding principle and cannot be overtaken by technology.

The relevance of the investigations to embodied modelling has not been discussed in the previous section. However, the approach to interactive artefacts may combine well with it because the basic insights into embodied machinery, motivated by the study of human experience, and combined with the richness of interactive resources derived from human conduct, may help overcome the problems and limitations inherent in representational and mentalist approaches to interactive artefacts.

Finally, potential problems with and limitations to combining a computational perspective and an interpretative sociology will be briefly outlined. Does this mean divorce?

- From a humanistic perspective the issue of socially inappropriate technology seems to lead to an impasse for a human science and technology partnership. Even more, a careful consideration of possible insidious uses in society must remain in mind.

- A deep assumption that needs to be questioned is that of using a person as a model for emulation or aspiration. It is not at all clear if this is a good thing, or if it is unavoidable. Wynn (1980) argues that many characteristics are not required.

- What will happen to CA and the empirical descriptive enterprise? Formalisation may lead to emasculation and a diversion of resources onto restricted features of human dialogue. Human communicative action, like conversation, may suffer from everyday contact with talking machines.

- The representational metaphor in embodied modelling has obviously gone too far in some cases, but the possibility of avoiding a 'representation' has not yet been resolved. Only further experimentation to find re-explanations or rational reconstructions of phenomena that have been appropriated in the name of cognitive science will determine this issue. For example, just as Coulter (1979) recovers the social construction of cognitive terms.

- Just before the final question, the following argument by Woolgar (1985, pp.566-7) must be kept in mind as it forms the crucial backbone of debate. A sociology of machines, human-machines and humans should try not to adopt a stance on the debate over the distinction and primacy of human over machine in terms of concepts such as 'action' or 'social'. This should be true for research on artificial life and artificial intelligence, where the entrenched idea of the natural carbon-based nature of life and singularity of intelligence and sociality will need to be examined again and again.

- Finally, an interesting question to consider is: will people realise that conversation is important and something to be valued and respected – not idle chit-chat – once the talking machine is commonplace and can demonstrate its own simplicity?

Appendix

Example 1

(2-2) KP

This example illustrates the appearance of the visual communicative space from the perspective of the participants. It is taken from the later part of one experiment at a particular instant, viz. [M5: at 21'26"], and records exactly what appeared on the screen. There is no analytic transcription. (Only the result of the participant's self-transcription when constructing typed responses is displayed.) The top half of the display screen is windowed for participants D and M, and the bottom for J and A. The two windows are identical in function.

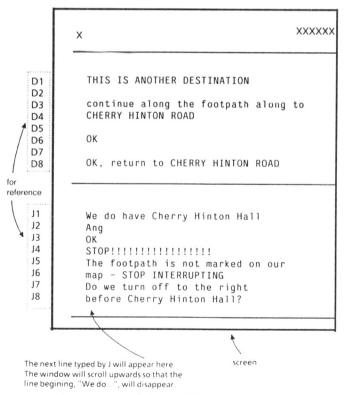

Figure 5.2

Example 2
(2-2) KP

This example illustrates the dialogue sequence leading to the display state in Example 1, e.g. [M5: at 21'26"]. D is typing for the pair D and M, and J is typing for both J and A. The transcription is abstract sequential with some chronos overlap. Notice that it reads like a normal line-by-line transcript record. However, much is lost by using this simple form of transcript for doing analysis in this case.

Note that lines 3 and 4 do not appear on the screen display. They were scrolled off the display by D's double spacing of responses. Line 5 was erased by D before typing line 7.

Example 3 *

Only two participants 'face' each other across the modality. Normally only the wider band that records the keyboard communication events is notated, but in this case and by accident, the gaze of one of the participants was recorded on video and is also transcribed. The flow of time runs from left to right. Notations of important time intervals, like pauses, are marked between vertical bars.

[M5: 19'04"-21'26"].

```
 1     J: We do have Cherry Hinton Hall
 2     J: Ang
 3     D: [The nusery is to the east
 4        of Cherry hinton hall.
 5     D: Ang?
 6     J: OK
 7     D: THIS IS ANOTHER DESTINATION
 8        continue along the footpath
 9        along to CHERRY HINTON ROAD
10     J: [STOP    !!!!!!!!!!!!!!!!!!
11     D: OK
12     J: The footpath is not marked on our
13        map -
14     D: [OK, return to CHERRY HINTON ROAD
15                          [STOP INTERRUPTING
16     J: Do we turn off to the right
17        before Cherry Hinton Hall?
```

Figure 5.3

---

*   The examples that follow in this appendix are quite complex. A little explanation of the format of the records will help in reading them.

Examples 4 and 5

These examples notate the features of two pairs of co-participants collaborating on a textual map surface, and communicating with the other pair through the computer-mediated modality. Unlike most CA transcription records there are 5 horizontal bars in the (2-2)KP record, and they are collected together in a bundle that represents the following simultaneous features. The middle bar represents the shared communicative space mediated through the keyboard. Above and below the middle bar are two pairs of bands that notate the speech, gesture and gaze of each co-participant pair. All 5 bars represent the flow of time from right to left. A slice through the 5 bars represents a moment in time, by which synchronies and concurrences can be mapped across modalities and participants. At the far left of each bundle of bands lie the letters: g, c and t. They notate the bands in the following way: g is for gaze; c is for conversation; and k is for keyboard. The seating positions and layout of the devices for examples 4 and 5 are illustrated in the plan in Figure 5.4. It is especially important in order to understand the concurrent pointing gestures in example 5.

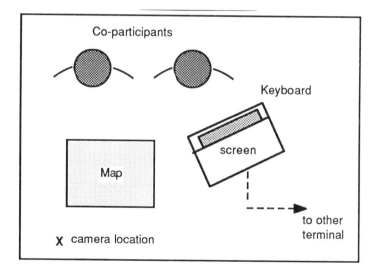

Figure 5.4

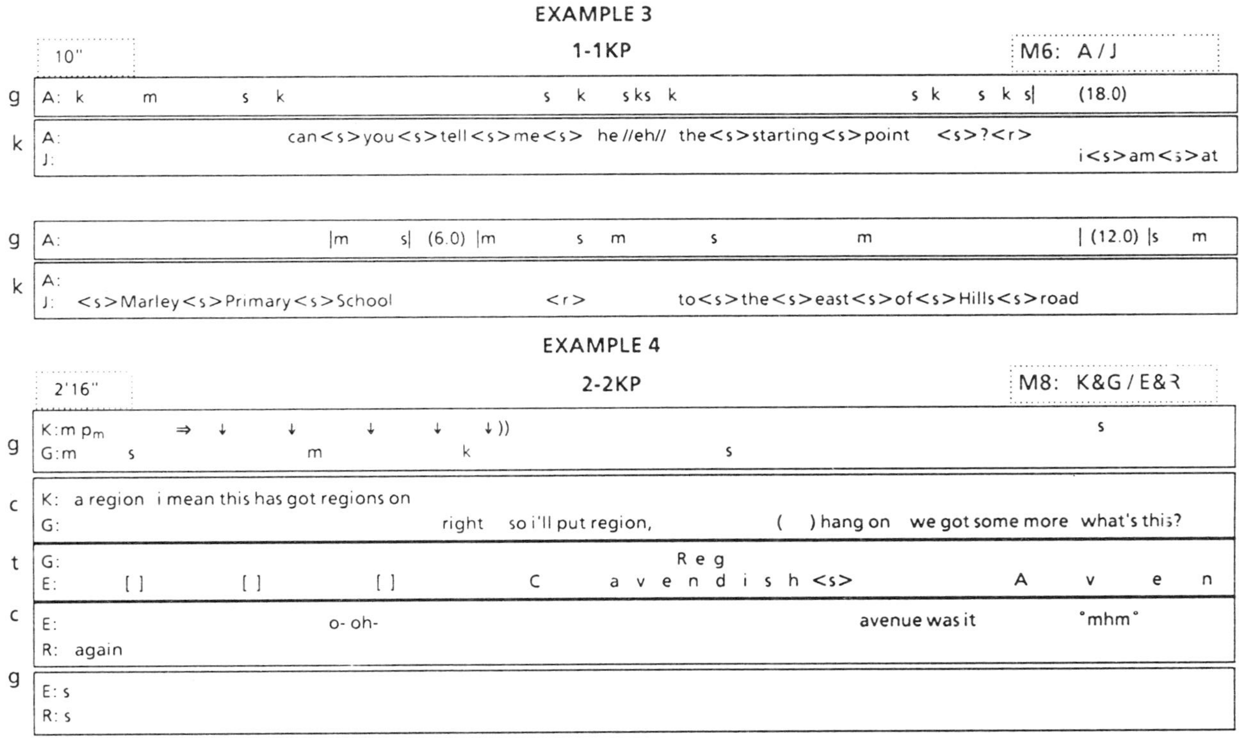

EXAMPLE 3

1-1KP

M6: A/J

10"

g   A: k   m   s   k   s   k   sks k   s   k   s   k   s| (18.0)

k   A: can <s> you <s> tell <s> me <s> he //eh// the <s> starting <s> point   <s> ? <r>   i <s> am <i> > at
    J:

g   A: |m   s| (6.0) |m   s   m   s   m | (12.0) |s   m

k   A: <s> Marley <s> Primary <s> School   <r>   to <s> the <s> east <s> of <s> Hills <s> road

EXAMPLE 4

2-2KP

M8: K&G / E&R

2'16"

g   K: m p_m   s   ⇑   →   →   →   →   →))   s   s
    G: m   m   k

c   K: a region i mean this has got regions on   right   so i'll put region,   ( ) hang on   we got some more   what's this?
    G:

                                      R e g
t   G: [ ]   [ ]   C   a v e n d i s h <s>   A   v   e   n
    E:

c   E: o- oh-   avenue was it   °mhm°
    R: again

g   E: s
    R: s

Figure 5.5

EXAMPLE 5
2-2 C(KP)

This is a complicated example with many illustrative features. However, only two will be discussed in the main text. The whole fragment contains a complex coordination of speech and gesture by J and R in managing a disagreement sequence - repairing misinterpretation and achieving agreement. At the beginning of this fragment, both J and R are working on constructing a communicative response. However, while J types the response, R attends to the other party's simultaneous current response. The problem is that J is still attending to the construction of an appropriate response when R talks on the other party's response. Two potential interpretations are relevant because of the differential in orientation. Consequently, J misinterprets R and a disagreement occurs. During the disagreement sequence and the repair of misunderstanding by R, neither party manages to coordinate mutual monitoring very well, even though they appear at a superficial level to be attending to each other.

The strips of conduct between the dash-dotted bars are the main focus in the text, with a particular interest in J&R. Remember g is for gaze; c is for conversation; k is for keyboard.

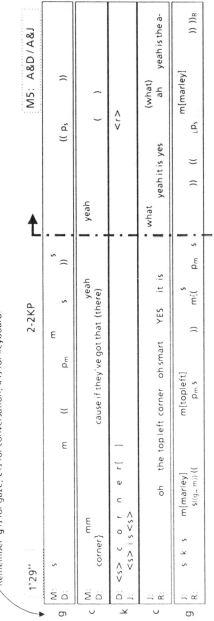

Figure 5.6

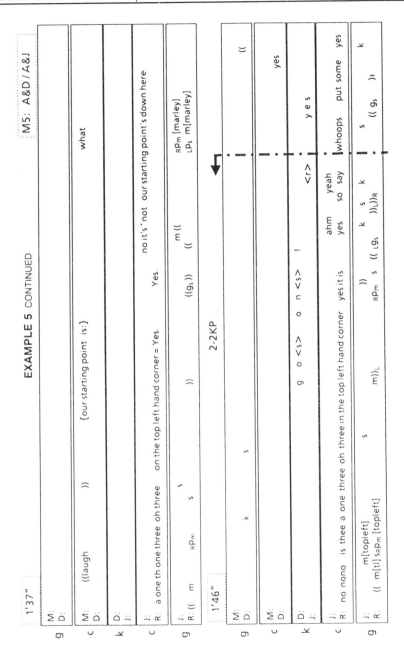

Figure 5.7

Acknowledgements

This research was supported in part by a grant from SERC, and was undertaken in the Department of Artificial Intelligence and the Department of Linguistics, University of Edinburgh. Thanks to my supervisor, Jim Miller, for his support and advice, and to Pirkko Raudaskoski and Colin Williams for helpful comments on draft versions. They helped reveal the background once again that is now all too transparent to me. Thanks to David Frohlich for suggestions on reorganising the draft, and to Anthony Finkelstein and Michael Wilson for insightful comments on the chapter. Ta to Graham Button, Rob Wooffitt and others for helpful discussions. Of course, all remaining errors are all mine. Draft document preparation facilities were generously provided by the Rank Xerox University Grants Programme. The final version was prepared using Mac Word 4.0 provided by the Humanities Faculty, Oulu University.

Chapter 6

Repair and Cooperation in Conversation

David Good

6.1 Introduction

It is not unusual, in human social interaction, for a conversation to go awry and for the contribution of a speaker to be misunderstood. Nor for that matter, is it unusual for the participants to decide that what was said should have been expressed differently. These mishaps and adjustments are reflected in conversation by the presence of what has been termed a repair-system (Schegloff, Jefferson and Sacks 1977). This enables either speaker or hearer to say something which is readily understood as amending what has already been said and not as furthering the existing line of a conversation. There is a preference for self-repair, i.e. for a speaker to amend what he or she has just said, but self-repair is not inevitable and the addressee may complete the repair if given the opportunity. Similarly, either self or other may initiate the repair sequence in which the amendment is offered. Repair sequences are ubiquitous in conversation and are handled with apparent ease. They rarely seem to cause any difficulties. This system is important for the development of natural language interfaces in a variety of different ways (see Raudaskoski this volume), and it is my intention in this chapter to add to that catalogue.

In developing an interface, a designer will make use of whichever pragmatic theories seem best suited to the task at hand. There are many different theories to choose between, but, in a rather crude way, they can all be placed into one of two groups. On the one hand, there are those which work with a very narrow view of what utterances contain, presume that the hearer can make a large number of assumptions about the speech situation, and propose that the hearer is able and willing to do an excessive amount of inferential work in interpreting an utterance. On the other, there are those approaches which stress the wealth of detail and information in what is said above and beyond the simple lexical content and syntactic structure, but pay little or no attention to the cognitive or computational capacities which underpin the use of this detail.

The former type has an obvious attraction for the computationally-minded system designer for a number of reasons. First, a number of theories of this type are couched in terms which reveal the pervasive influence which the computational metaphor has had in many of the human sciences since the mid-sixties. Second, they directly address processing issues on the assumption that all the basic syntactic and semantic processing has been done. This is usually the point at which pragmatic issues are considered within interface design. Third, the latter class of theory does not usually have much theory to offer, nor does it have a large number of findings in comparison to the proposed complexity of the conversational world. This attractiveness is, however, misleading and it is this misleading nature which I intend to illustrate by using a simple case drawn from my recent work on repair in a class of conversation which is normally associated with certain psychopathologies.

In what follows, I will begin by arguing that the use of data drawn from such environments can be extremely valuable for the study of normal conversational processes. I will then examine one case where the repair system is taken to an extreme, and draw various implications from it for the value of certain kinds of pragmatic theory in the development of computers that are competent conversationalists. In particular, I will consider a perspective which is widely adopted in the pragmatics literature. This perspective proposes that in the face of seemingly wayward, untrue or unhelpful utterances the hearer does not assume a corresponding attitude or state of mind on the part of the speaker, but assumes the opposite, and draws inferences which are in line with, and thus support, this assumption. In contrast my general proposal is that the assumption that the conversational other is a cooperative or rational person is not an inviolable part of the context and is created through what we do in the course of our social interaction. More specifically, I would propose that how the repair system is managed by the participants is crucial for the assumption that each will hold about the other being a cooperative or rational participant. Finally, I will conclude with some observations on the wider issues associated with repair in interface design.

6.2   Slips, schizophrenia and everyday conversation

The main empirical content of this chapter is a single brief interchange between a thought disordered schizophrenic and a clinical psychologist. On first consideration, such a small and difficult database would appear to offer little of relevance to the study of repair or cooperation. Almost by definition, it would seem to lack both elements, but I believe that deviant or extreme cases of this type can be extremely valuable in the study of dialogue in general, and these topics in particular. This belief is partly inspired by the example of work on slips of the tongue and aphasic syndromes, which has demonstrated the value of both pathological and normal errors to the study of language use and structure (Fromkin 1974; Cutler 1983). In other spheres too, the study of system failures has been well-rewarded, and there is no reason to believe that dialogic errors will not offer useful insights into normal conversational processes.

Among the first to suggest that cases of conversational breakdown might be useful for research into normal conversational processes was Labov. He and many other writers once argued that the most promising model for the analysis of conversational structure was a syntactic one based on the methods and formalisms which were being used to characterise the individual sentences in a language (see, for example, Labov 1972). If a syntactic analysis is to be successful, it must be possible to specify 'ungrammatical' conversational strings. Labov recognised this requirement, and offered cases (1) and (2) below as *prima facie* examples of 'ungrammaticality'. These cases came from patients who were said to be suffering from schizophrenic thought disorder and were taken from Laffal's earlier work on schizophrenia (Laffal 1965).

```
(1)
A:     I'm hot today
B:     No.
```

(2)

A: What is your name?
B: Well let's say you might have thought you
        had something from before but you haven't
        got it anymore.
A: I'm going to call you Dean.

(Labov 1972, pp.252-253)

As I have argued elsewhere (Good 1989) the examples of unacceptable conversational strings which he offered are not unacceptable in the same sense as an ungrammatical sentence and the notion of an ungrammatical conversation is itself incoherent. However, it is not incoherent to suggest that conversations might break down, we all know that they often do, nor that these breakdowns might be revealing about conversational structure and process.

The occasional speech errors of the normal speaker, and the chronic language deficits of the aphasic have both provided valuable data for the construction and evaluation of psycholinguistic models of normal phonological, lexical, syntactic and semantic processes. The restriction of this research strategy to these levels is probably as much a matter of historical accident as of reasoned choice. There are no obvious reasons for believing that analogous conversational breakdowns will not provide useful data, but nor is it obvious how one might simply extend this research strategy into this area. Our understanding of, and descriptive schemes for, these other linguistic levels is far more sophisticated and extensive than that which is available for conversation. Consequently, any use of conversational breakdowns must be more cautious and more clearly focussed on an existing claim or claims about some phenomenon. For this reason, it is likely that the specific difficulties which arise in conversations with thought disordered schizophrenics might be particularly interesting. Amongst these difficulties is a sense one gains that the schizophrenic participant in a conversation is not being particularly helpful or cooperative. This failing relates to a perspective which recurs in the pragmatics literature and which I noted in the introduction above.

While few authors still hold to the exact letter of Grice's original proposals on conversational implicature, the general spirit behind his framework is still held to be correct. He demonstrated how an apparent violation of the Cooperative Principle and its associated maxims could give rise to various inferences through a hearer's attempt to build a context which neutralises the transgression. Various authors have offered revisions of the maxims, and have sought to replace the quasi-contractual Cooperative Principle with

Rationality Principles and the like (see, for example, Kasher 1982; Leech 1983; Levinson 1987; Sperber and Wilson 1986), but the essential idea has been preserved. When faced with an utterance which apparently breaches the bounds of sensibility, the hearer should make whatever assumptions are necessary to bring it back into the fold of acceptability, and should not assume that the speaker is, in fact, not engaging in an intentional communicative act. However, most interlocutors find themselves unable to recontextualise many of the deviant utterances provided by schizophrenics, even though this may be possible when the utterances are removed from their original conversational setting.

All those who have followed the Gricean initiative have at one time or another cast a wary eye at those cases where an attempt to recontextualise an utterance is ill-founded, because there is, in fact, a breakdown in communication which is caused by the irrationality, uncooperativeness or similar shortcoming on the part of the speaker. For example, Kasher 1982, in defining his rationality principle includes the clause "When there is no reason to presume the contrary, take the speaker to be a rational agent", and others include similar caveats. An examination, though, of those cases where there is reason to suppose the contrary could prove to be an extremely useful way of highlighting the conditions an utterance must satisfy if it is to be taken as a legitimate conversational contribution. The schizophrenic often provides such material, and it would only seem sensible to attempt an analysis of why difficulties arise in those cases.

6.3   An extended repair sequence

The example I will be discussing below is taken from an interview between a a clinical psychologist and a patient who had been diagnosed as schizophrenic, and is a case taken from a much larger investigation. All the patients taking part in this study were given a copy of the story in (3), taken from Rochester and Martin (1977), and asked to read it. They were asked if they understood it and, when they said they had, they were asked to put it down and tell it to the interviewer from memory. If the story was deviant in some way or other, the interviewer would invite them to elaborate or be more specific in whatever way seemed necessary. They would continue the discussion of the story until it reached a natural conclusion.

(3)

A donkey loaded with bags of salt had to wade across a river. He slipped and fell and remained lying comfortably in the cool water for a few moments. Standing up, he noticed how much lighter his load had become because the salt had dissolved in the water. The donkey noticed this advantage and decided to use it the following day when he was carrying a load of sponges across the same river. This time, he fell deliberately but was badly disappointed. The sponges had soaked up a great deal of water and were far heavier than before. Indeed the load was so heavy that it drowned him.

(Rochester and Martin 1977, p.64)

The conversation between the clinical psychologist and the patient in the case I am presenting went on for a number of minutes and the section I wish to focus on was drawn from the early part of the conversation. A transcript of it is given in the appendix at the end of this chapter. There are several things to notice about this exchange.

First, and quite obviously, A's rendition of the story in lines 8-12 is less than perfect, and it displays various omissions, errors and obscure references which make it hard to understand as a repeat of the original. Also, as can be seen from the turns which follow his re-telling, it is interpreted in a very personal way. In short, A does not conform to our usual expectations of performance on a task like this.

Second, in other respects A is performing like any other competent conversationalist. Turn-taking seems unproblematic, adjacency pair structures are preserved (e.g. 14-17 and 18-21) and the recycling of 18-21 in a reduced form in 23-25 causes no problems.

Third, a more interesting and more important way in which A's ability to participate competently is revealed in the sequence which follows the problems caused for B by his reply to 26-27 in 28. B follows 28 with a query that claims that she did not understand A's reply. She initiates a sequence in which she seeks an amendment, alteration or elaboration of what A has said and he recognises the nature of her query by providing the reason in 31.

Jefferson (1972, p.304) studied repairs of this type under the heading of *misapprehension sequences*. The elements of such a sequence following a problematic item are: first, a demonstration by an addressee that the item was either misunderstood or not fully understood; second, a clarification or repair; and, finally, an acknowledgement of the acceptability of the repair and thus a closing of the sequence. The cycle may be extended by the first two items being reiterated if the clarification does not provide the person who initiated the sequence with what he or she needs. The three part nature of the sequence means that closing of the sequence is the responsibility of the addressee who initiated it and so that individual can recycle the sequence for as long as the original speaker is willing or able to cooperate.

In the turns which follow 31, we see a recycling of the initiation phase by use of a full restatement of 29 in 40, and by use of a simple but not fully accepting affirmation by B in 32, 42 and 44. 46 does not produce a response from A, but his preceding turns have claimed a self-evident quality to the explanation of everything by his status as genesis. 47 is hearable as a silence on his part which claims there is nothing more which can be said. This is supported by the angry quality to his reply in 51-57 in response to B's further extended recycling of the initiation in 48-49. As a result of this, we gain a comparatively clear, if somewhat strange, picture of the basis for his interpretation of the story and the context of his subsequent remarks.

This sequence suggests that A is at one level being a cooperative conversational partner. He can interpret B's initiation of a repair sequence based on the difficulties she reports with his contributions, and bears with her recycling of it over what is, by any standard, an extended period. It is by this performance that he establishes his cooperativity because it is in other-initiated repair sequences that the social fabric hangs in the balance. A failure to comply with the demand of a repair initiation places in jeopardy the whole basis of the exchange. Unfortunately, the way in which he complies with the request preserves only the structural characteristics of the exchange.

His problem appears to lie in the strange beliefs he holds about himself and his relation to the world and the fact that he cannot appreciate the problems his beliefs raise for the addressee when he or she is trying to comprehend what he says. While his speech shows many of the weaknesses which others such as Rochester and Martin have described, it is clear that he can recognise the need for a remedy to the problems he is creating when prompted to do so. His failing to take account of the addressee is not an all-or-nothing matter, as is shown by the extended repair sequence discussed above.

6.4   Relevance to the study of ordinary conversation

There are four observations which are prompted by this case and which are relevant to the choice of perspective in the development of natural language interfaces.

First, Grice himself suggested that the Cooperative Principle would have stronger and more interesting foundations if it could be reduced to being the consequence of a rational action on the part of the speaker, and several subsequent authors have agreed with him. Sperber and Wilson (1986) follow this line in part with their principle of relevance and argue that Grice's account overestimates the degree of cooperativity which must necessarily exist for communication to be successful. The case reported in the appendix and discussed above does, superficially, seem to support their view. Whereas Grice proposed that speakers should "make your contribution such as is required, at the stage at which it occurs, by the accepted purpose or direction of the talk exchange in which you are engaged" (Grice 1975, p.45), Sperber and Wilson argue that the only common purpose necessary for a genuine communicator and a willing audience is to have the communicator's informative intention recognised by the audience (1986, p.161). A and B, in their conversation following A's assertion that the story is about him, cooperate in the construction of a readily identifiable side sequence, and operate in a seemingly independent way at the level of the *ostensive stimuli*, to borrow Sperber and Wilson's term. However, this separation of activities would deny two important points. One, without a sequence the ostensive stimuli would have no medium within which they could be articulated. Therefore, imagined one-turn conversations aside, sequences are the *sine qua non* of communication. Second, there are good grounds for arguing that the expectations formed by the preceding turn or turns in a sequence are part and parcel of the ostensive stimulus. Generally, Sperber and Wilson work to a very impoverished notion of the character of an utterance and this is one more instance of this failing. Thus, while different domains of cooperation may be delimitable for the theorist, their separation for the participant interpreting an utterance may not be possible or even desirable.

In a spirit more in keeping with Grice's own suspicions, Kasher (1982) reduces the Cooperative Principle directly to his Rationality Principle in his analysis of the essential capacities of the minimal speaker. In restricting the object of study to the minimal speaker, he rules out various issues normally addressed within sociolinguistics, but it is not clear how sequential aspects of talk are to be handled. If they are included within the capacities of the minimal speaker, then the problem arises of how the cooperation they represent can be reduced to his rationality principle. If they are not, then the first point made against Sperber and Wilson would seem to apply.

However these objections are handled, the implication from the case discussed here is that there are at least two and possibly more ways in which Grice's Cooperative Principle is manifested in conversation, and that it is important for us to keep the different levels in view for analytic purposes, but to not reify the distinctions which follow.

Second, many readers will recognise (4) below, which has been referred to, rather appropriately given the current chapter, as the "Mad Passer-by Example". For those who do not recognise it, it is taken from Sperber and Wilson (1986).

```
(4)
Flag-seller:    Would you like to buy a flag
                for the Royal National
                Lifeboat Institution?
Passer-by:      No thanks, I always spend my
                holidays with my sister in
                Birmingham.
```
(Sperber and Wilson, 1986, p.121)

From cases such as these they offer an analysis of the class of cognitive activity in which hearers must engage to comprehend all sorts of communicative acts. A major contribution of their approach, they suggest, is the radical revision it offers for the psychology of utterance interpretation on how context is specified and deployed during comprehension,

> ....it suggests a complete reversal of the order of events in comprehension. It is not that first the context is determined, and then relevance is assessed. On the contrary, people hope that the assumption being processed is relevant (or else they would not bother to process it at all), and then try to select a context which will justify that hope: a context which will maximise relevance. In verbal comprehension in particular, it is relevance which is treated as given, and context which is treated as variable.

(Sperber and Wilson 1986, p.142)

In many respects, the Passer-by's utterance in (4) presented the Flag-seller with the same problems as B faced when hearing lines 28 or 32 in the Genesis transcript. We do not know how the Flag-seller understood and reacted to this justification for sales resistance, but the implication in Sperber and Wilson's work is that it is quite possible, if not probable, that the full import of the utterance was understood (i.e. that anyone who spends their holidays in Birmingham will not go near the sea, and therefore will not need the services of the RNLI). Similarly, if B had reflected on 28 or 32 then it is quite conceivable that something like the material A offered subsequently could have been brought to mind; not necessarily in that exact form, but certainly of that ilk. Indeed, a small sample of administrative personnel in my home department were able to do so when presented with a transcription of the dialogue up to that point. Therefore, one would not wish to quibble with their proposal that it is possible to do this, because it is. However, it is equally true that B did not act in response to 28 or 32 in a manner which suggested immediate comprehension of the full possible import of those turns. It might be suggested that she did not do so because those turns still had a large measure of ambiguity, even when one has created the appropriate context. Consider, though, the exchange in (5) between my wife and myself.

> (5)
>
> A1:   Did you know Mary McAndrew?
>
> B1:   Yes, she was the first medical student I met in Dublin.
>
> A2:   Well, we've got a new graduate student in the department who's the spitting image of her.

The key things which A and B know about each other and which are relevant to an interpretation of this dialogue are given in (6).

> (6)
>
> (1) B knows that A has never met Mary McAndrew, and does not know what she looks like.
>
> (2) B knows that MM has an identical twin called Rachel and does not know that A knows this.
>
> (3) B knows that A knows 1 and 2.

This is a relatively well-defined, small context and the possible interpretations of A2 are very few. Indeed, the only one which comes to my mind is that Mary McAndrew's twin sister is this new graduate student, but B did not produce any of the alternatives in (7) as her next turn, instead she offered (8). There then followed a lengthy exchange in which A revealed the identity of the new graduate student, and the basis of A2.

```
(7)
- How is she getting on?
- Did she say how Mary is?
- I didn't know her sister was doing
  psychology.
```

```
(8)
- Uhnnh?
```

Thus, the failure of B to infer the identity of the new graduate student cannot be attributed to any indeterminacy or uncertainty as to the inferred proposition. These failures, though, in the transcript I have presented, and the dialogue in (5) are not clear counter-examples to the Sperber and Wilson position. They are aware that communication is prone to failure (1986, p.45) and that intuitions as to the interpretation of particular examples are difficult to interpret as evidence (1986, p.119). One might say, therefore, that cases such as these are uninteresting, because they simply represent instances where the full potential for processing the utterance had not been exploited. To say this would be to miss two important points about utterance processing which are apparent from these cases.

First, writers such as Sperber and Wilson place great emphasis on the internal cognitive aspects of utterance interpretation and pay little attention to the external interactional aspects. Clearly, though, context may be found as much through the latter route as through the former, and both are undoubtedly important in the communicative process. The possibilities afforded by both routes reflect the fact that speakers and addressees are under various constraints which at times work in opposite directions. For example, if I hear some oracular utterance I may indeed wish to ponder its significance and take time before I reply to it. But if I am to be the next speaker, then I may not be able to delay because the previous speaker has addressed me directly, and I do not wish to delay. The demand to speak sooner rather than later will run counter to that desire to reflect on the utterance. The way out of this impasse is to explore the context and relevance of the previous turn by interrogating that previous speaker. Thus the interactional and intellectual demands would be reconciled. How these internal and external strategies relate to one another is obviously an open matter, but it would not be too unrealistic to suggest that through the acquisition process children learn about the creation of frameworks for interpretation and how to create them by being participants in conversations where these things are done externally.

Second, if we focus only on those internal processes, this may lead us to radically over estimate the scale of the problem which faces the hearer as a real-time participant in a dialogue. This may only mean that we propose a larger or more powerful processor than is actually required, and not that we make some fundamental error in our description of its characteristics. However, the history of cognitive psychology and related disciplines is replete with examples of lines of enquiry where this kind of over-estimation has arisen. As a result, fundamentally different types of process have been proposed to solve problems which in practice do not exist. This was a recurrent theme in a number of the early attempts at simulating cognitive processes such as vision and problem solving. There is no reason why an incomplete or incorrect specification of the task which confronts some cognitive system designed for utterance interpretation should not suffer the same difficulty.

The third main point follows from the second and is essentially the methodological side of the coin. As we have already noted, Sperber and Wilson and others are aware that pragmatic intuitions are fraught with difficulty. However, simply admitting the difficulty does not produce some mantra which when chanted will ward off the evil spirits of methodological inadequacy. The fact that I can perform certain intellectual operations when prompted with a printed example in a suitable theoretical context does not mean that my sense of those operations is of any interest at all. To emphasise this point, consider (9).

(9)

Sugary pobbles.

I first saw (9) in the London Times beneath a grid with some of the squares blacked out, and the indexing system stated that (9) indicated a word of seven letters. In short, (9) was a cryptic crossword clue. At that time I enjoyed doing this kind of crossword, and was for a while tolerably good at them. Consequently, I immediately knew that the answer was "lactose". Now if anyone suggested that this skill provided direct evidence for the rôle of contextual factors in the lexical access process in the comprehension of spoken language, I am sure it would be the case that some methodological pedants would raise more than the odd eyebrow. But in the study of utterance pragmatics we seem to entertain something of this nature. This is not to say that our intuitions and sense of the character of various forms may not be used widely in the analysis of the concepts we use and may borrow from ordinary language. But theorists such as Sperber and Wilson propose themselves as offering a psychological performance theory where they are specifying the character of psychological processes and they curse the connotations that the ordinary language term 'relevance' may bring to mind. If one is concerned with a performance theory then performance data, be it of humans or computational simulations, should be given much greater precedence.

Finally, it has proved very popular in theories of pragmatic processing to view conversation as made up of a series of turns which fully determine their interactional status and are unchangeable once offered. Some authors have argued, see for example Turner (1970), that this view is fundamentally mistaken and that the status of a turn and its significance can evolve and develop in the light of the subsequent turns in a dialogue. Cases such as the one considered here reinforce this position and demonstrate that the relevance and interactional significance of an utterance, no matter whether that term is construed ordinarily or in some technical way, is often achieved over a stretch of conversation, and that identifying the cognitive demands with a single turn is quite misleading. A, in the light of B's questioning, makes line 28 intelligible and relevant (if a little unusual) in the subsequent exchange and it seems more sensible to see that exchange as part and parcel of the accomplishment of the significance of a stretch of dialogue rather than individual turns.

6.5   Conclusion

In an earlier paper (Good 1985) I proposed that computational approaches to conversation would be well-advised to attend to the lesson provided by attempts to develop machines which could perceive the visual world. Initially, that work ignored the wealth of information in normal scenes, and worked on the assumption that informationally impoverished environments such as the 'blocks world' coupled to high-powered computational machinery provided an appropriate exemplification of the normal case in which prototypes could be developed. This resulted in a considerable over-estimation of the computational needs of a visual system at different levels of the processing system, an incorrect formulation of the problems to be solved and the procedures required. This point automatically directs one to more empirically based studies of conversation for an account of the content of that information-rich conversational world and a recognition that *post-hoc* pragmatic intuitions can be misleading as an indicator of the real-time on-line demands which face the ordinary speaker or hearer.

In this chapter I have developed this argument using the case of repair. Much of it has focussed on the work of Sperber and Wilson, but, hopefully, it is clear that the points which have been made are relevant to the class and manner of theorising which their approach represents. The other chapters in this volume also demonstrate that the environment in which any competent computational conversationalist is situated, is quite different from a linguistic blocks world and that the development of adequate systems will depend on understanding the complexity of that environment.

Appendix

```
1   A:  Right
            |
2   B:      Alright

3           (.)

4   A:  Yeh

5           (..)

6   B:  Okay can you tell me (0.1) whats in the story.

7           (1.4)

8   A:  It tells me that the donkey had a problem about is

9       foot (.) and er::: it had sand in it and 'nd as he

10      crossed the water it made it easier.  When he wanted

11      to come back it made it (.) harder (1.4) erm (3.2)

12      thats about it really.

13          (2.2)

14  B:  Righ::t can you remember- anything that was there

15      were two crossings weren't there?

16          (.)

17  A:  Yeh=

18  B:  =can you remember what was different about the two

19      crossings?

20          (.)

21  A:  ur:::m (7.6) no

22          (2.8)

23  B:  not at all
```

```
24          (.)

25 A: no=

26 B: =hmm (.) Did-and what do you think the story might be

27    about?=

28 A: =me

29 B: in what way?

30          (1.3)

31 A: er:::: (.) because I'm genesis.

32 B: mye:::h

33          (0.9)

34 A: so the story relates to what I'm saying, that p-

35    whole para- all of that (hh) is me.

36          (.)

37 B: can you s-
                  |
38 A:             -every sentence everything there is there is

39    me=

40 B: =can you say in what way

41 A: genesis, it speaks for itself genesis

42 B: yehp=

43 A: =tshh::: the smashing of glass

44 B: yehp

45 A: explains genesis

46 B: yehp

47          (3.1)
```

```
48 B: 'n can you tell me- I mean just because I dont (.)

49     understand (.) how this story relates to that.

50        (1.4)

51 A: because if you say a word like it (1.3) thats a-

52     thats genesis you see everything relates to each

53     other it doesnt matter if that was the story if you

54     gave me another story or a packet a cigarettes (.)

55     I'd just say yeh its a packet a cigarettes. we all

56     have that in common so we- it makes genesis coz

57     everything is- relating to everything else.

58 B: right=

59 A: =atoms understand atoms

60 B: right

61        (3.4)

62 B: and the smashing of glass?

63 A: tsch:::: theyre like aha the singers aha hah::::

64     tsch::: genesis pink floyd the wall yno all the

65     groups supertramp.

66 B: hmm

67        (3.7)

68 B: 'n (.) did you find this interesting?

69        (1.6)

70 A: find what interesting?

71 B: the story

72 A: no not at all.  I found it pretty dull and boring
```

73   (3.9)

74 B: what would make it more interesting?

75 A: (hh) I dont know

76   (5.6)

77 B: Alright can we try something else?

Chapter 7

Repair Work in Human-Computer Interaction

A Conversation Analytic Perspective

Pirkko Raudaskoski

7.1 Introduction

The chapter begins with a short review of repair in different areas of study. Two views are contrasted: the artificial intelligence (AI) approach taken in human-computer interaction (HCI) and the approach taken in Conversation Analysis (CA). Following this introduction, an implementation of some repair strategies is described in the domain of a telephone dialogue system. An experiment to evaluate the implementation is described and some results from the experiment are given. Finally, some general conclusions on the applicability of the approach taken are drawn.

7.1.1 What is repair work?

Usually, repair is seen as something not wanted; the smooth progress of the interaction has been disturbed and communication has broken down. This is the view that most artificial intelligence and human-computer interaction researchers take of repair work. Linguists have taken little interest in repair work. Instead, they have concentrated on the syntax or semantics of individual utterances studied in isolation from their context. The pragmatic approach to aspects of linguistic studies, for example discourse analysis (DA), has brought the structure of conversations and interactions under analysis although repair has not been studied as such. There are many methods of study in DA, varying from the syntax-like analysis of discourse segments to sociolinguistic (cross-cultural) studies of different discourse styles.

Conversation Analysis is an interpretative approach to studying conversational phenomena with no predefined model for conversation. In CA, repair is understood to be something essential for successful human communication; one of the resources for managing meaning in conversation. Within this perspective, repair becomes a condition, not a hindrance, for a successful conversation. It is not something extra but an essential part of the way humans communicate.

7.2   Two perspectives on repair work

7.2.1   A CA approach

Misunderstanding, and the repair work that follows it, have been a major concern of CA studies. It is understood as part of a larger phenomenon, for example as part of a problem of intergroup communication involving gender and cultural differences. These social reasons are important when the target of study is the injustice caused by different usage of language. Although the reasons might differ, it is well-known that misunderstandings occur in almost every interaction. Studies of the structure of misunderstandings and the way they are repaired have found that there are preferred types of repair. Most preferred is 'self-initiated self-repair', then 'other-initiated self-repair' and, finally, 'other-initiated other-repair'. This implies that it is mostly the person who causes the misunderstanding who does the repair in conversations. One way of avoiding explicit correction of the speaker is to help them to self-repair.[1] There are **transition spaces**, or transition relevance places (TRPs), in talk

---

[1]   The hearer cannot always be sure if there is anything to be corrected.

where another person can yield the floor and start a turn. These transition spaces are very short time periods during which the change of the speaker is possible. If a speaker attempts to take a turn outside these spaces then it is understood as an interruption. Repair initiators are found at certain places in conversation relative to these transition spaces. Self-initiated self-repair is ordered in two groups. The most preferred place to initiate self-repair is within a turn, rather than at a transition space before the other interlocutor(s) manages to take a turn. In the following (hypothetical) example, speaker A self-initiates self-repair in the transition space and, in the following turn, speaker B replies with an attempt to other-initiate self-repair.

```
(1)
A:      I'm going to see a film by Bergman
        tonight - no, by Pasolini.
B:      By who?
```

These example repair initiations occur either in the same turn or in the following one, but there are instances of third and even fourth turn repair that result from the sequential nature of conversation. The analysis of a turn-at-talk given in the next speaker's turn can show misunderstanding and it can then be repaired in the third turn. In fourth turn repair it takes longer for the repair initiator to realise misunderstanding has occurred. For example, a question is asked and an answer is given. This answer may fit at the local point in conversation although it does not show that the speakers have a different idea about what is going on. Only in the next turn does the questioner show the answerer the misunderstanding of the original question. Here is a fictional example of this phenomenon.

```
(2)
A:      Do you want to go out?
B:      Yes.
A:      Here's your coat.
B:      Oh, I thought you meant tonight.
```

In this example B's first turn does not show any misunderstanding of A's original question. It is only after A's second turn that B realizes the misunderstanding, shown by B's second turn.

Repair is obviously the result of some kind of misunderstanding but as CA analysts attempt not to make presuppositions before analysing conversations what triggers this recurrent phenomenon is not self-evident.[2]

However, Schegloff has studied the reasons for repair work (Schegloff 1981). He sees the sources of trouble to be divided into two groups: problematic reference and problematic sequential implicativeness. Reference problems are what are usually understood as repair initiators, that is, it is not clear what an expression is referring to (cf. the HCI work on repair). Sequential implicativeness refers to the adjacent positioning of turns-at-talk and how this is used to make sense of the interaction. Every next turn shows an analysis of the previous one, giving the producer of the prior turn a chance to comment on the analysis. If it shows misunderstanding, a repair can be initiated in the following turn. In terms of sequential implicativeness, Schegloff found four different types of misunderstanding (where next, third and fourth turn repair are at issue).

(1) Misinterpreting jokes as serious or vice versa (resulting in either the "I was just kidding you" or "No, I mean really" type of repair initiator).

(2) Taking the action the turn-at-talk was meant to do as something else (especially interpreting anything as a complaint. This is something people are very sensitive to in interaction).

(3) Mixing the constructive and composite readings of an utterance (e.g. "What are you afraid of?" can be understood as a request for information or a reassurance. Each have different requirements for the next turn).

(4) A joke-at-first, where a misunderstanding is feigned to make a joke before giving the actual serious answer or turn.

The last of these makes use of a common source of real misunderstanding. It shows that achieving misunderstanding actually requires **understanding** misunderstanding.

---

2   Even mishearings can sometimes be used strategically.

For example.

```
(3)
A:      Are you into Artificial Intelligence,
        too?
B:      No, I prefer the genuine thing!
```

Though the reasons for repair can be looked at, most CA researchers think that there is no clear connection between the source of trouble and the type of repair work adhered to (Schegloff et al. 1977). The recurrent patterns of repair are thus not bound to what triggered the repair. Jefferson sees the structure of repair as a side-sequence where the following usually happens: (1) the source of trouble is identified (e.g. "Do what?" or even more interesting syntactic constructions: "You did what where?"), (2) the source of trouble is clarified, (3) the repair initiator shows the repair has been understood, for instance: "Oh, I see..." (Jefferson 1972). Similarly, Schegloff has found recurring items of speech in repair sequences, like "No, I mean..." starting a third turn repair, followed by some additional material depending on the meaning of the turns (whether they have been complaints etc.). Repair work is thus structured when it occurs, but predicting the points in a conversation where it is most likely to emerge is impossible.

7.2.2   An HCI approach

In AI models of dialogue, repair work tends to be connected with misunderstanding and the computer system not working "intelligibly". This leads to the view that the computer's model of the user is not good enough. Miscommunication results from the fact that the computer system is unable to infer well-specified plans from what the speaker says. Some HCI researchers have drawn similar conclusions from experiments undertaken with human subjects. In these, experts usually have to tell novices how to perform a specified task (e.g. to build a working tool from its pieces). If, from the recorded conversations between the participants, the hearer does not understand what is going on, it is seen as some deficiency in the hearer's capability to infer the plans of the speaker (e.g. Goodman 1986). This type of result is quite easily obtained from a task-oriented dialogue which involves frequent reference to objects in the world and where reference confusion is bound to occur.[3]

---

[3]   See also Robinson (this volume) for a criticism of task orientation in HCI.

The importance of observing real conversations (both between humans and between humans and machines) is usually acknowledged by HCI researchers. Notions similar to the results derived from CA studies have also been expressed. McAllister (1987), for example, gives an account of a third turn repair when she is modelling what is happening in a certain type of misunderstanding, though she does not use CA terminology. She is interested in what she calls spontaneous explanations, i.e. third turn repair giving users information they do not explicitly ask for. This recognition is then used as a basis for user (and system) modelling, where the aim is to describe the actual (cognitive) process of what is happening when a turn is analysed. McAllister sees this as a conflict between the models of the world that the participants have and gives a computationally effective solution to match these models and generate user dependent answers.

Understandably, the situation most commonly observed in HCI studies is that of users at a terminal and the difficulties that occur. Mostly, these studies concentrate on the system failing to understand the user. However, a dividing line between user and system misunderstandings is not so easy to draw. Schuster and Finin (1983) are interested in the users' potential for misunderstanding the system's advice or instructions. Their solution is to enable the machine to detect what kind of misunderstandings the user has about the system. In CA terms, the system should be able to initiate a third turn repair. As in human-human interaction, this is the way Schuster and Finin want the computer to share the responsibility of making sense. Therefore, HCI research has realised the importance of examining real conversations and, though conversations are not analysed, CA methods are being combined with traditional plan-based approaches (cf. Cawsey, Norman and Thomas, Finkelstein and Fuks this volume).

7.2.3   Basic differences

One of the differences between the HCI and the CA approach is how the trouble source is classified (which again depends on the general analysis of interaction). In CA the emphasis is on the sequential organisation of talk into turns and the local nature of conversation. In HCI the division is made on the basis of what kind of communication failure is in question, i.e. whether it is a reference failure, a model failure or a difficulty in a belief model (cf. Ringle and Bruce 1982). Thus, CA researchers concentrate on the patterns of the conversation sequences which handle misunderstanding and HCI researchers   are   more   concerned   about   the   cause   of miscommunication, looking at natural conversations to discover types of trouble sources.

HCI researchers, like Goodman, claim that spoken communication should be studied in order to find out what is happening in natural language which is full of "complex, imprecise, or ill-devised utterances" (Goodman 1986, p.273). This attitude is quite common among HCI research. The language that people use in their everyday environment is something "impure" and "untamed"! What the computer then does in human-computer interaction is "the transformation of sequences of complex, imprecise, or ill-devised utterances into well-specified plans that might be carried out by dialogue participants" (Goodman 1986, p.273). Conversational language is, of course, ill-formed if it is looked at from the point of view of a parser in a computer system. When humans converse they have, in addition to brainpower, the whole context of the interaction to draw clues from, whereas a computer has to rely on the limited verbal input it gets from the user. When this limited source of information is then translated into plans, goals and beliefs, errors are bound to occur. Though understanding events as actions with intentions behind them may not be what people do to make make sense of one another.

Both CA and user modelling are concerned with the interpretation of a speaker's turn. It is in the process of analysing a turn that misunderstandings occur. In user modelling the process itself is the centre of interest, whereas from the point of view of CA the misunderstanding is manifested in the sequential organisation of conversation.

7.2.4 Meaning and repair work

The claim HCI research makes about conversation is that we are aware of the beliefs and goals of our interlocutors. Misunderstandings are thus explicable within the framework of world models of all the participants. It is obvious that we have to understand what another person says if we are going to have a successful discussion with them or know what a speaker is saying in a monologue or even understand words spoken in isolation. However, this process of understanding is far from simple. Although meaning is affected by syntax (e.g. questions are different from assertions), speech act theory showed that the mapping of meaning onto sentence form is not enough (as in the case of indirect speech acts). When words are put together to form utterances the meaning is not compositional (i.e. it is not the sum of the meanings of the words because context even affects what is meant by a word).

CA shows that very little, if anything, can be said about the meaning of an utterance outside the conversational context, **meaning is continually negotiated**. Thus, repair work is part of a negotiation process. This includes cases when something particular to a speaker's turn is not clear to the other speaker (next turn repair initiator), cases when the original speaker realises that the participant has misunderstood something (third turn repair), and cases where one of the participants understands later that he or she has misunderstood something (fourth turn repair). Repair is a reflection of the continuous monitoring and **interactional reconstruction** that is going on in conversation (Fox 1987). It is a tool for reconstructing the meaning all the time that we are conversing. Whatever the reason for repair, once initiated, the way it is done is very predictable, e.g. "No, I mean..." usually starts a third and "Oh..." a fourth turn repair. A fourth turn repair indicates not so much a misunderstanding of something specific about the other speaker's turn, but that the first interpretation, or understanding, was wrong.[4]

If conversation involves achieving understanding then repair work is an essential part of the apparatus, enabling the participants to check their interpretations or correct the other person's interpretations. As was mentioned in an earlier section, there are certain preferences as to how this is done which seem to be a result of the social nature of spoken communication (e.g. you want to protect your 'face' and save your co-speaker's 'face' by preferring self-repair to other-repair). As there are recurrent patterns in the way, in general, the resources of a conversational situation are used and, in particular, for repair, these findings should also be useful for designing human-computer interfaces. According to Frohlich and Luff "it is feasible to model some of the dynamics of natural conversations in a human-computer interaction by local management of the dialogue" (Frohlich and Luff 1989). The 'Advice System' they describe gives the user the possibility, at certain structural points (transition relevance points), to take the floor and initiate a repair sequence. This results in other-initiated self-repair by the system. By selecting "What?" the user is given an explanation of the meaning of the system's previous turn

---

4   Jefferson calls a next turn repair initiator "misapprehension", which starts a
      side sequence of talk, and claims that "Oh" starts a turn where the side
      sequence is terminated ("Oh" indicating that the hearer has understood what
      the speaker means, as in fourth turn repair). According to Jefferson
      continuation of the original talk is done with "so" (Jefferson 1972).

and by answering "No" to the system's prompt "OK?" the user has a means of showing misunderstanding. These devices allow the user to initiate 'system' repair and so are a form of 'other-initiated self-repair'. It should not matter to the computer system if it got an other-initiated other-repair (last in the preference list), but a user, familiar with certain types of repair initiators, should find the self-repair initiators more natural and convenient.

The checking of understanding implemented in the Advice System is a specific way of dealing with miscommunication, viz. the speakers check to make sure that the other person is following, and if not, actively search for sources of trouble. However, in human-human communication this type of prompting is used for a social purpose, to show that the speaker is interested in the hearer, and not necessarily as a prompt for misunderstanding.

7.3 Choosing and implementing the domain for the study

The CA approach was chosen as the starting point of the study to be described in this chapter. On the one hand, the approach taken here does not imply that CA findings can easily be transferred into a formulation of rules that a computer program could apply. On the other hand, it is not as critical as that of Button's in this volume, rather it aims to bring the CA perspective to the whole concept of HCI (see, for example, McIlvenny's contribution in this volume on the pragmatic use of CA for the design of interactive artefacts).

One of the requirements for a domain for this study was that it should be one where the pressures of human-human conversation would be present and where it would be possible to anticipate the repair work that could emerge (at least from the point of view of system design). Therefore, it was important to choose the domain carefully. Of course, the domain had to be computationally feasible. The domain had to be kept simple, so that it would be possible to concentrate on exploring certain features of a system. Rather than show global plan-based behaviour, it was important to show the localness of dialogue in a dialogue system where possible misunderstandings would be clear. This was not a strong constraint because situated action is productively troublesome and contingent. In every dialogue the course of the dialogue is decided on the spot with repair as an essential part of the interaction.

Choosing a domain also restricts the type of dialogue phenomena that can occur. The first restriction was to human-computer interaction; HCI interfaces include keyboard systems, menu-based keyboard systems (which either allow users to choose a command from a menu or build up sentences the computer can understand) and speech systems. Speech and keyboard systems offer very different kinds of interactional resource. Work has been done to compare the two modes of typing and talking, either directly to the computer or to a human interpreter (Hauptmann and Rudincky 1988). As the approach taken in this chapter is conversation analytic the most natural choice for the domain was where spoken language would be used. Studies like Hauptmann and Rudincky's show that there are "significant differences in the usage of spoken language compared to typed language, and several phenomena which are unique to spoken or typed input respectively". The main differences are that a larger range of words are spoken and spoken utterances are longer (Hauptmann and Rudincky 1988:, p.83). Although the language that people use when talking to a computer system differs from that of everyday talk, CA methods can still be used to analyse it. In fact, one common view, expressed by Frohlich and Luff (this volume), is that the organisation of spoken language would not be appropriate for visible language. The choice of spoken language also meant that problems that occur when users manipulate menu-based systems can be ignored.

The chosen domain was a telephone answering system that could send messages and store them for play-back. Being a voice system it would reflect the pressures of a real-time conversation. For the evaluation session of the system it was also important to have a domain which would be as natural as possible. In the near future, computer systems could be built that allow users to check and leave messages (e.g. the Sundial Project described by Gilbert et al. in this volume).

7.3.1   The repair strategies implemented

Only next turn repair initiators were considered. This was because, first, localness was a major theme of this research and, second, because it was interesting, in terms of CA, to see how people manage and make sense of repair work in human-computer interaction.

The devices chosen for the system's repair initiation were the following:

(1)   Specify the source of trouble: "Leave what?".

(2)   Imply not hearing or understanding the user: "Sorry?".

(3) Have a guess what the user tries to do (on the basis of synonymous expressions): "Do you mean leave a message?".

(4) Give specific choices for the user: "You can leave messages or listen to messages – select either".

(5) Precheck everything is alright: "So you want to ---- is that right?".

Devices (1)-(3) can be expressed in CA terms as other-initiated self-repairs. Whereas (4) only implicitly repairs; it explicitly states what the user can do within the system. It might be regarded as a next turn other-initiated self-repair or, less likely, as a third turn repair-initiator (cf. "No, I mean you can..."). Device (5) cannot be regarded as a repair initiator in CA terms; it is a mere check of understanding.[5]

While the users are given opportunities for repair, it has to be noted that there is no way of telling **where** in the dialogue they would adopt these repair opportunities. The meaning of the turns of a carefully predesigned system might turn out to be something totally new for individual users. It is impossible to foretell what kind of dialogue precedes or follows some point in a dialogue system. It is not predictable whether the user will make sense (or nonsense) of a system's turn. Therefore, only general repair initiators can be made available to a user. The following repair initiators were allotted to the user:

(1) Specify the source of trouble: "Do what?".

(2) Imply mishearing: "Sorry?", "What was that?" etc.

The user was allowed to use these two initiators anywhere in the dialogue. As simple misunderstandings might arise anywhere in the interaction with an experimental voice system this is a plausible assumption to make.

7.4 Evaluation

The importance of evaluation to the design of human-computer interfaces is acknowledged by HCI researchers. It is necessary to study

---

5   In fact this type of utterance can begin with "so" (which also precedes a fourth turn repair). As it would look like a summing up of what was said before it would be a kind of preclosing for the whole encounter.

not only how people communicate between themselves, but also the specific nature of human-computer communication and the pressures of (spoken) communication. Systems have to be designed in cycles where evaluation and reimplementation are as important to the final artifact as was the original design.

Carroll and McKendree (1987) stress an empirical methodology for designing expert systems from the point of view of behavioural psychology. They see evaluation as being important for developing advice giving systems "for even if current questions of technical possibility were to be settled with overwhelmingly impressive software, we would still be gambling that the type of advisory facilities developed would be usable by, and desirable to, real people" (Carroll and McKendree 1987, p.28). This also holds true for evaluation from the CA point of view. Even if a system had all the knowledge of the user it could possibly have it still would have to be able to manage the contingencies of conversation in a human-like way to be user friendly. In their evaluation of a telephone information system, van Katwijk et al. (1979) showed that the users found the most annoying features of the system to be its unnaturalness, bluntness and lack of clarity.

Thus, it was both because of the general importance of evaluation to the design of computer interfaces and to answer specific questions of the extent to which resources of repair work could be used in a computer dialogue system that the investigative experiment was necessary. The evaluation was carried out in order to study the overall pressures of spoken conversation and whether the repair strategies worked in practice; for example, the evaluation should show how users analysed the system's repair initiators *in situ* and whether they adopted any of the possible repair initiator resources provided.

7.4.1   The method

For the evaluation an experiment was designed where the system was simulated on the phone. What the users said was typed into the system by a simulator who also read the system's answers to the user. Of course, this meant there was a delay in answering.

Two preliminary tests were done before the actual evaluation session: one where a student used the system in a keyboard mode and one where a student used a telephone to call the system (i.e. his turns were typed in for him). The latter of these was to ensure that it was possible to realise the setting of the evaluation as it was planned. The final test was carried out with three secretaries who, after reading an instruction sheet, phoned the system, left and checked messages according to those instructions. The simulator was also the designer of the system and secretaries were chosen because they were used to the task. The subjects did not know exactly what would happen in the experiment, or its purpose. An office in the AI Department of Edinburgh University was used for the experiment and the system was run from a terminal in the office. The simulator answered the phone, and a microphone attached to it was used to record the session. When the phone rang in the office the system was started, the simulator switched the recording on, answered the phone with the system's first turn (holding the receiver on her shoulder) and was ready to type what the user said.

In addition to tape recording, a script was stored of the simulator's transaction with the system. This script was used as a basis for the transcription of what was actually said, though in the three sessions what was typed in was not identical to what was said on the phone. The names of the participants were changed to preserve anonymity and when the user did not use the anticipated form of "yes" or "no" this was replaced by the 'proper' form. This kind of manipulation of the system's turns was regarded as acceptable because the main purpose was to test repair strategies and not the matching procedure of the program.

To end the session, the subjects were asked two questions: how did they find the system in general and what did they think about the delays in the system's turns?

7.4.2   Main results of the evaluation

As the experiment was carried out in real time, it was interesting to see how, on the one hand, the subjects modified their general turn-taking strategies and, on the other, to what extent this basic feature of conversation was a source for misunderstandings (i.e. that it was not anticipated).

The readiness of the subjects to adapt to the system was no doubt due to their own working environment where they are familiar with writing down dictated text, communicating with foreign speakers of English, etc. – one of them actually dictated what she wanted to say when she heard the typing of her turns on the phone. All the subjects coped easily with the delays. The only thing that they found difficult was not being allowed to use pronouns (this may have been due to the fact that it was mentioned separately in the instruction sheet). All subjects knew that they had talked to a simulated system.

Two of the five possible repair strategies for the system and two for the user were not used in the sessions. The reason for this could either be that the expectations in the program design were wrong or that the sessions were not long enough to elicit all the repair strategies.

A transcript, based on the script and tape, of one of the shortest telephone dialogues is given below. The transcription conventions were as follows:

The system's turns (S:)

UPPER CASE   What the system printed out and was read over the phone.

< >   Text in the system's responses that was not read over the phone.

[ ]   Overlapping speech, e.g.

> U: [What? S: Do] you...

where "What" and "Do" overlap.

The user's turns (U:)

UPPER CASE   What was said but not typed in (for various reasons) by the communicator.

lower case   The communicator's typed response on the basis of what was heard on the phone (even when starting a sentence).

" "   What was typed in but never said (either by mistake or not).

[ ]   Overlapping speech .

```
(4)
 1    S:   HELLO - WHAT DO YOU WANT TO DO?
 2    U1:  hello has it thats pirkko has HAS fred sent
 3         any messages [hello
 4    S:                    A MES]SAGE FROM WHO PLEASE?
 5    U1:  has fred sent any messages
 6    S:   SO YOU WANT TO LISTEN_TO A MESSAGE FROM
 7         <HELLO HAS> FRED <SENT ANY MESSAGES> - IS
 8         THAT RIGHT?
 9    U1:  yES CAN I LISTEN TO ANY MESSAGES FROM FRED
10         PLEASE
11    S:   SORRY NO MESSAGES
12         IS THIS ALL?
13    U1:  "no" has eve sent any messages
14    S:   LISTEN_TO A MESSAGE FROM WHO?
```

```
15   U1:  eve
16   S:   SO YOU WANT TO LISTEN_TO A MESSAGE FROM EVE
17        - IS THAT RIGHT?
18   U1:  yES PLEASE
19   S:   SORRY NO MESSAGES FROM EVE BUT THERE ARE
20        MESSAGES FROM THE FOLLOWING PERSONS (EMMA
21        EVELYN)
22        -- DO YOU PERHAPS MEAN ONE OF THEM?
23   U1:  no FRED OR EVE
24   S:   OK. IS THIS ALL?
25   U1:  no
26   S:   <WHAT ELSE DO YOU WANT TO DO?>
27   U1:  iD like to LEAVE a message "to" FOR eve -
28        CAN YOU SAY THAT JUDY IS AT HOME - A MESSAGE
29        FOR EVE
30   S:   YOU CAN LEAVE MESSAGES OR LISTEN TO MESSAGES
31        - SELECT EITHER
32   U1:  just to leave a message "to" FOR eve AND I'D
33        LIKE TO LEAVE A MESSAGE FOR FRED
34   S:   SO YOU WANT TO LEAVE A MESSAGE FOR EVE - IS
35        THAT RIGHT?
36   U1:  A message for eve that's correct
37   S:   WHAT IS IT THAT YOU WANT TO DO THEN?
38   U1:  CAN YOU SAY THAT   judy is at home
39   S:   DO WHAT?
40   U1:  judy is at home
41   S:   YOU CAN LEAVE MESSAGES OR LISTEN TO MESSAGES
42        - SELECT EITHER
43   U1:  i want to leave a message for fred
44   S:   SO YOU WANT TO LEAVE A MESSAGE FOR FRED - IS
45        THAT RIGHT?
46   U1:  "y" FOR FRED THAT'S CORRECT
47   S:   PLEASE GIVE THE MESSAGE
48   U1:  right judy is going
49   S:   ALLRIGHT -- THE MESSAGE ** <RIGHT> JUDY IS
50        GOING ** IS TO BE GIVEN FOR FRED. IS
51        [THIS ALL?
52   U1:  THAT'S RIGHT] yES
53   S:   BYE BYE THEN
```

It can be seen from this example the main reasons why what was typed differed from what the user actually said. These were:

- When something was simply not heard, or misheard, or something was left out by mistake (lines 2-3, 27, 32, 36).[6]

---

[6]   These communicator's misunderstandings were limited to mishearing prepositions and names.

- When what the user said would not have affected the system's reaction, and so the process could be made quicker (lines 9-10, 18, 23, 38).

- When there was something implicit in the user's turn that needed to be made explicit for the program (line 13).

- When the user's complete turn would have caused difficulties in the system's next turn, i.e. the user talked too much (lines 27-29, 32-33).

- When the content of the user's turn was not expressed in the form expected by the program (line 46). Note that the system's turn on line 23 was not read aloud. This was because it would have disturbed the flow of the dialogue (interrupting what the user was saying on line 27) and what the user said in her turn (line 27 actually fitted this unread question.

What the simulator left as unread from the system's turns was extra material (from the user's previous turn) that would have made it impossible for the user to understand the system's turn.

This transcript shows that the user was able to communicate with the system. The subject goes through the tasks given to her of checking and leaving messages.

The delays in the system's answers were quite quickly adapted to, especially as the sound of typing could be heard on the phone. All the participants thought this was not disturbing. The only point where the delay appeared to cause the user to repeat was at the beginning of the first test (lines 1-5 above). Here the user repeats her first turn, overlapping the beginning of the next system turn.

7.4.3   Channelling the user

One of the functions of the system's repair initiators was to narrow down the users so that they gave only the expected information (and gave it in elliptical sentences). On line 5 in example 4, the system's question was meant to channel the user to answer with a name or a preposition and a name. Instead, the user's answer was different. This answer resulted in a long turn from the system (lines 6-8). The difficulties of channelling show that humans can be verbose. It is difficult to channel them to answer with one word answers. For example, the user's answer to "A message from who please?" was never answered as shortly as was expected (see example 5). Usually it was answered without ellipsis. In comparison to the question, only "please" was left out, contrary to what was expected in the original design.

```
(5)     S:    A MESSAGE FROM WHO PLEASE?
        U2:   ER a message from "ali" ALISON
```

Even with yes-no questions, where short answers would be easy, expansion was more a rule than an exception. In a turn starting with "yes" this makes little difference, because what follows usually confirms the "yes" by repeating the command once more, and the system's reaction will fit in (as in lines 6-12 of example 4). Ignoring what comes after a "no" sometimes makes the system have the appearance of being blunt or unfriendly, as happens on lines 16-29 in example 4, repeated below.

```
(6)
16    S:    SO YOU WANT TO LISTEN TO A MESSAGE FROM EVE
17          - IS THAT RIGHT?
18    U1:   yES PLEASE
19    S:    SORRY NO MESSAGES FROM EVE BUT THERE ARE
20          MESSAGES FROM THE FOLLOWING PERSONS (EMMA
21          EVELYN)
22          -- DO YOU PERHAPS MEAN ONE OF THEM?
23    U1:   no FRED OR EVE
24    S:    OK. IS THIS ALL?
25    U1:   no
26    S:    <WHAT ELSE DO YOU WANT TO DO?>
27    U1:   iD like to LEAVE a message "to" FOR eve -
28          CAN YOU SAY THAT JUDY IS AT HOME - A MESSAGE
29          FOR EVE
```

In this example, the first expansion after "yes" is again harmless ("yes please"). What appears after the first "no" ("Fred or Eve") is obviously an attempt by the user to check if there are messages from either Fred or Eve. The system ignores this and goes on to inquire if the user wants to do anything else. Here again, the user continues right after the "no" (the system's turn is not read aloud). Although here, expansion after the "no" was anticipated by the program.

Of the system's repair initiators, (2), i.e. "Sorry?" and (3), i.e. "Do you mean...?" did not appear at all. The reason for this was simply that the system's repair strategies were randomly selected and these simulations were too short to elicit all the possible strategies. The users never used the repair mechanisms available to them, though it was mentioned in the instructions that this was possible. This may be due to the fact that users are very tolerant when they know that it is a computer system they are talking to. Therefore, they consider nothing from the system striking enough for them to show that they did not understand or that the system's turn is not appropriate to the context. It could also shows how flexible human beings are in making sense of a situation. They interpret the system's turns on the spot, sometimes giving a turn quite a new meaning from that intended when the system was designed.[7]

```
(7)
34   S:    SO YOU WANT TO LEAVE A MESSAGE FOR EVE - IS
35         THAT RIGHT?
36   U1:   A message for eve that's correct
37   S:    WHAT IS IT THAT YOU WANT TO DO THEN?
38   U1:   CAN YOU SAY THAT  judy is at home
39   S:    DO WHAT?
40   U1:   judy is at home
41   S:    YOU CAN LEAVE MESSAGES OR LISTEN TO MESSAGES
42         - SELECT EITHER
43   U1:   i want to leave a message for fred
```

In the excerpt shown in (7), from the dialogue in example 4, the user's first turn was not changed into a "yes" or any of the alternatives expected for an affirmative answer. The system therefore regarded it as a negation and went on to ask what the user wanted to do. The user, oriented towards the dialogue on the basis of what had happened and what she had said, gave the system's turn a new interpretation: that the system was asking her for the content of her message. Even the system's next turn, which was meant as a repair initiator indicating that the system did not understand what the user wanted to do, was reinterpreted as a request to clarify the message and the user obediently repeated the message. The following system's turn was a repair initiator again, but the user's interpretation was that the system had continued after sending a message to Eve, repeating the possible actions that can be performed by the system. The user then went onto her next task of giving a message to Fred. This imbalance between the user's and the system's abilities to make sense helped to create a smooth communication between a user and a computer, but this had dangers. In (7) the user thought that her task was done while the computer was still trying to elicit an 'understandable' turn from her. The task never was completed!

---

7   This statement can be made safely, though what the system actually answered was sometimes modified (i.e. something was left unread) on the phone. What was left out was always extra material that would have blurred what the purpose of the system's turn was.

7.4.4 Special features of the spoken dialogue

Another script of a session where a student used the basic core program in a terminal simulation (i.e. typed his turns) provided some data for contrasting the spoken and written mode. There was some overlapping of speech in the spoken mode, occurring when the system had a longer turn that ended with a request for confirmation or a yes-no question. For example, in (8) the user's "no" does not overlap with anything, but comes within the system's turn.

```
(8)
S:    SO YOU WANT TO LEAVE A MESSAGE FOR
      ALISON
U2:   NO
S:    - IS THAT RIGHT?
U2:   no I want to leave a message for eve
```

Another major difference between the spoken and written simulation was that speakers tended to expand their turn when a single "yes" or "no" was expected (the program allowed for expansion after "no").

```
(9)
S:    SO YOU WANT TO LEAVE A MESSAGE FOR <ID
      LIKE TO LEAVE A MESSAGE FOR> FRED - IS
      THAT [RIGHT?
U2:        yes] YES I WANT TO LEAVE A MESSAGE
      FOR FRED
```

Out of 35 yes-no questions, 23 were expanded; the remaining 12 answered with a single "yes", "no", or corresponding expression ("that's right" etc.). This lends evidence to the results of Hauptmann and Rudincky's study (1988) where they contrasted different modes of interaction and came to the conclusion that spoken utterances tend to be longer than typed ones. Answering with expansion was idiosyncratic: one subject almost always produced single word answers.

7.4.5 Initial ideas on redesign

The evaluation showed the most crucial changes needed for the program. These are:

(1) Understanding synonyms for "yes" (e.g. "that's correct") and the cases where the affirmative is not first in the turn.

(2) Adding "tell" and "say" as synonyms for "leave".

(3) Fnding the most powerful channelling forms of questions.

(4) Developing the system so that it initiates third turn repair. On lines 39-42 in example (4) something like "No, no, what is meant is that you can leave messages etc." should be said to make it clear to the user that her/his turn was not understood.

The first two of these were added to a later version of the program. More experimental work is needed before the third change could be made and basic research is required for the fourth one to be successfully implemented. However, it is important to implement a third turn repair initiator to ensure that users make sense of the system and do not have a wrong idea of what the system has done.[8] Fourth turn repair would demand human-like capability from the system. Its implementation is therefore not feasible in the near future.

As for the evaluation itself, the callers could hear the typing when they were waiting for the system to answer. It would be interesting to see what would happen if there was complete silence. From studies of normal conversation it would be expected that callers would not have kept silent during the delays but would interpret the delays as something going wrong, or preceding dispreferred turns. In the experiment described here, the sound of typing was a useful resource for callers, who used it to know when they were not meant to talk, indicating the usefulness of audio cues to telephone dialogues.

7.5 Conclusions

Not only is CA useful for HCI design but, as long as the restrictions of human-computer interaction are taken into consideration, computer systems can also be used to test the findings of CA. The design of natural language front-ends has been based on research into isolated utterances (from the tradition of syntactic and semantic research) and user modelling. Both of these are very individualistic. Isolated

---

[8] Another solution to the problem of making sure that the user correctly interprets the system's repair initiators is **not** to aim at human-like conversation with computer systems. Instead of adopting human-like repair strategies the system would simply state that it does not understand. This would help the users because they would know exactly what the system wanted.

sentences are even less context dependent than the idiosyncrasies of user modelling. Clearly, this chapter has an opposite approach, building on the social and public nature of language. The study of the ways in which humans communicate has shown that people are capable of exploration and finding the best way of getting themselves understood. This should be remembered in HCI studies. People change their style of speaking until the system understands, but this process needs resources like repair to enable the mutual achievement of meaning. These types of resource are even more important in human-computer dialogues because the system does not have the human capacity to 'understand' what is going on.

The domain of a telephone dialogue system is ideal for research into comparing human-human and human-computer communication, as the situation resembles, more than any other encounter with a computer, that of a human-human conversation. Therefore, further research into HCI using this specific domain would be useful. This is specially true as human conversational behaviour on the phone has been studied and has provided a lot of data for investigating this type of communication. If the point of departure in building experimental or real telephone dialogue systems is that misunderstanding is one part of understanding, it should be feasible to get more user friendly computer interfaces.

When the essential resources for human-computer interaction are discovered, the results will not only help in building better systems, but they will also pinpoint some basic features of human communication in general. Thus, interdisciplinary studies into conversation and dialogue will be fruitful to both research traditions.

Acknowledgements

I would like to address special thanks to the following persons: Dr Elisabet Engdahl and Dr Helen Pain, who supervised my M.Sc. dissertation, and further to Paul McIlvenny and Alison Cawsey for good advice and criticism.

Chapter 8

Conversation Analysis and Specification

Anthony Finkelstein and Hugo Fuks

8.1 Introduction

We may crudely distinguish two broad approaches to the software development process, each of which views specification in a slightly different way.

The dominant research approach is that of formal development. In this approach a high-level abstract specification is made in a precise and analysable form, generally using discrete mathematics or logic. The description is verified and validated through the application of automated reasoning. An executable system is derived by the use of correctness-preserving transformations, automatically applied where possible. Subsequent system maintenance is done by changing a high-level specification and replaying the transformations to re-generate the system.

The approach on which most industrial practice is based follows a staged model of the software development process in which there are distinct requirements and design phases, each of which is completed when a specification is delivered. 'Formatted' representations, generally diagrams, with loosely defined syntax and semantics are used to support each phase. Diagram editing and consistency checking tools can be used to verify the requirements and the design. Validation is by inspection and walkthrough.

What both approaches have in common is the central rôle that they ascribe to specification. The construction of an exact description of software services, and the constraints under which those services are provided, is critical to the effective development of that software.

'Specification-in-the-large', that is the development of specifications for systems of substantial complexity and scale, mirrors 'programming-in-the-large' in raising a variety of difficulties that lie beyond the (non-trivial) clerical problems of handling large amounts of information. One such difficulty is that of specification from multiple 'viewpoints'.

'Specification-in-the-large' is, an activity in which there are many participants – clients, systems analysts, engineers, domain experts and so on. Each has differing perspectives on and knowledge about the object system, as well as a variety of skills, rôles and so on. In some cases these perspectives may be based on contradictory understandings. To construct a specification the participants must cooperate, that is, contribute to the achievement of a joint goal.

Existing specification schemes, methods and tools are generally based on specification by a single participant and refined using examples that consolidate this weakness. Our research objective is to develop a detailed (and, where possible, formal) understanding of specification by multiple participants so that we can both support the construction of specifications and reason about the process of specification itself.

We have constructed a preliminary model of specification by multiple participants in which the development of a specification is viewed as a conversation. The model deploys some formal apparatus, dialogue/commitment logics, taken from work on the foundations of logic, and an approach, cooperation and negotiation, from work on distributed artificial intelligence. We are extending this model using techniques and insights drawn from conversation analysis.

In this paper we will briefly discuss why we believe an examination of conversation may shed light on the process of specification. We will illustrate the development of a dialogue (or discourse) analysis based model and give a sketch of how it can be extended using conversation analysis. A short account is given of observational studies and specification support tools related to our approach.

The paper is based around an extended example. The example is not taken from a live software development project but has been constructed to illustrate our approach. This will not be our only violation of the spirit of conversation analysis.

The example reflects our interest in what might be termed 'fine-grain' software development modelling. By fine-grain software development modelling we mean the analysis and description of the detailed structure and organisation of development activities. In general this structure and organisation is ignored by those who are concerned with modelling software development at the level of tool invocation and inter-working (Kaiser, Feiler and Popovich 1988). We suggest that many important gross features of software development such as verification, validation and cooperation (Finkelstein 1989a) arise from the complex interplay of fine-grain activities. These features of software development are not simply embedded in a matrix of routine 'house-keeping' tasks. Rather, they are emergent properties that derive from the underlying fine-grain organisation.

8.2 Why conversation?

Before introducing the model it may be useful to examine the intuitions that prompted us to look at conversation in the first place.

The most significant informal motivation for using an understanding of conversation to develop a model of the construction of specifications is readily available. If we observe, naively, what happens during the process of specification we notice three features: participants talking to each other, participants writing documents, participants exchanging documents.

The setting for these activities generally consists of client(s) and specifier(s) sitting face to face across a table – the client explaining the requirements and the specifier occasionally asking guiding questions, seeking clarification, pointing out inconsistencies and raising unanticipated consequences. Interleaved with this spoken interaction are periods during which the requirements are documented. Throughout the process documents are exchanged, some containing further details of requirements on the part of the client, others containing preliminary documentation prepared by the specifier.

The spoken interaction, which appears to occupy the bulk of time devoted to specification, is readily recognisable as conversation. It may in addition be interesting to view the exchange of documents as a silent (but expressive) dialogue.

The specification process described above uses natural language. Hence, building representation schemes and selecting the appropriate conceptual categories for them, based on the way in which requirements are expressed in natural language, appears to have been a good way to develop schemes with higher expressiveness (Balzer, Goldman and Wile 1978). The approach is exemplified by "Gist" and "Pure Tell" (Horai, Saeki and Enomoto 1987). It is not a great leap of the imagination to extrapolate from this to using the structure of conversation as an overall setting.

Conversations mirror specification in that they both display physical distribution and cooperation through the interaction of multiple physically and logically independent participants.

Conversation, like the specification process, is flexible and dynamic. The shape of a conversation is not typically determined in advance but evolves in the light of issues brought to the fore during the course of that conversation. Participants continuously make moves to realise their objectives based on the revealed state of play. Contributions to the conversation make 'sense' only in their immediate conversational context.

8.3 Example

Jeff, Tom, Mike and Sue are involved in the specification of software to support the preparation and assembly of user manuals for a range of widget production tools. Jeff is a technical editor and knows all about how documents are prepared. Tom is the librarian. He knows all about the categorisation, version control and storage of documents. Mike is a salesman. He knows all about how manuals are assembled from the collected documents to meet the requests of customers. Sue is a software engineer. She knows about the needs of the software designers and, because she is experienced in dealing with technical documentation systems, about some possible problems which may occur in such systems.

Jeff, Tom, Mike and Sue meet to write the specification. After introductions and preamble the meeting gets underway. We join it some time after its start. On occasion, we may need to present fragments of the conversation out of their temporal order so as to illustrate important features of our analyses.

8.4   Dialogue analysis

Our analysis of the example begins with a preliminary model based
on dialogue analysis. The techniques we use are largely drawn from
dialogue and commitment logics (for a more detailed discussion of
these, see Hamblin 1971 and Fuks, Ryan and Sadler 1989). Similar
approaches have been developed by Mackenzie (1981, 1985) whose
work has formed a basis for the model.

```
[A] Jeff:    Documents  can  either  cover  new
             features or be a modification of a
             document  that  has  already  been
             issued.
```

In our preliminary model we distinguish two parts of the locution
act [A]: a locution act modifier (in this example an assertion, it is the
case that documents can either...), and a statement (in this example,
documents can either cover new features or be a modification of a
document that has already been issued). Our model uses the
following modifiers:

```
assertions, to be read as "It is the case that
Statement";
denials, to be read as "I deny that it is the
case that Statement";
questions, to be read as "Is it the case that
Statement?"; withdrawals, to be read as " No
commitment to Statement";
challenges, to be read as "Why is it to be
supposed that Statement";
resolution demands, to be read as "Resolve
whether Statement" .or "Resolve a potential
inconsistency in your commitments".
```

Statements are constructed in a propositional language which
includes negation, conditional propositions and conjunctions of
statements.

```
[B] Tom:     All documents are assigned a
             category.
```

[B] can also be broken down into a statement and a locution act
modifier, but we can make some further observations. Tom follows
Jeff and there has been a change in rôles. Jeff, who was the speaker, is

now the hearer (assuming he has not left the room) and Tom has
assumed the rôle of speaker. We model this as a succession of
locution events in which each locution event is represented by a
triple:

```
<Stage [marks the progress of the dialogue, stage,
stage+1 and so on], Name [of the current speaker],
Locution Act>
        [C] Sue:     Are modified documents assigned a
                     category?
        [D] Tom:     No, modified documents are not
                     assigned a category.
```

In [C] Sue asks a question, is it the case that...?. It is immediately
followed by an answer in the form of a denial. We note that there are
syntactic relations between these locution events. It would not make
any sense for Tom to follow Sue's question by a statement on some
completely different topic, or in certain circumstances by another
question. We model these syntactic relations in the form of dialogue
rules. Thus in the example above, the following rule applies:

```
Dialogue rule Quest (Questions):
After the questioning of a statement
(questions(Statement)), the next locution event
must be either the confirmation of that statement, or
the withdrawal or the denial of that statement
(asserts(Statement), withdraws(Statement) or
denies(Statement)).
No legal dialogue of length stage+1 contains a
locution event
<stage-1,hearer,questions(Statement)> unless it
also contains an event
<stage,speaker,asserts(Statement)> v
<stage,speaker,denies(Statement)> v
<stage,speaker,withdraws(Statement)>.
```

```
        [E] Tom:     There may be many current releases
                     of any given document.

        [F] Mike:    A manual consists of all the
                     current releases of documents in
                     the categories associated with the
                     tool owned by the client making the
                     request.

        [G] Sue:     So, duplicate documents are allowed
                     in a manual!
```

What is happening in this exchange? Tom makes a statement [E] which is heard by Mike, Sue and Jeff. Nobody objects and Sue feels it is safe to assume that everybody is committed to that statement and its consequences – duplicate current releases. In other words, Sue feels that Tom, Mike and Jeff have 'signed-off' the statement and taken some responsibility for its consequences (Winograd and Flores 1986; Thimbleby 1988). We note that locution acts, such as the assertion of a statement, establish (and remove) commitments. This is modelled in the form of commitment rules which define the relation between locution acts and commitments. A simple instance of such a rule might be:

```
Commitment rule W:

After a withdrawal the statement is removed from the
speaker's commitment store, the hearers store remains
unchanged.
After <stage,speaker,withdraws(Statement)>
    committed(stage+1,speaker)=
        committed(stage,speaker) - {Statement}
    committed(stage+1,hearer)=
        committed(stage,hearer)
```

Mike now makes a statement about how a manual is constructed [F]. Sue thinks she has spotted a potential inconsistency and tries to probe it by attempting to get Mike to commit himself to the statement that duplicate documents are allowed in a document [G]. The conversation continues.

```
[H] Mike:   No, I am not committed to duplicate
            documents being allowed in a
            manual.
[I] Sue:    Well in that case resolve your
            inconsistency with Tom.
[J] Mike:   I no longer hold that there may be
            many current releases of any given
            document.
```

In [H] Mike refuses to accept (effectively withdraws) the direct consequences of his commitments and Sue pounces by demanding that Mike resolves his inconsistency as in the following rule:

```
Dialogue rule Resolution (abbreviated):

The participant must adjust his commitments if s/he
withdraws/challenges an immediate consequent of
his/her commitments.
No legal dialogue of length stage+1 contains a
locution event
<stage-1,hearer,resolve(ConjunctionOfStatements)>
unless it contains an event <stage,speaker,Act> and
either:
Locution Act is withdraws(Statement) and statement
is one of the conjuncts of ConjunctionOfStatements.
or
Locution Act is withdraws(Statement) and statement
is one of the conjuncts of the antecedent of
ConjunctionOfStatements.
or
Locution Act is asserts(Statement) and statement is
the consequent of ConjunctionOfStatements.
```

Mike resiles from his previous position [J]. This now leaves Mike free to challenge Tom and sort out the confusion over current releases.

```
[K] Sue:    Why are modified documents not
            assigned a category?


[L] Tom:    Because modified documents are
            automatically given the category of
            the originating document.
```

In [K] we can observe Sue challenging, a special way of requesting an explanation of, a statement about document modification. Tom provides an answer to the challenge [L]. Sue now knows (and is committed to) that modified documents are not assigned a category and that modified documents are automatically given the category of the originating document. She also knows that the two are logically related: the fact that modified documents are not assigned a category implies that modified documents are automatically given the category of the originating document. In our preliminary model, the way in which these logical relations are established and maintained is given in argument forms which are embedded in special commitment rules. For instance:

```
Commitment rule G:
```
After an assertion (AnotherStatement) which occurs as
a reply to a challenge (**why**(Statement)) both
participants are committed to the reply
(AnotherStatement) and to the conditional
(AnotherStatement -> Statement).
After <stage,speaker,**asserts**(AnotherStatement)>
where the preceding locution event was
<stage-1,speaker,**why**(Statement)>

> **committed**(stage+1,speaker) =
>   **committed**(stage,speaker) U
>   {AnotherStatement, AnotherStatement -> Statement}
> **committed**(stage+1,hearer) =
>   committed(stage,hearer) U
>   {AnotherStatement, AnotherStatement -> Statement}

> [M] Sue: Why are modified documents
>   automatically given the category of
>   the originating document?

Our preliminary model is extremely sparse. By basing our
approach on what is in essence a formal model of argumentation
there are, aside from the well known difficulties of dialogue analysis,
practical limitations in both the underlying language and the features
of conversation we can capture. It is possible to build *ad-hoc*
extensions. For example, in [M] we can see Sue making another
challenge. This repeated request for an explanation, familiar to
parents of small children, is a typical elicitation tactic. Tactics of this
form could be modelled as special program-like scripts. For instance:

```
procedure refine;
begin
     repeat
            why;
            assert
     until
            goal
end;
```

Unfortunately, extensions of this form tend to introduce more
problems than they solve, such as, in the case of this example, how
are tactics identified, and what constructs are appropriate for such a
scripting language.

8.5   Conversation analysis

It has been an interesting, and unexpected, result of our work on applying dialogue analysis to specification conversations that a very limited model can account for a large range of gross features of that activity. These include simple elaboration and verification tasks. The formal basis of our preliminary model has given us a systematic foundation for understanding specification.

What we seek from conversation analysis is not an alternative to the approach established above but rather a principled basis for its extension, in particular, to take account of conversational strategies and the more complex features of turn-taking in multi-party conversation. We believe the conversation analytic approach has a useful contribution to make in this area and seems to fit well with the 'philosophy' of what we have termed fine-grain software development modelling.

Contrary to the assertions of conversation analysts, for example Levinson (1983), we see no necessary contradiction between conversation analysis and dialogue analysis. It is worthwhile briefly examining the two major methodological points of departure between the approaches to clarify our position.

Conversation analysis is primarily an inductive enterprise which works directly from observational data, while dialogue analysis tends to impose a rigid external theoretical framework on those data.

It seems clear that software development, and specification specifically, is a particularly complex human activity (in this regard it can usefully be compared with the day-to-day talk that has usually been the subject of conversation analysis). Empirical studies must therefore attempt to balance carefully the dangers of coercing data to fit a model which is inappropriate, with the alternative of generating vast amounts of data (typically, verbal protocols) with no analytical framework within which to interpret it. Our judgement is that the pendulum in studies of software development has swung too far towards the latter. There is, however, a well developed canon of general principles and concepts derived from observation in the conversation analysis style which, we contend, may be safely applied to specification independently of direct investigation and observation.

Although it is true in principle that dialogue analysis theories are essentially unfalsifiable, there being no explicit procedure for assigning a particular modifier to an observed locution act, the importance of this depends crucially on the primary objective of our work. Our objective is not explanation or prediction but rather developing automated support for specification conversations (this is very much in the same spirit as Frohlich and Luff and of Cawsey, in this volume). We are, in the long term, concerned with prescribing, constraining or guiding specifiers to act in accordance with suggested best practice in the conduct of the specification activity. The 'cost' of falsely or inappropriately identifying a sequence of events as ill-formed is simply the marginal cost of acting in a less than optimal way. Continuing the example:

> [N] Sue: So, all old document versions are
>   stored because they may be needed
>   in the future.

It is not clear that conversation analysts have successfully answered the argument that conversation analysis is based on an implicit categorisation of locution acts. However, the findings of conversation analysis point to a richer and highly task dependent and social situation dependent categorisation of such acts. In [N], rather than simply viewing what Sue says as an assertion, we could classify it as a summarisation with an associated commitment rule (possibly derived from that assertion). Other examples of such a categorisation might include criticism, posting an alternative, and so on.

> [O] Tom: Each modification of a document
>   creates a new version of that
>   document and the most recent
>   version of the document is the
>   current release of that category.

Our preliminary model assumes that each locution act has associated with it a statement which is a formula, which itself may consist of a conjunction of formulæ. In principle (note that some redefinition of the concept of immediate consequence may be required) each formula would constitute a turn constructional unit with an associated transition relevance point. This can be seen in [O]. Given this approach we can adopt turn-taking rules derived from conversation analysis (see Heritage 1987) more or less wholesale rather than the naive 'turn and turn about' rules in our preliminary model. At our current level of concern, complex features of turn-taking such as overlaps can, we feel, safely be ignored.

Conditional relevance follows naturally from any systematic study of conversation. In our preliminary model it is embedded in the dialogue rules. The conventional conversation analysis adjacency pair organisation (question [C] – answer [D], and so on) will also be subsumed in the dialogue rules. Insertion sequences, of the type commonly identified in conversation analysis, are not explicitly recognised in our preliminary model. We include these by enriching our simple notion of locution event with the relative location of the locution act.

```
[P] Jeff:    I write all documentation.
```

Perhaps the most interesting feature of conversation analysis is the concept of preference organisation. In everyday conversation (inviting people to dinner, and so on) a preferred locution is one which builds, or tends to build, social solidarity while a dispreferred locution act destroys, or tends to destroy, social solidarity. Participants will delay dispreferred locutions. We might build an equivalent organisation in specification conversations. A dispreferred locution destroys, or tends to destroy, 'specification solidity' while a preferred locution promotes it. Instances of dispreferred locutions might be the introduction of exceptions, withdrawals and demands for the resolution of an inconsistency. Preferred locutions might be the "white lies" observed by Balzer (1985) in which a simplified statement is made to give the specifier a basic understanding and subsequently corrected to give a more accurate description. [P] is an example of this. We know that Jeff does not write all the documents, for he often modifies existing documents. Jeff cuts out this unnecessary complication by telling a white lie.

```
[Q] Jeff:    Well actually...
```

Specification as an activity is concerned with very precise communication and assurance of mutual understanding. In this context the suggested preference organisation is the skeleton on which sophisticated repair work can take place (see Raudaskoski in this volume). In the case of white lies the repair may be self-initiated [Q] while in verification-style repair it is other-initiated.

Where a dispreferred locution (or in special cases a non-normative locution) occurs, conversation analysis suggests that an account or explanation follows. This can be readily accommodated within the argument form framework above.

We have sought wherever possible to keep clear of the semantic analysis required to understand and use topic coherence (Hobbs 1982) in the control and organisation of conversation. By using a more expressive logical scheme as the underlying language in which statements are built we may provide the hooks for a formal analysis of discourse structure.

8.6 Automated support

We aim, as software engineers, to provide automated support for developing specifications.

Such support has both a short-term and a long-term rôle to play in our work. Our short-term goal is to use it as a workbench while developing an improved understanding of the analytical tools and enhancing the descriptive schemes. Without support even relatively simple examples are awkward to handle. Our long-term goal is to use it as the core of a specification support environment (Finkelstein 1989b). In such an environment replaying a 'development history' would be equivalent to running through a record of conversation events (this can be compared to the approach of Conklin 1989).

We have developed two dialogue support systems (IC~DC One and IC~DC Two) which animate, albeit in a simple-minded way, the preliminary model. These tools allow the user to develop simple 'conversations' and then replay them in whole or in part. IC~DC One is written in Prolog and has been used to help us to understand and enhance the dialogue rules. IC~DC Two is written in Smalltalk-80 and has been used to investigate an appropriate architecture for a specification support environment. It is the vehicle for the proposed conversation analysis extensions to the model.

In both tools the dialogues are monitored for legality, and illegal dialogues can be explained and rolled back to a legal state. Users may view the commitments of the participants and may change the course of the dialogue by editing these commitments directly.

8.7 Observational studies

To date we have carried out no extended observational study of specification in its natural, that is industrial, setting, though we have carried out informal studies of university research teams developing small specifications of lift systems, central heating controllers and the like. Because of the commercial sensitivity of software specification, organising studies in natural settings is extremely difficult. Other major methodological barriers are that: specification often takes place over a prolonged period; the most interesting exchanges take place some time after the specification phase is considered finished, that is, during implementation and post-installation maintenance; and conversations often hinge on documents, documentary references, back-of-envelope sketches and diagrams.

We have found it useful to refer to studies of specification practice in the literature, for example, that by Fickas, Collins and Olivier (1987). There is still some·way for us to go using this data before the need to carry out our own studies becomes pressing.

8.8 Conclusion

We have seen in very crude outline how we might begin to model the 'fine-grain' of specification using a dialogue analysis model (for more detail, some fully worked examples and an account of the limitations and shortcomings of our preliminary model, see Finkelstein and Fuks 1989) and have given a sketch of the extensions that conversation analysis suggests.

As yet our work is at a preliminary stage. It should be stressed that there remains a substantial amount of foundation work to be done in order to make extended models of conversation that are both computationally tractable and formally sound. Future work includes the construction of a dialogue-based framework for theorem proving and a detailed analysis of the structure of elicitation and verification strategies.

Acknowledgements

The authors would like to thank their colleagues and students who have contributed significantly, through lively critical discussion, to the work this paper reports. Hugo Fuks is supported by the Brazilian National Research Council CNPq, grant 202471/86-cc. Anthony Finkelstein is supported by EC Esprit, DTI IED and SERC.

Chapter 9

Applying the Technology of Conversation to the Technology for Conversation

David Frohlich and Paul Luff

9.1 Introduction

In this chapter we aim to show how the insights of conversation analysis (CA) have been useful to us as designers of interactive technology, and how, in our opinion, they have helped us to make the technology itself more interactive. We begin with a description of the particular approach we have adopted towards interaction design and go on to discuss its implementation in a demonstration expert system called the Advice System.

There is a specific way in which we have made use of the findings of CA. It can be illustrated with reference to the CA programme as described by Sacks,

> The gross aim of the work I am doing is to see how
> finely the details of actual, naturally occurring
> conversation can be subjected to analysis that will yield
> the technology of conversation. The idea is to take
> singular sequences of conversation and tear them apart
> in such a way as to find rules, techniques, procedures,
> methods, maxims... that can be used to generate the
> orderly features we find in the conversations we
> examine.
>
> (Sacks 1984, p.13 [1971])

Sacks suggests a programme of analysis of the details of individual sequences of talk, directed towards the discovery of what he calls a *technology of conversation*; a kind of common machinery and know-how for the manufacture of conversational contributions within a particular culture.   The direction of the process here is from phenomena to *technology*.

Our own programme has been one in which we have attempted to apply Sack's programme of analysis in reverse. That is, we have taken various aspects of the *technology of conversation* as it has been described in the CA literature and tried to build them into the operation of a computer in such a way as to generate and support orderly sequences of talk. The direction of the process here is from *technology* to phenomena.

Thus, we can say that the gross aim of the work we are doing is to see how productively the technology of conversation can be used to reproduce the details of actual, naturally occurring conversations between people, in conversations between people and computers. The idea is to take the rules, techniques, procedures, methods, maxims... that have been proposed to account for the orderly features of conversation and to put them together in such a way to support "singular sequences of conversation".

Of course, it is possible to object to this programme on a number of theoretical grounds. First, current descriptions of the *technology of conversation* are based on the analysis of human conversations, whereas the conversations we wish to support are those between humans and computers.   Perhaps the same conversational machinery will not work when one party is a machine. Second, CA is based on recordings and transcriptions of predominantly verbal exchanges, whereas the exchanges we wish to support are (in the first instance) textual. Perhaps the organisation of spoken language will not be appropriate for visible language. Third, the accounts of conversational order offered by conversation analysts are non-deterministic, whereas we wish to instantiate them within a deterministic mechanism. Perhaps this cannot be done (see Button this volume).

In reply to the first objection, we note that there is as yet no human-computer conversation analysis which has delivered insights on the sequential organisation of human-computer interactions. In the absence of such insights it seems reasonable to model human-computer conversations on human-human conversations. This is not only because the quality of human-human conversation is generally superior to that of current human-computer conversation (e.g. Hayes and Reddy 1983; Nickerson 1981), but also because the possible ineffectiveness of the human-human model will be made explicit by using it in the human-computer domain. In fact, the data generated by people interacting with such machines constitute a rich resource for just that enterprise whose absence we noted above.

In reply to the second objection, we believe that many of the peculiar features of textual interactions derive from the fact that they often take place through an essentially static medium over long periods of time (e.g. Frohlich 1986). In contrast, modern interactive computers support textual interactions in real-time and there is no convincing evidence to suggest that these interactions should not be organised along the lines of spoken interactions. Again, it would be interesting to discover any differences which do exist by analysing textual interactions organised as if spoken.

Finally, a brief reply to the third objection, that accounts of conversational order cannot be instantiated using a deterministic mechanism, would be to say that we have done it. Although we might have made greater use of CA accounts, those we did use gave us a principled way of making a large number of dialogue design decisions and eventually a method of implementing those decisions in rules. The fact that we could do this relatively directly from the accounts themselves is a credit to their quality and seems to us to confirm Sack's hope for a sociology which can deal with the details of actual events both formally and informatively (Sacks 1984 [1971]). To take the objection more seriously would be to acknowledge that we may have misrepresented the accounts in the process of formalising them for design. We leave this for the reader to judge, but note that our primary purpose in applying the *technology of conversation* has been to build better technology for conversation. The value of the approach should be measured by the extent to which it has allowed us to do this.

In the following sections we outline the requirements of the particular system we have designed, before going on to describe the selection and implementation of a *local management* style of dialogue control based on various findings in the CA literature.

9.2   The Advice System

The Advice System is one of four demonstration computer systems constructed by the Alvey DHSS Demonstrator Project (see Gilbert 1988). The purpose of the Advice System is to show how computer technology might be used to give welfare rights advice directly to members of the general public. Although it is not intended to fulfil all the roles performed by a trained advice worker, the system should possess much of the knowledge of benefits which advice workers have and be able to share this knowledge effectively with clients. In this sense, the Advice System could be seen as an expert system for non-experts.

In designing such a system, we have found ourselves attempting to overcome well recognised problems with traditional expert systems (Buckland et al. 1987). Compared with human advisers, expert systems are unsatisfactory since they fail to answer a sufficiently broad range of questions, they do not allow the user an active rôle in problem solving, they do not help the user to formulate his or her problem, and do not adequately explain the advice given (Coombes and Alty 1984; Kidd and Cooper 1985; Kidd 1987; Morris 1987; Pollack, Hirschberg and Webber 1982). These shortcomings are clearly undesirable for all classes of user. However, their effects are most severe for non-experts who lack a professional context within which to interpret the 'advice' from such systems.

To overcome some of these problems, we have attempted to construct a system capable of answering a wide variety of user questions on benefits within an open-ended dialogue (Robinson et al. 1988). We hope that a question answering model of interaction will help to ensure that the system always addresses the problems users themselves want to solve, and that opening up the interaction will give users more responsibility for directing the focus of the dialogue and for negotiating with the system about the meaning of answers to questions.

Three technical innovations have been needed. First, we have had to enhance the capabilities of the underlying expert system to generate many types of answers to users' questions (Buckland et. al. 1987; Gilbert 1987c; Gilbert and Jirotka 1989). For example, users can ask *case level* questions about their own or another person's eligibility for benefit, *domain level* questions about the rules governing eligibility for target groups of people, and *theory level* questions about the reasons for the rules on eligibility. Second, it has been necessary to provide users with a method of volunteering statements or asking questions at any time in the interaction, as well as a method of providing answers to system questions. This has been done through the development of a menu-based natural language input interface (Robinson et. al. 1988). Users construct questions or statements by first choosing the topic of their utterance from a series of topic menus and then choosing the wording of the utterance from a series of phrase menus (see the right-hand side of Figure 9.1). These "dynamic menus" allows users to communicate with the machine in natural language rather than in a specialised command language whilst ensuring high levels of input recognition (Tennant et al. 1983). Third, and most important for this chapter, we have had to derive and implement a set of dialogue control policies, capable of constraining the question, statement and answer exchanges made

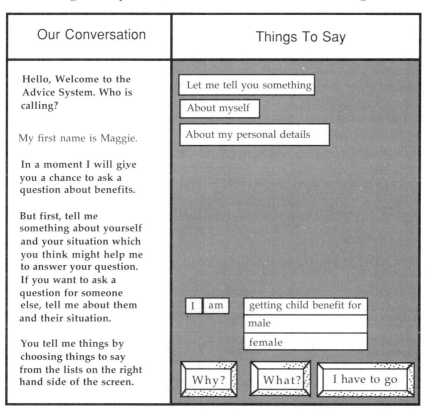

Figure 9.1 Screen display from the Advice System.

possible within the above framework. These dialogue policies are expressed as a set of *interaction rules*, held in an *interaction module* of the Advice System.

9.3 Dialogue control requirements

The requirements for dialogue control become clear if we consider the possibilities for utterance exchange. The system is capable of providing 17 different kinds of system answers (SA) in response to about 70 different forms of user questions (UQ). It can also volunteer certain types of information to the user in system statements (SS). Some system answers can be provided immediately after the user's question, but others require further information from the user. There are around 200 different pieces of information which are relevant to the calculation of system answers. Whenever a piece of information becomes relevant to the provision of an individual answer, the system can ask the user for the information in a system question (SQ) and the user can provide it in a user answer (UA). In addition, the user is able to volunteer most of the 200 pieces of information in a user statement (US). This potentially leads to a dialogue comprised of combinations of UQ, US, UA, SQ, SS, and SA, in which the basic dialogic unit is a UQ-SA pair, liable to separation by any number of SQ-UA pairs. There are no inherent constraints on the placement of SS or US utterances, since these serve primarily to pre-empt certain UQ or SQ utterances and could therefore occur at any time before such utterances become relevant.

Dialogue control policies are therefore required to handle the various utterance sequences made possible by this scheme. Some of these sequences can be illustrated with reference to Table 9.1, which shows all the pair-wise combinations of utterance types which could be supported by the system. Note that no pair is ruled out by the technical constraints described above.

We can see from Table 9.1 that in half the pairs, both utterances are made by the same speaker, allowing multi-utterance turns both by the user (Row 1, Columns 1,2,3; Row 2, Columns 1,2,3; Row 3, Columns 1,2,3) and the system (Row 4, Columns 4,5,6; Row 5, Columns 4,5,6; Row 6, Columns 4,5,6). This means that either party could hold the 'floor' indefinitely by producing further pairs in the same group. Control policies are required to determine whether or not this should be allowed and if so, how, when and by whom. In particular, allowing repetition of the same utterance type by the system (Row 4, Column 4; Row 5, Column 5; Row 6, Column 6) creates special problems of how to order complex system questions, statements and answers made up of multiple parts.

The possibility of supporting multi-utterance turns highlights a general problem with controlling the taking of turns in the dialogue. If turns do not simply switch between parties each time an utterance is made, on what other basis should the switch occur? For example, should the switch be made when the speaker runs out of things to say, automatically following certain utterance types, or by interruption from the other party?

Repetition of questions by either party (Row 1, Column 1; Row 4, Column 4) raises a difficult problem in controlling the order of question answering in the dialogue. Whenever additional questions are asked before prior questions have been answered, a decision must be made about which of the outstanding questions to answer first. If the user is asking the questions, the system might answer on a first-asked-first or last-asked-first basis, although the dialogue as a whole might become extremely convoluted if too many outstanding user questions are permitted. If the system is asking the questions, it must determine both the order in which to ask them and the order in which to present users with the options to answer them. The ordering of system questions remains a significant dialogue control problem, even if only one question is asked at a time, because of the effect that ordering will have on the user's perceived 'sense' of any line of questioning.

2nd part :	Column	1	2	3	4	5	6
		UQ	US	UA	SQ	SS	SA
1st part: Row							
1	UQ	UQ-UQ	UQ-US	UQ-UA	UQ-SQ	UQ-SS	UQ-SA
2	US	US-UQ	US-US	US-UA	US-SQ	US-SS	US-SA
3	UA	UA-UQ	UA-US	UA-UA	UA-SQ	UA-SS	UA-SA
4	SQ	SQ-UQ	SQ-US	SQ-UA	SQ-SQ	SQ-SS	SQ-SA
5	SS	SS-UQ	SS-US	SS-UA	SS-SQ	SS-SS	SS-SA
6	SA	SA-UQ	SA-US	SA-UA	SA-SQ	SA-SS	SA-SA

Table 9.1   Matrix of possible pair-wise combinations of utterances allowed by the Advice System. The basic utterance types are user question (UQ), user statement (US), user answer (UA), system question (SS), system statement (SS) and system answer (SA).

A special set of dialogue control problems are created by the need to deal with various kinds of 'incomprehensible' user statements (Row 2 and Column 2) or answers (Row 3 and Column 3). Although keyboard input is kept to a minimum through the menu-based interface to the Advice System, it is still possible for users to enter certain kinds of numeric information in a format which the machine cannot recognise, for example, typing a date into a text box intended for the "number of children". Furthermore, users can reply with a 'Don't know' answer to most system questions, and go on to contradict previous answers or statements. Policies are required to control the system's response to these events.

Finally, the dialogue as a whole must begin with a sequence in which the user asks a first question of the system, continue with a sequence in which the user asks a further question, and end with a sequence in which the system provides a last answer to the user. Control policies are required to do this.

In the next section, we will outline a number of alternative approaches to dialogue control based on different underlying models of discourse. The aim of all the approaches is to facilitate meaningful conversation between participants by somehow constraining their individual contributions. Although no single approach provides control policies to meet all the requirements we have outlined above, we suggest that a CA approach is most likely to fit the expectations about the meaning and structure of conversational behaviour which users themselves will bring to the system.

9.4   Selecting a CA approach to dialogue control

Insights into the organisation and control of dialogue are provided by at least eight different disciplines. Philosophy, linguistics, psychology and sociology are concerned with explaining the way in which language is used in the context of social interaction between people, and suggest a number of models of dialogue. Cognitive science (CS), artificial intelligence (AI), human computer interaction (HCI) and software engineering (SE) are concerned with the construction of computational devices to support interaction between human and/or artificial agents, and suggest a number of approaches to dialogue management. Complex interactions exist between the insights offered by each discipline, such that any individual piece of work is likely to combine insights from several sources. Table 9.2 is an attempt to structure this complexity, at the risk of oversimplification, in order to show some of the relationships between important pieces of work carried out in recent years. The categories are our own and do not reflect the categories in which the authors might see themselves.

The work shown in Table 9.2 has been chosen to exemplify the development of four major approaches to dialogue management, stemming from theoretical traditions in each of the four pure disciplines (see columns). Various underlying models of dialogue have been used to develop techniques in CS and AI which have then been adapted and applied within the fields of SE and HCI; a process which itself generates feedback and development of ideas in the other direction. We briefly review these developments here in order to show how we came to adopt a CA approach to dialogue design and also to illustrate the relationship of CA to other approaches.

Within a philosophical tradition begun by Austin (1962), dialogue is viewed as sequence of *speech acts*, uttered by each party to achieve certain goals. Austin recognised that sentences can be used not only to say things that are true or false, but also to do things which serve some social function, like promising, convincing, ordering and so forth. Searle (1969) developed this idea by attempting to establish the (felicity) conditions under which certain acts can be used. Recent work by Sperber and Wilson (1986) is a continuation of that of Grice (1975), presenting a theory of how a hearer can understand an utterance by relating it to what is relevant in a given context. Gorayska and Lindsay (1989) have attempted to formalise this notion of *relevance* in terms of the goals of the speaker and hearer in a dialogue.

The speech act model of dialogue has been further developed into a technique for inferring the plans of a speaker (Cohen and Perrault 1979; Perrault and Allen 1980; Allen 1983). Cohen, Perrault and Allen have seen that the notion of speech acts parallels the characterisation of actions in AI planners, in which individual actions are defined in terms of preconditions and effects, and sequences of actions are described as plans to achieve some goal. They have developed an algorithm for inferring the plans behind what a speaker is saying, by making use of mappings between beliefs, knowledge and goals, and various types of speech acts. This is the same kind of inference made in certain kinds of dynamic user modelling when the system tries to infer the user's level of knowledge and current goals and/or plans from the actions performed at the interface (e.g. Genesereth 1982). It is also similar to the inferences made in cooperative question-answering systems (e.g. Kaplan 1983; Kiss 1987).

	Philosophy	Linguistics	Psychology	Sociology
Theory	*Speech act*	*Discourse grammar*	*Social Skill*	*Interactional achievement*
	Austin, Searle	van Dijk, Hinds	Argyle, Bartlett	Sacks, Schegloff & Jefferson

	Relevance Sperber & Wilson, Gorayska & Lindsay			
Technique (CS / AI)	*Plan inference* Cohen, Perrault & Allen	*Focus register* Grosz, Sidner	*Script* Shank & Abelson	*Local management* Frohlich & Luff
		Context spaces Reichman	*Schemata* McKeown	*SDL* Young
Application (HCI / SE)	*User modelling* Genesereth	*Natural language interfaces* Reilly, McTear	*Task analysis* e.g, GOMS Card et al.	*Advice discourse* Gilbert et al.
	High level dialogues Kiss		*Structured dialogue* Coombs & Alty	*Repair* McTear, Raudaskoski
	Cooperative question answering Kaplan			*Explanations* Cawsey, Moore & Swartout
Recent Critiques	Gilbert	Winograd & Flores, Levinson	Suchman, Agre	Luff & Frohlich

Table 9.2 Classification of work on the organisation and management of dialogue.

We define a linguistic tradition category as that founded on the work of Chomsky (1957) on transformational grammar. Chomsky attempts to explain how speakers of a language come to generate regular (rather than irregular) sentences in terms of a shared knowledge of grammatical rules. The rules are said to generate a deep structure relating the form and meaning of groups of words. Discourse analysts such as van Dijk (1977) and Hinds (1979) have extended the notion of a sentence grammar to dialogue, suggesting that the form and meaning of sentences themselves might be governed by a shared set of *discourse grammar* rules.

Discourse grammars form the basis of several techniques developed in computational linguistics to understand or generate natural language utterances in context. Reichman (1985) for example, proposes the idea of a *context space* describing the current set of things being talked about in any dialogue. She then defines various *conversational moves*, sometimes marked by clue words such as "so", "anyway" and "now", which can be made to effect transitions between context spaces. The work of Sidner (1983), Grosz (1986) and Grosz and Sidner (1986) is a related development in which various *focus registers* and *spaces* are proposed to represent the focus of attention in a dialogue. Shifts in focus are made by speakers making utterances which add or subtract items from the current focus registers. Some of these techniques have been adapted for the construction of natural language interfaces to computers (e.g. Reilly 1987; McTear 1987).

In contrast to philosophical and linguistic theories of dialogue, psychological and sociological theories are more deeply rooted in the empirical observation of conversational organisation. However the purposes for which psychologists and sociologists have collected conversational data are quite different, and have affected the way their findings have been analysed and explained. Psychologists have tended to study dialogue as a *social skill*, which individual participants possess to varying degrees (e.g. Argyle and Kendon 1967). Particular attention has been paid to professional social skills such as interviewing, selling, teaching and counselling in order to uncover the hallmarks of communicative competence in these settings. Analysis is directed toward the measurement of competence, and theory is often developed to inform programmes of social skills training intended to improve it. On the other hand, sociologists have tended to study dialogue as an *interactional achievement*, the product of two or more parties interacting cooperatively over time. In this view, dialogue is seen as an inherently social phenomenon which is worthy of investigation in its own right. Thus, it has been described as the 'primordial site of sociality' (Schegloff 1988b) and the primary medium in which social life is created and sustained (Sacks 1984 [1971]). The central concern of this approach has been to uncover the sequential organisation of utterances over time and to propose a common sense machinery which can generate it (see Section 9.1).

A significant consequence of these different orientations towards dialogue is that the psychological tradition has tended to be more context-dependent, while the sociological tradition has been more context-independent. This can be seen most clearly in the computational techniques which have been developed and applied from the models suggested by each discipline.

Within the psychological tradition, Schank and Abelson (1977) suggest that a dialogue can be viewed as an episodic pattern of events carried out by a set of characters with the aid of props. They call this pattern a *script*. Different scripts must be used to characterise the episodic structure of different types of dialogue. The notion of a script is descended from the concept of a *schema*, which itself has a long history in the psychology of perception and skill, but which has generally been used to refer to a stereotypical pattern of stimulation or behaviour represented in memory (e.g. Bartlett 1935; Hebb 1949; Posner and Keele 1968; Pew 1974). McKeown's (1985) work on *schemata* is an extension of the same idea applied to the generation of coherent textual descriptions. Numerous methods of task analysis within software engineering are based on the abstraction of stereotypical patterns in dialogue (e.g. Card, Moran and Newell 1983), and much of the practice of dialogue design in human-computer interaction consists of building in such abstractions into interactive software (e.g. Coombs and Alty 1980).

We have already noted that our own work lies within the sociological tradition and involves the development of a dialogue control technique based on the *local management* of turns (Frohlich and Luff 1989 and this chapter). A similar technique appears to have been developed in a specification dialogue language called SDL by the COSMOS Project (Young 1988) to control the taking of user turns in a computer conferencing system. Both techniques are general to a wide variety of different types of dialogue, as we will go on to explain. Local management of dialogue has been applied in the Advice System (Gilbert et al. 1989), while a number of authors have begun to apply the sociological model of dialogue as an interactional achievement to the design of explanation facilities (e.g. Cawsey 1989 and this volume; Moore and Swartout 1989a) and repair strategies (e.g. Raudaskoski this volume; McTear 1985) for interactive systems.

Before adopting the CA model of dialogue as a basis for designing dialogue control policies for the Advice System, we considered the suitability of many of the above insights (Luff and Frohlich 1987). We found that the insights derived from philosophy and psychology were less useful and generally more difficult to apply in our domain than those derived from linguistics and sociology. In particular, the findings of CA spoke directly to problems of turn organisation with an authority quite lacking in other accounts. We began to see how the same solutions which people appear to adopt to these problems in spontaneous spoken conversation could be used in the management of dialogue between users and the Advice System; a strategy of double benefit if it also meant that users would be able to carry over to this interaction the same expectations about conversational organisation they usually employ.

Our decision to explore a sociological approach to dialogue management has been corroborated in several recent critiques of other approaches. For example, Suchman (1987) criticises a planning model of action for overlooking the situated or *ad hoc* nature of people's interactions with the world. This can be seen as an attack both on the speech act model of dialogue and on the social skill model, since the evidence on which it is based is taken from an analysis of user interaction with a help system based on a dialogue schema. Gilbert (1987b) attacks the strategy of plan inference and dynamic user modelling on similar grounds, arguing that users may not formulate highly developed plans when interacting with computers (see also Young and Simon 1987). Levinson (1983) shows how speech act and discourse grammar approaches cannot account for a variety of phenomena in pragmatics, while Winograd and Flores (1986) join Suchman in criticising rationalistic views of man. All these critiques promote insights from sociology, although Winograd and Flores (curiously) return to the speech act model as a basis for dialogue design. A common theme is the advocacy of what might be called an *interactionist approach* to the understanding of social interaction, in which interactional phenomena are treated as properties which emerge out of the ongoing behaviour of more than one agent, rather than as properties which are explicitly represented or generated by individual agents (see Agre 1989).

In the next section we show how such an approach can be adopted towards interactive system design, by applying some of the insights of CA to the formulation of dialogue control policies.

9.5 Dialogue control policies

Returning to the dialogue control requirements outlined in Section 9.3, we are now in a position to consider two things. First, what specific dialogue control policies are suggested (if any) in the CA literature as being characteristic of the way people satisfy similar requirements? Second, how might these policies be implemented in the Advice System? We turn first to the problem of multiple same-party utterances and the taking of turns.

9.5.1   Control of turn-taking

The possibility of multi-utterance turns in the Advice System was illustrated by Table 9.1, in which both parts of half the utterance pairs were made by the same party. A general problem in turn-taking was said to result from this possibility since an exchange policy based on single utterance turns cannot work and must be replaced by something more sophisticated.

Sacks, Schegloff and Jefferson (1974) have described a simple but sophisticated system of turn-taking which appears to be used in spontaneous spoken conversation. They observe that turns at talk typically vary in length, content, order and distribution throughout a conversation, but that turn transitions with no gap and no overlap are common. To account for this state of affairs they suggest that both speakers and listeners are sensitive to the possible completion points of any turn, such that speakers themselves can organise their talk so as to provide opportunities for listeners to 'interrupt' them and listeners can anticipate possible places where such interruption can be done. This led to the idea that talk is organised in turn constructional units (TCU) divided by transition relevance places (TRP) at which turn transitions can take place. Two methods of turn-taking are said to operate in this situation. The current speaker can select the next speaker with a TCU which expects a response, or the next speaker can self-select by beginning to speak at a TRP.

Use of a TCU which expects a response results in an adjacency pair structure (e.g. Schegloff and Sacks 1973; Schegloff 1968, 1972). The adjacency pair can be seen as a fundamental unit of conversational organisation comprising two parts; a first pair-part such as a question, greeting or invitation and a second pair-part acting as a response to the first, such as an answer, greeting or acceptance. The first pair-parts of adjacency pairs set constraints on what should be done in the next turn by making a second pair-part immediately relevant and expectable.

This scheme lends itself naturally to implementation in the Advice System. This is because the question answering dialogue proposed for the system is already organised around question-answer adjacency pairs and segmented into TCU-like utterances of questions, answers and statements. Furthermore, the system is a rule-based system which already uses inferencing techniques to apply rules to answer questions. For both these reasons we decided to attempt to implement the scheme in rules which operate to constrain or select the next user or system utterance in the interaction. The result is what we call a *local management* style of dialogue management (after

Sacks et al. 1974), designed to recreate some of the dynamics of ordinary conversation. The turn-taking rules on which it is based act as a foundation for supporting other kinds of conversational organisation observed in the CA literature.

Table 9.3 contains a sample set of interaction rules for turn-taking and adjacency. The rules as a whole comprise a declarative definition of the interaction between user and system and are applied locally, on a turn-by-turn basis. This means that what can happen next depends on what has happened previously, as recorded in an *interaction history*. Although, the conversational planning activity of the Advice System is limited to one conversational move ahead of the current turn, it is informed by an interaction history which stretches back to the beginning of the conversation. There are two types of interaction rules: *action rules* which specify the next system move or the next set of possible user moves, and *history rules* which update information in the interaction history. Only action rules are shown in Table 9.3.

Each individual action rule is made up of a move label or name on its left-hand side and a move description on its right hand side. The description specifies a further sequence of moves which may or may not be conditional upon some state of affairs in the interaction history. Moves can either be terminal moves, moves that are made by user or system at the interface, or defined by other rules in the interaction rule base. Terminal moves come in three types: statements, questions and answers, and at two levels: 'substantive', about the domain of the Advice System, welfare benefits, and 'meta', about the interaction. Meta-utterances will described in more detail in Section 9.5.2.

The `conversation` and `body` rules in Table 9.3 show that the entire interaction between users and the Advice System is based on an adjacency pair structure lying between an opening and a preclosing sequence. Within the main `body` of the conversation, what happens next is determined by the `adjacency-pair` rule (and sub-rules) and depends on whether there are any outstanding user or system questions in the interaction history registers. As we will describe in subsequent sections, the opening and preclosing sequences are designed specifically to generate user questions, so that the body of talk can continue to be extended through the operation of adjacency pairing.

The `adjacency-pair` and `body` rules are mutually recursive. The `adjacency-pair` rule is comprised of a user turn followed by a system turn. These are followed by a return to the `body` rule to see if there are any outstanding user or system questions. This ordering reflects the fact that the user always drives the interaction with questions for the system, although the system can itself generate questions for the user to answer in subsequent turns.

For brevity, only the user-open-floor rule is expanded in Table 9.3. If the system has asked a question in the last turn then the user gets a chance to perform the terminal moves described within the user-answer-turn rule. Otherwise the user enters a user-statement-turn. From the definition of the user-answer-turn it is possible to see the variety of things the user could do in response to a system question. The rules show that the user can either provide a substantive answer to the question or ask a further question. Furthermore, the answer can be provided with additional utterances defined within the user-statement-turn rule. This allows the user to follow an answer with a series of statements, so long as there are no problems with the user's turn, checked for in the check-to-continue rule at the bottom of Table 9.3. In this way the user can try to hold the floor by continuing to speak, or give it back to the system.

The holding or passing of turns is done by the user selecting punctuation marks at the end of utterances constructed, using the dynamic menus on the screen. Selection of a full stop sends an endTurn signal to the interaction module which means that the first user-answer-turn rule shown in Table 9.3 has been chosen and completed. It also means that the containing user-open-floor move has been completed. Selection of three full-stops ("...") sends an endTCU signal to the interaction module and is an attempt to retain the user-open-floor for a user-statement-turn. (A third check? signal can be chosen with an answer to end the current turn, this is a repair initiation device and will be discussed in the next section.)

```
conversation <- opening
               body

body <- if (OR (user-questions) (system-questions))
          then adjacency-pair
          else preclosing1

adjacency-pair <-    user-open-floor
                     system-floor
                     body

user-open-floor <- if (system-questions)
                     then user-answer-turn
                     else user-statement-turn


user-answer-turn <-
   answer(user substantive endTurn (possible-answer))
user-answer-turn <-
   answer(user substantive endTCU (possible-answer))
   check-to-continue
user-answer-turn <-
   answer(user substantive check? (possible-answer))
user-answer-turn <- question(user substantive)
user-answer-turn <- question(user meta ri)
user-answer-turn <- question(user meta ntri)

user-statement-turn <- question(user substantive)
user-statement-turn <-
               statement(user substantive endTurn)
user-statement-turn <-
               statement(user substantive endTCU)
               check-to-continue
user-statement-turn <- statement(user substantive check?)
user-statement-turn <- statement(user meta endSession)
               check-end-of-session

check-to-continue <-
   if (OR contradiction
      (dont-know (top past-utterance-stack))
      (NOT (valid(top past-utterance-stack))))
      then possible-system-interrupt
      else user-statement-turn
```

Table 9.3 Interaction rules for turn-taking and adjacency.

The endTCU signal does not guarantee the user continued use of the floor since the end of every TCU in the interaction is an opportunity for the other party to self-select. Here, the system will self-select only if the answer given by the user is incomprehensible for some reason. As users can combine text input with menu selection when constructing utterances, it is possible for them to enter invalid information, make a contradiction or say that they do not know the answer to a system question. These are problems common to other interactive systems and 'self-selection' provides the system with an ideal opportunity to deal with the 'error' as soon as it arises, rather than waiting until later when further errors might have occurred. Also, anything the system says in the interaction is open to misunderstanding by the user. The interaction rules also allow self-selection to be done by the user between every TCU uttered by the system. This means that users can also attempt to deal with 'error' immediately it arises. At the interface, users are given the opportunity to self-select by the presentation of a "Let me speak" button on the screen in a pause interval following the display of every system answer or statement. They must 'select' this button with the mouse driven cursor before it disappears if they want to interrupt the system.

Three other options are available to users in the user-answer-turn. Users can ask a substantive question (about the benefit system) or one of two different meta-questions (about the conversation itself). For now, it is sufficient to note that this scheme provides a good deal of flexibility to users in the way they might handle system questions whilst at the same time constraining what might be done according to principles derived from CA.

For example, the opportunity for users to make a statement following a system question is deliberately barred by the interaction rules and their implementation at the interface. This is because the asking of questions is said to create a *conditional relevance* in the conversation such that any statement made in the next turn is likely to be heard as an answer to the question (Schegloff 1968). We have been able to mimic this by writing interaction rules that selectively identify which options should be presented at the interface; in this case omitting to specify statement options in the user-answer-turn rule and so removing these as possibilities. Furthermore, although the interaction rules show user questions to be legitimate seconds to system questions, the design of the interface ensures that it is easier for the user to provide an answer first. The user must effectively back out of an initial answer menu to get access to substantive question topic menus. By presenting answers as the first set of options to select from, it has been possible to mimic the *preference organisation* surrounding the second pair-parts to questions (cf. Levinson 1983). The same kind of preference organisation governs the system's response to a user's question, although this is implemented differently. Whenever the system has a choice of things to say which involve statements, questions and answers, interaction rules operate to organise them in a three part A-S-Q turn such as that observed by Sacks et al. (1974, p.722). In their language, the first part (A) addresses the relation of a turn to a prior, the second (S) is involved with what is occupying the turn, and the third (Q) addresses the relation of the turn to a succeeding one.

The influence of CA constraints on the possibilities for turn-taking and turn construction can be illustrated with reference to Table 9.4. This is a reproduction of the matrix in Table 9.1 with eleven cells missing. The missing cells show exactly which utterance pairs are ruled out by the style of turn-taking observed in human conversations and its implementation through the local management of dialogue by interaction rules. The gaps in Row 1 and Row 4 show that there is always a turn transition whenever the user or the system asks a question, and that it is never appropriate for an unrelated statement to follow a question. The gaps in Row 2, Column 3 and Row 5, Column 6 show that it is inappropriate for a statement to precede an answer for the same reason. All other utterance combinations appear to be legitimate within the scheme, although one or two appear unusual at first sight. For example, the SA-SA combination (in Row 6, Column 6) arises not in response to the asking of multiple questions, which is disallowed, but as a method of structuring complex answers composed of a number of parts. Thus by implementing this scheme, it has been possible to apply a powerful set of constraints to the set of possible utterance sequences which are supported by the Advice System in a way which is consistent with the very flexible style of turn-taking characteristic of ordinary conversation. Furthermore, it is just this style which has allowed us to build in additional dialogue control policies to support other conversational phenomena.

9.5.2 Control of repair

It was mentioned above that the opportunity for self-selection available to user and system through the turn-taking scheme is useful to both participants as a resource for dealing with 'error' or, more generally, *failure* in the interaction. Failure, and its corollary *repair*, are routine occurrences in ordinary conversation and have been the subject of considerable research in CA. A number of findings on the sequential organisation of repair sequences have been useful to us in designing the dialogue control policies required by the system to deal with incomprehensible user input (see Section 9.3). The fact that many of these policies are symmetrical has meant that they also help

2nd part Column :	1	2	3	4	5	6
1st part: Row	UQ	US	UA	SQ	SS	SA
1 UQ	–	–	–	UQ-SQ	–	UQ-SA
2 US	US-UQ	US-US	–	US-SQ	US-SS	US-SA
3 UA	UA-UQ	UA-US	UA-UA	UA-SQ	UA-SS	UA-SA
4 SQ	SQ-UQ	–	SQ-UA	–	–	–
5 SS	SS-UQ	SS-US	SS-UA	SS-SQ	SS-SS	–
6 SA	SA-UQ	SA-US	SA-UA	SA-SQ	SA-SS	SA-SA

Table 9.4   Matrix of pair-wise combinations of utterances constrained by the rules for turn-taking and adjacency.

the user to deal with incomprehensible system output.

The function of repair in conversation appears to facilitate mutual understanding between participants. The turn-by-turn organisation of conversation is such that participants must repeatedly exhibit their own understanding of prior utterances, especially when those utterances expect some direct response, as with adjacency pairs. A kind of *other-initiated repair* is forced upon speakers whenever other participants indicate in their own turns some trouble in understanding (cf. Schegloff, Jefferson and Sacks 1977). However, a preference for self-initiation of repair can be seen to be the result of a cooperative minimisation of failure by participants. Speakers attempt to anticipate failure by continuous monitoring of listener's understandings in backchannel cues or via checking moves like "you know". Listeners comply by providing such clues, responding to checks and delaying their responses to problematic utterances. The fact that repair is itself subject to the same kind of monitoring means that mutual misunderstanding can almost always be resolved to allow the conversation to proceed.

Error correction of this kind is an extremely powerful interactional resource (Jefferson 1974) and one which we have tried to support in the Advice System. We used several interactional devices and numerous interaction rules to do this, only some of which will be described here. A key design decision was to recognise that failure and repair behaviour often involves talk about talk rather than talk about some substantive topic. This led to the notion of *meta-utterances* in the form of meta questions, meta statements and meta-answers, which although subject to the same sequential organisation as substantive utterances, can be used to exchange information about the understandings each party currently holds about the other's talk. Meta-utterances could then be used to support the two kinds of repair initiation shown in Table 9.5, and the kind of repair work performed by the rules shown in Table 9.6.

How many children do you have?
Once.
What?
One.
...
From the information you have given you should be able to get £46.75 a week from the main benefits for lone parents...
OK?
No.
You may get less than £46.75 in Income Support if you claim it with other benefits.

Table 9.5 Kinds of repair initiation.

The first method of repair initiation is for the user or the system to utter the meta-question "What?". In the example shown in Table 9.5, it is used by the system to initiate repair of invalid input by the user. However, it is also available to the user at each TRP following a system statement or answer as a labelled icon on the screen. Since "What?" is a question, it results in a turn transition and demands a response from the other party. In ordinary conversation, the response expected by such an utterance seems to be a re-doing of the original speaker's utterance, and the user can be seen to oblige in the next turn. These kind of utterances are called appropriately, *next-turn-repair-initiators* (Levinson 1983); and we use this name as a label (ntri) in the meta-questions (see Table 9.3).

The second method of repair initiation is to utter the meta-answer "No" to the meta-question "OK?". This can be seen to be done by the user in the second example of Table 9.5 and results in the same kind of repair work as triggered by a "What?". Here the system attempts a rephrasing of its last substantive utterance. The 'OK?' meta-question constitutes the first pair-part of a *checking move* (Ringle and Bruce 1981), which is itself a verbal device for monitoring a listener's level of understanding. This is identified with a check? label in substantive user questions (see Table 9.3). Checking moves can also be initiated by users to give the system a chance to begin repair. To do this, users select "OK?" from the punctuation options displayed at the end of substantive answers or statements.

Both methods of repair initiation lead to a kind of other-initiated-self-repair in which the responsibility for repair work is passed from the offended to the offending party. The system can constrain how the user chooses to follow up system repair turns and has a variety of interaction rules for determining its own follow-up of user repair. These are organised into distinct sets of rules governing different kinds of follow-up sequences, depending on the original type of failure. Sets of rules exist for dealing with invalid input, 'don't know' answers and contradictions in what might be called *side sequences* of the main conversation (after Jefferson 1972). A selection of rules used in the `invalid-answer-side-sequence` is shown in Table 9.6.

The `check-invalid-answer` rule is used to control the sequencing of user and system meta-utterances in a repair side sequence initiated by the system. This rule calls the `invalid-answer-side-scquence` rule if the last input by the user is found to be `NOT(valid)`. Otherwise the system must see if a confirmation meta-answer is required in the `check-user-checking-move-yes` move. This rule outputs the system meta-answer "Yes" if the user has just initiated a checking move with an 'OK?' meta-question.

Within the `invalid-answer-side-sequence`, what happens in the next turn depends on whether the repair was initiated through a checking move or not. The `check-user-checking-move-no` rule works to output the system meta-answer 'No' if the user initiated a checking move with an 'OK?' meta-question. If there was no checking move, the system goes straight on to the `system-initiate-invalid-sequence` rule and utters the meta-question "What?" before doing an `invalid-response-check`. This rule, not expanded in the figure, checks to see if the user replies with an utterance that the system can understand. If there is still a problem, the system will give more information about the problem. Some of the repair sequences that could be possible, given the interaction rules in Table 9.6, are shown in Table 9.7.

```
check-invalid-answer <-
    if (NOT (valid (top past-utterance-stack)))
        then
            invalid-answer-side-sequence
        else
            check-user-checking-move-yes

invalid-answer-side-sequence <-
    if (NOT (user-check))
        then
            question(system meta ntri)
            invalid-response-check
        else
            check-user-checking-move-no
            statement(system meta notUnderstand)
            invalid-response-check


check-user-checking-move-yes <-
    if (user-check)
        then
            statement(system meta yes)

check-user-checking-move-no <-
    if (user-check)
        then
            statement(system meta no)
```

Table 9.6 Interaction rules for invalid answer side sequences.

The effect of all this is always to give the user two chances to repair an invalid utterance, with increasingly detailed advice about what is wrong, *unless* the user has already indicated a possible problem with the utterance by terminating it with an 'OK?' meta- question. In the latter case the user receives only one chance to repair and is immediately given the most detailed advice on the problem.

This example serves to show how the interaction rules can be used to exert fine control over the development of relatively long sequences of turns in the conversation. Control is always exerted locally on a turn-by-turn basis and therefore remains sensitive to the moment-by-moment activities of each party. Managing the dialogue in this way provides scope to support conversational phenomena not found in human conversations, as well as those which are. In the next two sections we show how the observed opening and closing sequences of telephone conversations have been adapted for use in the context of starting, continuing and stopping the interaction with the Advice System.

User makes a 'valid' utterance followed by a checking move

```
System        How old are you?
User          Thirty OK?
System        Yes.
              Are you living in England, Scotland
              or Wales?
```

User makes a 'invalid' utterance followed by a checking move

```
System        How old are you?
User          Thurty OK?
System        No.
              I don't understand that. Please try
              again.
User          Thirty.
System        Are you living in England, Scotland
              or Wales?
```

User makes a 'invalid' utterance and then repairs it

```
System        How old are you?
User          Thurty.
System        What?
User          Thirty.
System        Are you living in England, Scotland
              or Wales?
```

User makes a 'invalid' utterance and then fails to repair it in the
next turn

```
System        How old are you?
User          Thurty.
System        What?
User          Thurty.
System        I don't understand that. Please try
              again.
User          ((second chance to repair))
```

Table 9.7 Repair in the Advice System.

9.5.3   Control of the opening sequence

The adjacency pair organisation of the interaction between user and
system implies that the user drives the system with questions. As
was mentioned in Section 9.3, there is a dialogue control requirement
to get the user to ask a first question so that the main body of talk may
begin. This is a non-trivial problem for which there appears to be an
elegant solution in spontaneous spoken conversation.

Schegloff (1968) has proposed a summons-answer sequence as a general mechanism for opening conversations. This is a three part sequence in which a first speaker 'calls' a second speaker whose answer obliges the first speaker to provide a reason for calling. In effect, the three parts of this sequence are composed of two adjacency pairs arranged back to back thus:

```
Summons              a  John?
Answer/ Question     b  Yeah?
Answer               a  Pass the water wouldja?
                     (from Levinson 1983, p.310)
```

An extended version of this sequence appears in the organisation of telephone call openings (e.g. Schegloff 1979). Essentially, an identification sequence is inserted between the receiver's first answer and the caller's reason for calling, if the telephone's ring is treated as the caller's summons. This insert often takes the form of a greeting-greeting adjacency pair.

The same basic form is reproduced in the opening sequence of conversations with the Advice System. The user is treated as the caller and begins the interaction by pressing a button labelled "Let me call the Advice System". What follows is shown on the left hand side of Figure 9.1. The opening sequence is completed when the user provides a reason for calling in the form of a first user question. Since this is itself the first pair part of an adjacency pair, it also constitutes the first utterance of the body of the conversation (see again Table 9.3).

```
conversation <-    opening
                   body

opening <-   statement(user meta summons)
             question(system meta identification)
             answer(user meta (identification $User))
             statement(system meta scope)
             user-opening-floor
             get-first-question
             system-floor

user-opening-floor <-    user-opening-statements
                         check-whether-more-opening

user-opening-statements <-
     statement(user substantive endTCU)
     check-to-continue-on-opening
user-opening-statements <-
     statement(user substantive endTurn)
     possible-system-interrupt
user-opening-statements <-
     statement(user substantive check?)
     possible-system-interrupt
user-opening-statements -
     statement(user meta endSession)
     check-end-of-session

check-to-continue-on-opening <-
     if (OR contradiction
           (dont-know (top past-utterance-stack))
           (NOT (valid(top past-utterance-stack))))
     then possible-system-interrupt
     else user-opening-statements

check-whether-more-opening <-
     question(system meta anyMore)
     answer(user meta yesno)
     check-opening-answer

check-opening-answer <-
     if (yes (top past-utterance-stack))
          then statement(system meta continue)
               user-opening-floor

get-first-question <-
     statement(system meta firstQuestion)
     question(user substantive)
```

Table 9.8 Interaction rules for opening.

The interaction rules for opening are shown in Table 9.8. They show how the basic form is both preserved and extended in the computer context. A series of specific exchanges between user and system is defined in the opening rule of the opening sequence. The user begins the interaction with a summons meta-statement ("Let me call the Advice System"). In fact this is a special kind of statement which expects an identification system meta-question as an answer, which in turn expects an identification user meta-answer. Note that, unlike in the main body of the interaction, there are no possibilities for either the system or the user to depart from the sequence specified in this single rule. At this point we introduce a sequence designed to give users practice at using the interface to construct utterances, by using a system meta-statement called scope to trigger a user-opening-floor. From the system's point of view, this can be seen as a getting-to-know-you period in which the user volunteers statements about him or herself. Later, these may be useful in calculating the answers to future user questions. After these opening statements have been made the user will be encouraged to ask an initial question (in get-first-question) and the system will try to answer it (in system-floor).

Within the user-opening-floor the user can make user-opening-statements in single or multi-utterance turns. This is done by the utterance of substantive statements terminated either by a single full stop (endTurn signal), three full-stops (endTCU signal) or an "OK?" (check? signal). At this point only the statement menus are available at the interface, together with a button displayed on the screen labelled "I have to go". Users can select this button to make the meta-statement endSession and initiate a closing sequence (see next section). At the end of each substantive user statement turn in the user-opening-statements move, a check-whether-more-opening is done. This involves the system asking the user whether he or she wants to provide anymore statements, to which the user must give a yesno meta-answer. If the answer is "Yes", the check-opening-answer rule fires to generate a system meta-statement inviting the user to continue. Otherwise (if the answer is "No") control returns to the opening move at get-first-question. Here the user is invited to provide a firstQuestion in a system meta-statement, and the user must formulate a substantive question in response. Now, only the question menus are available to users at the interface. The interaction then passes into the main body of talk via the next system-floor move.

9.5.4   Control of continuation and closing

Once the user's first substantive question has been answered by the Advice System, there is a requirement to get the user to supply another question or to close the interaction (see Section 9.3). Continuations and closings, like openings, are non-trivial control problems. Just as participants cannot simply begin a conversation by beginning to speak, so they cannot simply continue a conversation by continuing to speak or close it by ceasing to speak. The problem with continuing is that it may involve the introduction of new topics in turns which are unrelated to prior talk. The problem with closing is that there is usually a TRP after every turn, which expects further talk. Fortunately, there is a sequence in ordinary conversation which appears to be used to assist both continuing and closing functions. It is called a *preclosing* (Schegloff and Sacks 1973).

Preclosings may typically be found before the closing exchange of a conversation and involve the mutual 'passing' of chances to produce further talk. Similar sequences can also be found in the main body of conversations at topic boundaries. This suggests that passing turns are used as a device for participants to offer each other opportunities either to raise topics which may not cohere with the prior topic, or to agree to close. Closing is done after each party has declined at least one opportunity to continue talking. This is usually achieved in a *terminal exchange* with a 'Bye-Bye' adjacency pair.

A variety of interaction rules operate to engage the user in up to three preclosing sequences after the Advice System has answered the first substantive user question. These sequences have been designed asymmetrically to encourage the user to ask a further question on the same topic, on a related topic or on any other topic before the conversation closes. Passing up these opportunities is a way for the user to close the current topic, its related topic and the conversation respectively (see Figure 9.2). An exception to this graduated closing is provided by the "I have to go" button mentioned in Section 9.5.3. This returns an `endSession` signal which causes the system to check once for a confirmation to close before uttering the first pair-part of the terminal exchange. In this way, closings can be initiated by both the system (through preclosings) and the user (through the `endSession` statement).

Our Conversation

Do you want to ask another question about the amount of Housing Benefit?

No.

You may be able to get Child Benefit and Family Credit and One-Parent Benefit.
Do you want to ask a question about one of these?

No.

We can stop talking now unless you want to ask anything else. If we stop talking I won't remember what you have told me if you come back later.
Do you want to ask anything else?

No.

OK, bye.

Bye

Figure 9.2 The preclosings in the Advice System.

Preclosings have turned out to be even more useful for dialogue control than we first thought. In addition to providing a framework for the management of continuation and closing, they also provide a location in the dialogue at which the system can volunteer useful information to users and refer back to previous utterances. This can be illustrated with reference to the interaction rules for `preclosing1` which are shown in Table 9.7. These rules are a good example of how CA findings can be applied to support essentially the same kind of local sequencing of talk as they describe, but in a form which is adapted specifically to the computer context in which the talk occurs.

```
preclosing1 <- deduction-side-sequence
               first-topic-suggestion

deduction-side-sequence <-
    if(deductions)
       then
          statement(system substantive deduction)
          deduction-side-sequence

first-topic-suggestion <-
    if (not-empty same-held-over-questions)
       then
             question(system meta
             (sameHeldOver(same-held-over-text)))
             check-held-over-response-to-preclosing1
       else
             question(system meta
                (sameTopic
                    (top-topic
                       (top-path
                          (top last-question-stack)))))
                check-same-topic-response-to-preclosing1

check-held-over-response-to-preclosing1 <-
    answer(user meta yesno)
    check-answer-to-held-over1

check-answer-to-held-over1 <-
    if (no (top past-utterance-stack)
       then preclosing2
       else get-same-held-over-question

get-same-held-over-question <-
    statement(system meta chooseOne)
    question(user substantive
                (sameHeldOver(same-held-over)))
    system-floor
    body

check-same-topic-response-to-preclosing1 <-
    answer(user meta yesno)
    check-answer-to-same-topic

check-answer-to-same-topic <-
       if (no (top past-utterance-stack))
       then preclosing2
       else get-same-topic-question
```

Table 9.7 Interaction rules for preclosing1.

Since the first preclosing begins directly after presentation of a substantive system answer, it can be used as a place for the system to volunteer substantive statements on the same topic. This is done in a deduction-side-sequence located in the first position of the preclosing1 move. Any 'interesting' deductions which the system has made while calculating the answer to the user's last question are reported to the user here. For example, if the system works out that a user is able to get One-Parent Benefit in the process of answering a question on eligibility for Child Benefit, it can relay this fact to the user in a deduction statement.

After the outstanding deductions are presented, the system makes the first-topic-suggestion. This is an opportunity to refer back to what we call "held over questions". These are complex questions the user asked while the system was trying to answer the user's initial question, but which the system refused to answer. A complex question is defined to be one that cannot be answered in the next turn. They are held over to limit the nesting of insertion sequences within the conversation's main body. If there are any held over questions in the interaction history about the same topic as the last major user question (same-held-over-questions), then the first-topic-suggestion of the system is to present the text of such questions for re-selection at the interface. Otherwise, the system asks the user if he or she wants to ask a question about the topic of their last-question. Topics are defined in relation to the topic trees used to construct utterances at the interface. The topic of the user's last-question is the final selection they made on the topic menus when the user constructed his or her last substantive question. In fact, the topic trees used at the interface to generate topic options for user's statements and questions have proved a useful resource in the management of topic. Here, a classification of questions to question topic tree branches is used to determine 'same' and 'related' topics to the topic of the last-question. A similar classification of statements to statement topic tree branches and sub-branches is used to order the asking of system questions by 'same' topic.

If the option of selecting a same-held-over-question was presented to the user through the first-topic-suggestion move, the user's meta-answer in check-held-over-response-to-preclosing1 is considered in check-answer-to-held-over1. A 'No' answer is taken to signify a rejection of the offer by the user, causing preclosing2 to begin. A 'Yes' answer calls the get-same-held-over-question rule in which the system explicitly invites the user to chooseOne of the same-held-over questions which are displayed in a menu on the right hand side of the screen. Selection of the meta-sameHeldOver question label by the user has the same effect as entering the substantive question itself. This is then taken as the next question in the interaction which the system will reply to in the system-floor move.

If there were no held-over questions, the option of selecting a question of the sameTopic would be presented to the user by the first-topic-suggestion move. The user's meta-answer in check-same-topic-response-to-preclosing1 is considered in check-answer-to-same-topic. As before, a 'No' answer is taken to signify a rejection of the offer by the user causing preclosing2 to begin. However, this time, a 'Yes' answer calls the get-next-question rule, in which the system invites the user to construct a next substantive question. At this point the topic options are preselected down to the topic of the last user question on the right hand side of the screen, with the first phrase options awaiting selection. Although get-same-topic-question is not defined in Table 9.7, it allows the user sufficient flexibility to back out of the same topic options to any other question topic. Thus, users are directed but not forced to continue the current topic of conversation. The conversation will continue as soon as they enter another substantive question of any kind.

9.6 Conclusions

Returning to the aim of our programme we can say that applying the *technology of conversation* has allowed us to generate and support many of the properties of conversation identified by Sacks et al. (1974).

Thus, dialogue between users and the Advice System is characterised by alternating turns at talk which vary in size, content and distribution over time. Turn constructional units are employed to segment what each party says, and turn allocation techniques are used to control turn transitions between segments. Continuous or discontinuous talk can result from this, depending on whether or not the pauses between TCUs are filled with talk by the other party. Finally, the overall length of the conversation is not specified in advance and repair mechanisms exist for dealing with various kinds of error. In short, we have found conversation analysis to be a valuable resource for conversation design in a context where good design can mean the difference between a useful and a useless system.

Throughout the chapter we have stressed the usefulness of the design to the system. For example, the control of turn-taking was said to provide an explicit way of handling the construction and termination of multiple sentences by the same party, and the ordering of questions and answers; the control of repair was said to provide a method of dealing with invalid user input, 'Don't know' responses and contradictory user statements; the control of openings was said to provide the system with a first user question and some statements which might help answer it; while the control of preclosings and closing was said to supply the system with either a further user question or an explicit signal to end the interaction.

However, the conversation's design is also useful to the user. For example, the turn allocation techniques enable a user to give or take the initiative in the interaction, and through this to direct its focus; repair devices can be used to get the system to redo any of its previous utterances; openings provide an opportunity to learn how to use the interface and to volunteer important information to the system; while preclosings and closings suggest possible follow-up questions to ask before ending the conversation.

In conclusion, the dynamics of the conversation provide resources for both parties to carry out conversational work relevant to the exchange of questions and answers (Frohlich and Luff 1989). We hope that the ability to do such work will lead to a truly mixed initiative dialogue in which users will attempt to direct the conversation towards the answering of questions of local and immediate concern to them, whilst cooperating with the system's own demands for relevant and comprehensible information. 'Advice', like 'explanation', in this context can be seen as something the user gets out of the system over a large number of turns in the interaction, rather than as something the system gives the user in a single turn; as an emergent property of the conversation rather than as a particular fragment of talk (Frohlich 1988). The fact that the user is able to play an active part in obtaining information from the system should increase the likelihood of the system delivering satisfactory advice.

The next stage in our programme is to evaluate the usability and utility of the Advice System to users. In this we intend to exploit some of the methodological insights of CA in analysing the sequential organisation of conversation. In particular, we hope to discover how the dynamic properties of spoken conversation transfer to the written medium of interactive text, and to see whether or not they conform to the expectations people have about how to talk to a computer. A preliminary analysis of the mixed initiative aspects of interactions with 25 users is available in Luff and Frohlich (forthcoming).

While we may find that certain aspects of the technology of ordinary conversation do not transfer well to the technology for conversation, we are confident that the model of dialogue on which it is based will prove more appropriate than any other for the design of human computer conversations. By viewing the orderly features of dialogue as an interactional achievement, it will be possible to move away from the design of 'order' *per se* to the design of appropriate devices, resources, indeed *technology*, which active participants can use to create it. The technique of local management we have described is one general way in which this might be done.

Acknowledgements

This work was carried out as part of the Alvey DHSS Demonstrator Project, which was supported by the UK Science and Engineering Research Council and the Alvey Directorate of the Department of Trade and Industry. The project collaborators were ICL, Logica, Imperial College London, and the Universities of Lancaster, Surrey and Liverpool. We gratefully acknowledge the collaboration of Marina Jirotka, Sarah Buckland and Nigel Gilbert of the Social and Computer Sciences Research Group, and of Kevin Johnstone and David Goodwin of ICL, Manchester; the contributions of Christian Heath of the Department of Sociology, University of Surrey; and the support of many others on the Demonstrator Project.

Chapter 10

A Computational Model of Explanatory Discourse

Local Interactions in a Plan-Based Explanation

Alison Cawsey*

10.1 Introduction

There is considerable evidence that effective explanations and advice involve dialogue. Pollack et al., for example, found that advice-giving dialogues are best regarded as a negotiation process, where both the problem to be solved and the solution are jointly worked out in an extended dialogue (Pollack et al. 1982). Gilbert makes similar observations, but emphasises how local coherence constrains the organisation of the dialogue (Gilbert 1987). As the novice continues to talk about the problem, the expert attempts to find things to say which are coherent with the last utterance, yet contribute to the overall goal of the conversation. Draper, on the other hand, suggests that dialogue is important because the speaker cannot see into the hearer's mind, and so a planned explanation is unlikely to 'succeed' at first attempt (Draper 1987) as there may be missing background knowledge.

* Supported by a studentship from the Science and Engineering Research Council

In general the following types of interactions seem to be important if an explanation is to proceed smoothly:

- Negotiation to establish what explanation is sought and how much the novice knows (Rymaszewski 1987; Pollack 1982). This will be especially important at the beginning of an explanatory dialogue.

- Checking moves and opportunities for interruption and repair within the explanation (Ringle and Bruce 1981).

- Follow-up questions at the end of an explanation (Draper 1987).

The work mentioned above has emphasised the importance of dialogue in explanation. However, Draper also discusses how an explanation can be planned to include necessary background information. Much of the recent research on explanation generation has concentrated on just this issue – planning an explanation that is appropriate, given assumptions about the prior knowledge of the hearer (e.g. Paris 1987; Wallis and Shortliffe 1984). The majority of this work fails to take into account the interactive nature of explanation – though an exception is Moore and Swartout's work on follow-up questions after a plan-based explanation (Moore and Swartout 1988b). On the other hand, recent work on local management of interaction in an advice system (Frohlich 1988; Frohlich and Luff 1989) has emphasised interactivity to the exclusion of higher level planning. This chapter argues that a combined approach is necessary, where an explanation may be planned, given assumptions about the user, but interactions such as those described above are allowed. Such interactive, plan-based explanations enable the responsibility for generating appropriate explanations to be shared. The expert should generate the best possible explanation, given assumptions about what the user knows, but allow the novice (or user) opportunities to interrupt and redirect the explanation, obtaining any necessary clarifications.

Another advantage of a joint approach is that the interactions may be used by the content planning/user modelling component to infer what the user may know, while the content plans may be used by the discourse planner (which has responsibility for structuring interactions) to generate appropriate meta-comments and discourse markers.

The content planning and user modelling components of the system have been described elsewhere (Cawsey 1989a; Cawsey 1989b).

The rest of this paper will therefore concentrate on describing how interactions may be structured in a plan-based explanation.

10.2 Structuring interactions within plan-based explanations

The following discussion will consider how a wide range of types of interactions are used within plan-based explanations. The discussion will largely be organised according to ideas from conversation and discourse analysis.

10.2.1 Opening and closing exchanges

Explanations involve opening and closing sequences which are used to negotiate the opening and closing of the topic. The structure of these opening and closing sequences will depend on the social rôles of the participants. For example, when studying formal classroom discourse, Sinclair and Coulthard suggest that topics are frequently begun with a discourse marker and meta-comment, and ended with a concluding statement (Sinclair and Coulthard 1975). Because the teacher has the dominant rôle, there is little or no negotiation. In less formal explanations the novice and expert may jointly negotiate the topic.

In the EDGE[1] model, opening and closing sequences are planned by the system. Opening sequences (at the beginning of a topic) involve discourse markers and meta-comments, while closing sequences involve checking that the novice is ready to leave the topic. These types of opening and closing sequences were taken from an analysis of a corpus of human explanatory dialogues. However, as these explanations were given in an artificial situation, with the initial topic set by the experimenter, this reveals relatively little about how openings are normally managed, so they should be viewed only as example, rather than definitive openings and closings. The 'rules' used in planning these sequences are somewhat similar to those used by Frohlich and Luff (this volume). For example, the following rules (Figure 10.1) show how the opening and closing sequences are planned:

---

[1]   EDGE stands for "Explanatory Discourse Generator".

```
informing.transaction(Teaching-goal)  -
    boundary.exchange(Teaching-goal, open)
    teaching.exchanges(Teaching-goal)
    boundary.exchange(Teaching-goal, close)

boundary.exchange(Teaching-goal, open)  -
    framing.move(open)                    ; discourse marker
    focussing.move(Teaching-goal)         ; meta-comment

boundary.exchange(Teaching-goal, close)  -   ; preclosing
    request-close.move(Teaching-goal)
    answer-close.move
```

Figure 10.1 Planning opening and closing sequences.

The 'teaching exchanges' rule will pass control to the main explanation planner, to determine the content of the explanation. The explanation is incrementally planned, so that planning decisions take into account the unpredictably changing situation. When there is a proposition to convey, control passes back to the interaction/discourse planner, and the content is conveyed as a sequence of exchanges with the user. Within each exchange there are opportunities for interruption by the user. This is discussed further in the next section.

If novices ask a question after a 'preclosing' sequence (maintaining the topic) another preclosing is planned. The approach mixes high-level planning (deciding on the structure of opening and closing sequences) with local responses (allowing topics to be continued, and adding preclosings to the plan when a topic is ending).

The following example of interactions with the system (Figure 10.2) illustrates such opening and closing sequences. These (and later) examples are taken from the evaluation sessions. In the first example the planned opener is the first statement. The following sequence results from the content planner needing to know something about the user's knowledge. The combined sequence illustrates how both topic and understanding are negotiated. The second example illustrates the use of preclosings and follow-up questions.

Opening meta-comments and questions

```
E:            OK, we're going to be explaining
              how the heat detector works.    Do
              you know what a heat detector
              circuit is?
N:            --- No
E:            A heat detector circuit is a sort
              of potential divider circuit.
```

Closing sequences and follow-ups

```
E:            Is that enough about how the low
              heat warning circuit works.
N:            --- What does the comparator do?
E:            OK, When the input voltage (V2) of
              the comparator is quite high
              (towards 9V) the output voltage
              (V5) will be low (0V).    When it is
              quite low (towards 0V) the output
              voltage (V5) will be high (9V).
              Anyway, is that enough about that?
N:            --- How does the comparator work?
E:            OK, suppose the input voltage is
              quite high (towards 9V). .....
E:            Anyway, is that enough about that.
N:            --- OK
```

Figure 10.2 Example opening and closing sequences

10.2.2   Informing exchanges and TRPs

In human verbal explanations the explainee or novice may interrupt at any point to seek clarification or to redirect the discourse. The points at which they may interrupt correspond to the 'transition relevance points' (TRPs) discussed in conversation analysis (Sacks et al. 1974).   Failure to interrupt is generally viewed as an implicit acknowledgement that the previous utterance was understood and that the discourse is progressing satisfactorily.

It is unclear how such opportunities for interruption (and hence for implicit acknowledgement) should be incorporated into human-computer interaction. The different mode of communication means that certain direct models of human interaction may be unnatural. For example, Frohlich and Luff have suggested that text should be generated at a "slow reading speed" with opportunities to interrupt at certain points (Frohlich and Luff 1989) (though they have since abandoned this approach). Yet many users would almost certainly prefer a different style of interaction, where large sections of text are presented with opportunities for interruption at the end. It is an open question what the 'ideal' style of interaction is, or whether it depends entirely on the preferences and experience of the users. This can only be resolved by empirical evaluation of a range of systems.

The EDGE model requires explicit acknowledgement after each utterance (typically a sentence in length). At these points, clicking with the   'mouse' indicates that the user is happy with the explanation, and wants the system to continue. This corresponds to the 'lack of interruption' and visual cues at a TRP which, in verbal interaction, indicates that the hearer is willing for the speaker to continue. If the user wants to ask questions or make requests at these points, then instead of 'clicking' in the text window they can select an item from a menu.   The items in the menu include relevant questions about the domain, and options to repeat or quit discourse segments (sub-topics). For example, the user could ask a domain question such as "What does a light dependent resistor do?" or ask the system to "Stop explaining what a light dependent resistor does.". An extension to the basic model (discussed in the following section) would be to allow the user to signal general lack of comprehension at these points (corresponding to frowns in verbal discourse, or signals such as "huh" or "what").

The EDGE model views an 'informing exchange' as this statement-acknowledgement sequence, where the acknowledgement may consist in verbal discourse of minimal visual cues and the absence of interruption, and in human-computer discourse of signals such as clicking a mouse button. It therefore contrasts with some discourse analysis models, such as Sinclair and Coulthard's, which view an informing exchange as a sequence of informing statements and an explicit verbal acknowledgement.

10.2.3   Side sequences or interruptions

If the user asks a clarification question within an explanation, then this will generally initiate a side sequence or interruption (Jefferson, 1972). This may happen both after an informing statement, and after a question.   An interruption is structured so that the question is answered and then the preceding discourse is (actively) resumed. In the analysis of human explanations there are two main ways of resuming an explanation. The commonest was to repeat one or more utterances from where the explanation left off, but another approach was to give some meta-comment on the interrupted discourse. In the EDGE model it is straightforward to define either of these sorts of resumptions. However, the current system repeats questions if the interruption follows a question, but provides a meta-comment if the interruption follows a statement. Figure 10.3 illustrates some (short) interruptions and resumptions.

Answering a question with a question

E:	What's it going to be when the input light intensity (L1) is low (dark)
N:	--- What's a resistor?
E:	OK, this component here is a resistor. Anyway, what's the output voltage (V1) of the light detector circuit going to be when the input light intensity (L1) is low (dark)?
N:	--- Quite low (towards 0V)
E:	Precisely, excellent, it's quite low.

Interrupting at a TRP

E:	What's the output voltage (V5) of the comparator going to be when the input voltage (V2) is quite high (towards 9V).
N:	--- Quite high.
E:	No, thats not right, it's low.
N:	--- What's a comparator?
E:	OK, this circuit section here is a comparator. Anyway, we were in the middle of explaining how the low heat warning device works if it has the following inputs: heat-intensity high.

Figure 10.3 Example interruptions and resumptions

Interruptions are planned in the same way as the top level explanation, involving opening and closing exchanges, where the closing exchange may either involve a repetition of an utterance, or a meta-comment on the interrupted discourse. The appropriate meta-comment or repeated utterance may be found by examining the 'discourse model'. This is a hierarchical structure representing the past explanation and any future explanation planned, and corresponds loosely to Grosz and Sidner's model of 'intentional' and 'attentional' structure in discourse (Grosz and Sidner 1985). The use of meta-comments is important if the user is to understand the system's view of the discourse situation. Otherwise the user's interpretation of utterances may be incorrect because of problems in interpreting that situation. Appropriate use of meta-comments requires a global view of the discourse. This view seems to suggest that it is because of the situated nature of action and interpretation that a global model of discourse is required! In the EDGE model, not every question will be answered. The discourse model can be examined, and if the question is likely to be answered later, a postponement negotiated. For example, a simplified version of the discourse model near the beginning of a circuit explanation is given in Figure 10.4 (using indentation to represent the hierarchical structure of the discourse).

```
interaction informing.transaction
                ((teach how-it-works (light-detector)))
        interaction boundary.exchange ((teach......) open)
            interaction frame.move (open)
                interaction marker.act (open)
                interaction focussing.move ((teach...))
                    interaction meta-comment.act ((teach....))
        interaction teaching.exchanges ((teach....)))
            teach how-it-works (light-detector)
                teach causal-behaviour (light detector)
                    teach particular-causal-behaviour
                        (light-detector (light-intensity high))
                    interaction teaching-exchange
                        ((suppose light-detector
                            (light-intensity high)))
***                     interaction teacher-inform.exchange
                            ((suppose ...))
                    teach causal-bit
                    (light-detector (light-intensity ...))
                    teach particular-causal-behaviour
                        (light-detector (light-intensity low))
                teach what-it-does (light-detector)
        interaction boundary.exchange ((teach...) close)
```

Figure 10.4 Example discourse model.

The stars indicate the current point in the discourse goals – past this point are part of the partially defined future plan, while goals before this point are a more detailed representation of the past plan. Suppose the user then asks what the light detector does. The system may then reason that it is about to answer that anyway, resulting in the following sequence.

```
E:              Suppose the input light intensity
                is high.
N:              --- What does a light detector
                circuit do?
E:              I'll be getting on to that in a
                minute.
```

10.2.4   Remediation sequences

The particular discourse structures used in the EDGE system are based on 'tutorial' discourse. In this type of discourse the teacher or system may ask questions and provide remediation. These remediation sequences (triggered by incorrect answers to questions) are based on analysis of human tutorial explanations and related work on generating tutorial dialogues (e.g. Woolf and McDonald 1984). A remediation sequence is treated as an interruption or side sequence and the previous discourse resumed using repeats or meta-comments as shown above.

The particular content of a remediation sequence will depend on the domain and on the type of question just asked. However, the basic form is similar in all domains. A typical sequence may involve the teacher/system first providing some additional useful information which will enable the student to understand why his answer was incorrect, and then asking the question again. The following example (Figure 10.5) illustrates a case where, following the 'remediation', the user gets the correct answer to the question asked.

The remediation sequence is triggered by the specific local situation, and obviously cannot be planned in advance. It is a type of 'repair' sequence, where the system realises that the user has failed to understand, and needs to fix things so that the user is 'put back on the right track'. However, though it is the local situation which triggers the sequence, it takes place within a planned explanation. The content of the remediation sequence will be planned, and will depend both on system's assumptions about the user's knowledge and on the past planned explanation (represented in the discourse model).

10.2.5   Summary: plans and interactions

The above discussion should give a general picture of the sorts of explanations and interactions allowed in the EDGE model. These are globally planned, but may take into account aspects of the situation as recorded in a hierarchical discourse model. The planning itself is done only when required, and not in advance, so constraints on plans

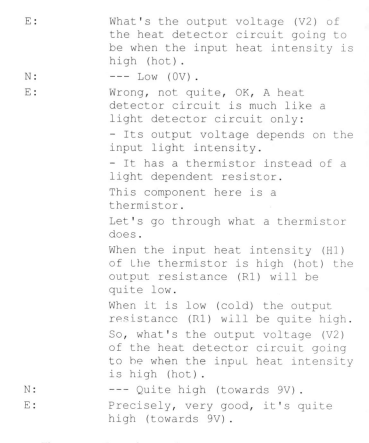

E: What's the output voltage (V2) of
            the heat detector circuit going to
            be when the input heat intensity is
            high (hot).
N: --- Low (0V).
E: Wrong, not quite, OK, A heat
            detector circuit is much like a
            light detector circuit only:
            - Its output voltage depends on the
            input light intensity.
            - It has a thermistor instead of a
            light dependent resistor.
            This component here is a
            thermistor.
            Let's go through what a thermistor
            does.
            When the input heat intensity (H1)
            of the thermistor is high (hot) the
            output resistance (R1) will be
            quite low.
            When it is low (cold) the output
            resistance (R1) will be quite high.
            So, what's the output voltage (V2)
            of the heat detector circuit going
            to be when the input heat intensity
            is high (hot).
N: --- Quite high (towards 9V).
E: Precisely, very good, it's quite
            high (towards 9V).

Figure 10.5 Example remediation sequence

access the actual current and not predicted situation. By allowing interruptions (side sequences), remediation sequences and follow-up questions, the local reactivity of explanatory dialogues is captured and the explanations made more robust.

The examples given above are all from actual users using the system (though some are slightly simplified). This evaluation consisted of having eight people (familiar with computers, but not with the domain) use the system to obtain explanations of the circuits given. From examining the scripts, answers to a simple questionnaire and comments made during the sessions, problems were identified which suggest areas for further work. The subjective view of users was generally that the mixed initiative style of interaction was helpful in an explanation system. However, not all user's were happy with being led through a planned explanation. One user, for example, assumed a far more dominant rôle, directing the discourse by asking many questions. This unexpected style of interaction meant, for example, that many of the inferences made by the user modelling component were incorrect. There is clearly much more work to be done on how different dialogue styles can be best accommodated, and how they interact with the other components of the system.

10.3 Local coherence and repair

One of the major questions in the type of mixed-initiative planned explanations discussed, is how the current (and past) situation should influence later discourse. For example, how should an explanation continue after an interruption, and how should the explanation given so far influence repair strategies adopted when the user fails to understand the explanation? This section will consider two main extensions planned for the EDGE discourse model which would make the explanation more truly reactive given the dynamically changing situation, while retaining the notion of planned discourse.

10.3.1 Partial ordering and local coherence

The first extension involves making the explanation content plans partially ordered. Currently, the content plans define both what to say and in what order to say it. Although there are some ordering constraints in explanation generation (arising chiefly from prerequisite and coherence relations between concepts being explained), there is also considerable flexibility. For example, the components of a system could be introduced in any order, but should generally be introduced before an explanation of system behaviour. Content plans must represent explicitly the constraints that exist, while allowing the freedom to re-order unconstrained content depending on the immediate situation.

Suppose, for example, it is necessary to know the symbols and behaviour of a transistor and a thermistor as prerequisites to understanding a description of how some circuit works. There would be prerequisite ordering constraints between the component descriptions and the explanation of how the circuit worked, and possibly coherence (focus) constraints that suggest that a component symbol and behaviour should be given together. However, there might not be any constraints on the order in which the components should be described. If the user then asked "What's the symbol for a transistor?", then the system should both be able to reason about whether this is a reasonable question at this point (are there any prerequisites that are unknown?) and if so, after answering the question, use local coherence or focus constraints to decide to next talk about the transistor's behaviour.

Using partially ordered plans and focus constraints is a straightforward extension of the system. It would make possible explanation or advice dialogues much like those described in (Gilbert 1987), where the adviser is constrained to give advice which, though satisfying the overall goal, is coherent with the advisee's questions. It is a step further towards integrating plan-based and interactive/locally defined systems.

10.3.2 Negotiation and repair

The second extension that will be discussed is perhaps essential for robust explanations, and concerns what to do when the user fails to understand an explanation. At this point, some kind of explanation repair is needed. We have already considered two cases where local interactions are initiated to deal with misunderstanding – the user may interrupt and ask a clarification question, or the system may initiate a clarification (remediation sequence) having detected that the user has not understood. Yet, in many cases, the system may not be able to detect the misunderstanding, and the user not be able to specify the source of trouble. In this case users may want to initiate a repair sequence by simply indicating that they have not understood. It is then up to the system to guess the source of trouble. Moore has done some work on this topic, allowing users to say "Huh?" at the end of an explanation (Moore 1989). Her system will then examine the plan of the explanation to find what constraints might not have been satisfied, and re-explain taking this into account.

However, there are two limitations with Moore's work. First, it is impossible to signal misunderstanding in the middle of an explanation (at a TRP). This makes it arguably less natural for the user, and certainly harder for the system to guess the source of trouble. Second, the system guesses what is wrong, but does not check with the user that it has correctly found the problem. Yet the user, though unable to express what the problem is, may be able to confirm which of the missing prerequisites they understand, for example.

A more robust approach to explanation repair might therefore be the following. At any TRP (where the EDGE system pauses for acknowledgement) the users could signal that they don't understand.

The system would then reason (from the explanation plan and user model) about possible problems with the explanation. Then would follow a negotiation phase to confirm the problem, and a repair, supplying the missing knowledge or re-explaining something in another way. The following sorts of dialogues should be possible (Figure 10.6):

```
         E:              .... so the output voltage is high.
         N:              --- Huh?
         E:              Don't you know what a potential
                         divider circuit is?
         N:              --- No.
         E:              OK, let's explain what the heat
                         detector circuit does another way.
or
         E:              OK, let's go through what a
                         potential divider circuit is.
```

Figure 10.6   Example repair sequences.

This is another extension which increases the interactivity of the explanation. Yet again, this requires a global model of the discourse to be maintained, including all the assumptions that might have been made about the user's knowledge.

The type of repair considered here is of course very limited, concentrating on the user's misunderstanding of complex information. There are many other sorts of repair important in human-computer interaction, initiated by system or user. Some of these are discussed by Raudaskoski (this volume).

10.4 Conclusion

The above sections have described how plan-based and interactive approaches to explanation generation may be combined, sharing responsibility between system and user in generating appropriate explanations. Section 10.2 describes how interactions are controlled in the implemented (and evaluated) system, while Section 10.3 describes some extensions which are needed to make the explanation truly responsive to the user's initiative. Plan-based and local or interactive approaches need not be contradictory; on the contrary, one provides resources for the other. Simple fixed-order hierarchical discourse models are insufficiently reactive to user input. But on the other hand, a local model gives an insufficient representation of discourse context and fails to exploit the possibility of planning an explanation which depends on the user's knowledge. Combined approaches such as the EDGE model give the advantages of both.

The planning of interactions is very similar to that described by Frohlich and Luff (this volume). However, because of the different type of application (tutorial explanations rather than advice), the rôles of system and user are very different. In the EDGE system, the system has the dominant rôle, and directs the progress of the discourse, while in the Advice System the user dominates the the interaction. It is partly because of this different rôle of the system that a plan-based approach is important in explanation generation. Yet without interaction, the plans are unlikely to succeed. By combining the two approaches, we get closer to a framework that can support a wide range of styles of interaction, from system-directed to user-directed explanation or advice.

Of course, any claims about the approach will not hold out without further evaluation! But evaluation is impossible without flexible systems to evaluate. The EDGE model is such a system, and represents a possible approach to practical explanation generation of the future.

Acknowledgements

This research was carried out while the author was supported by an SERC postgraduate studentship. It is continuing thanks to support under an SERC postdoctoral fellowship.

Chapter 11

Organising Computer Talk

Nigel Gilbert, Robin Wooffitt and Norman
Fraser

11.1 Introduction

Conversation analysts have for some twenty years been engaged in
the detailed study of naturally occurring talk. Workers within this
tradition have eschewed premature theorising and have focused
instead upon the inductive discovery of recurrent patterns in the
interactions which have been recorded and transcribed. This research
strategy has been outstandingly successful and productive. In the
light of this success we began to wonder whether the findings of
conversation analysis (CA) could be employed in the design of
human-computer interactions. With the continuing explosive
growth in computer use, there is a practical need for systems which
are "easy to use". One tempting design strategy is to look to the
interactional strategies which people use in their daily lives, and to
apply these to HCI. This could have two benefits. First, we may
assume that interactional procedures and strategies which are
grounded in everyday life are reasonably effective. Second, as people
are tacitly familiar with these strategies, they will have less difficulty
communicating with computers which have been designed to capture
the characteristics of these procedures.

Some work has been done on adapting the phenomena described
by CA to control the interaction of a user with an expert system. In
the 'Advice System' the choice of possible next turns available to the
user and to the system is controlled by a set of rules based on CA

descriptions of turns found in everyday question and answer sequences (see Frohlich and Luff 1989 and this volume).

The Advice System uses a conventional mouse, screen and keyboard interface. The findings of conversation analysis about human-human interaction would seem to be even more likely to be able to make a contribution to the design of voice-mediated human-computer dialogues, where the user speaks to the machine and the machine's responses are generated using a speech synthesiser. Speech understanding and synthesis systems have now been developed to the point where the technological infrastructures required to support such dialogues are within sight. Although they are still fragile laboratory prototypes, there are now systems which can recognise respectably large vocabularies, up to about 1000 words, while synthesis has progressed to the point where systems can not only pronounce individual words in an easily understandable fashion, but can also go someway towards providing appropriate co-articulation (elision at word boundaries) and prosody (changes in pitch).

Despite these opportunities, there has been some scepticism about applying CA findings to the design of computer systems and, more generally, of developing computational models of conversational phenomena (see Button this volume). In part, this scepticism may be due to a belief that models from linguistics are inappropriate for the analysis of conversation. For example, Levinson (1983), in a masterly survey of the pragmatics literature, first examines broadly computational approaches to discourse and, having found difficulties with each of them, turns to CA. But in doing so, he notes that "it is important to see, though, that the basis for rejection of [Discourse Analysis] is that the methods and theoretical tools advocated, namely those imported from mainstream theoretical linguistics, seem quite inappropriate to the domain of conversation. Conversation is not a structural product in the same way that a sentence is – it is rather the outcome of two or more independent, goal-directed individuals, with often divergent interests" (Levinson 1983, p.294).[1]

The aim of this chapter is to investigate whether this scepticism is wholly justified. While there is no doubt that the organisation of a conversation differs from the organisation of a sentence, this does not necessarily imply that none of the very sophisticated apparatus of linguistics could be applied to its analysis. In particular, some of the

---

1   This is in fact a somewhat tendentious description of a conversation: it is not
     clear how one could determine that the individuals were 'goal-directed' or what
     their 'interests' might be.

more recent advances in computational linguistics would seem to have some value in examining conversation. One advantage of the computational approach, both to linguistics and to understanding conversation, is that it forces the analyst to be clear and precise about what is being proposed. Another is that it provides a way to conceptualise and explore the consequences of the fact that conversation is "the outcome of two or more independent, goal-directed individuals". One can not only try to build computer programs which interact in a conversational way with human users, but also try to build programs which interact with each other and which, in doing so, appear to behave in 'goal-directed' ways (for examples, see Bond and Gasser 1988). The benefits of success in achieving working computational models of conversation are, however, not only academic. The models could be immediately put to practical use in computer-based speech systems.

To introduce the argument, we begin by briefly describing a current speech system project, the ESPRIT II Sundial project,[2] which aims to draw on some of the interactional strategies which have been revealed by CA. We intend to use these as resources to organise the computer's dialogue with the user. In the following section we consider some of the salient findings of CA as an introduction to this discussion. In the second half of the paper, we discuss a simple computational model which tries to take account of the points raised in these arguments to provide, as far as possible, an initial model of conversation which is faithful to the phenomena identified by CA. Finally, we discuss the shortcomings of this model to see whether the problems are such as to invalidate the enterprise or are merely difficulties which a more sophisticated model could overcome.

11.2   The architecture of a speech understanding system

The aim of the Sundial project is to develop a computer system which is capable of 'conversing' with members of the public over the telephone to answer simple queries such as the time of arrival of a particular airline flight or the times of trains. To be successful at the basic recognition task, the computer will need to be able to

---

[2]   Sundial, ESPRIT project P2218, is a collaborative research project involving Logica Cambridge Ltd. and the University of Surrey (UK), CAP-SESA, CNET, and IRISA (France), Daimler-Benz, Siemens and the University of Erlangen (FDR), and CSELT and Sarin (Italy).

understand connected word speech from callers using a moderately large vocabulary (about 1000 words). This goal is likely to be achieved within one to two years.

Most speech understanding systems can be divided for convenience into a number of functional modules.[3] Analogue electrical signals from a microphone or from the telephone line are conditioned to remove as much extraneous line noise ('crackles and pops') as possible and smoothed to eliminate gross amplitude variations. The analogue signal is then converted into digital form and passed into an 'acoustic-phonetic' module. The major tasks of this module are to chop the continuous signal into segments (corresponding roughly to phonemes, although different techniques use different units for segmentation) and then categorise the segments with labels. However, the process of segmentation and labelling is very prone to error.

The output of the acoustic-phonetic module provides the input to a lexical processor whose purpose is to extract words from the segment stream. This is a difficult task because speakers blur and change the pronunciation of words depending on the surrounding speech context. Speakers may omit phonemes, for example, when eliding two words together (cf. "That" and "Book" with "That book"), or insert phonemes (for example, 'how' as a single word is typically pronounced without a final /w/, but when it precedes 'are' as in 'how are you?', the /w/ is voiced). Words are also pronounced differently depending on their position in the sentence and their degree of stress.

For these reasons, the output from this module is not a simple sequence of words, but a 'word lattice' which gives the probability of any of a large number of combinations of words being the ones which the caller actually spoke. The word lattice is passed to syntactic and semantic parsers (sometimes these are distinct, but more often syntax and semantics are analysed using the same parser). This has the task of filtering the word lattice to reject those word combinations which are, firstly, syntactically unlikely according to its rules of grammar (e.g. 'Thread ream miss seating'), and secondly, semantically unlikely (e.g. 'The red dream is eating'). The result is one or more 'parses' of the caller's utterance.

Most existing speech understanding systems stop at this point. An information service system would have a 'back-end' program which takes the output from the speech recogniser (which might be, for instance, a semantic representation of a single question) and attempts

---

3   Introductions to current techniques for speech recognition can be found in Holmes (1988) and Ainsworth (1988).

to provide an answer from a database. In other applications, such as stock control, the user's utterance might be a statement about the number of items in stock and the corresponding semantic representation would be stored in the computer. In both these examples, the speech system deals with utterances one at a time, with little or no notion of context or of the development of a dialogue over a series of turns.

In contrast, a key component of the Sundial system will be a 'dialogue manager' which will superintend the computer's interaction with the user during the telephone call. The dialogue manager will receive the output from the parser, interact with an external program such as a database to obtain answers to callers' queries, and send instructions to a 'message generator' module. The latter has the task of translating these instructions into natural language for a speech synthesiser, the module which 'talks' to the caller. The dialogue manager has to handle a number of functions as well as interacting with the parser, message generator and database: it manages the conversation as a whole, ensuring that it opens and closes 'properly' and proceeds expeditiously to answer the caller's queries; it determines the questions that the caller should be asked; and it keeps a history of the interaction so far. Each of these functions are themselves quite complex and this paper will discuss in detail only the first, the management of the conversation.

With these objectives for the dialogue manager component, it seems natural to consider whether it would be possible to build some of the findings of conversation analysis into the design. For example, adjacency pairs (such as question - answer, greeting - greeting, offer - acceptance, assessment - agreement and so on) are claimed to be one of the fundamental units of conversational organisation (Levinson 1983, p.304). If so, a dialogue manager which is able to converse naturally with human users clearly needs to have knowledge of these phenomena.

11.3   Adjacency pairs: a central feature of conversational organisation

In conversational turn-taking one possibility is for the speaker to select the next speaker. This is typically achieved by uttering the first part of an adjacency pair (e.g. a question), with the expectation that the next speaker will provide the second part (e.g. an answer). However, the next speaker need not immediately offer a second part. In between there may be insertion sequences, often composed of embedded and nested adjacency pairs in which matters relevant to the first part are sorted out before the second part is produced. Thus, one obtains patterns of, for example, questions and answers of the following form:

```
A                         Hello
B                         Is Fred there?     Q1
A                         Who is calling?    Q2
B                         Is he there?       Q3
A                         Yes    A3
B                         This is Joe Henderson    A2
A                         Just a moment      A1
```

(Taken from Sacks, Lecture 3, 1972, p.23)

In fact, this is somewhat of an oversimplification. The first part of an adjacency pair merely sets up an expectation and relevance context for a second part. This means that, where possible, subsequent turns will be heard as being either the second part itself, some preliminary working up to the second part, or some announced failure to provide the second part. The last case is illustrated by the following example.

```
[13]  T1:SB:9588  (T)

1    A: flight information british airways good
2       day can I help you
3       (.)
4    C: 'h erm yes I wonder if you could tell
5       me I haven't actually got the flight
6       number but there should be a flight
7       coming in from crete this morning (.3)
8       and I'm wondering what time it arrives
9    A: right where at gatwick
10      (.)
11   C: er yeah (.) -sorry
12   A:              -any idea of a time
13   C: 'hh I think it's roughly ten o'clock
14   A: right hold on
15      (43)
16   A: you're probably find it's an
17      airtours flight
18      (1)
19   C: right
```

```
20   A: a charter flight erm: (.3) but I'm just
21      trying to find out for y-ou
22   C:                            -huhh hah
23       ·hh
24   A: it's definitely into gatwick at ten
25      it may not be a flight we handle
26      at all just a moment
27   C: okay
28      (73)
29   A: well I'm sorry I've looked up (.)
30      heraculen which is crete
31   C: yeah
32      (.)
33   A: and chania we don't seem to have
34      any thing you y:* you may well find
35      it's another carrier
```

In this extract the agent is unable to provide the information requested by the caller in lines 4 to 8. Her utterance in lines 29 to 35 is an account for why an answer, made 'conditionally relevant' by the production of the question, is not forthcoming. As this example shows, second parts, or the participants' displayed orientation to expectations generated by first parts, may be located at some distance from the first parts.

The concept of adjacency pairs, and the many other phenomena noted by conversation analysts which are described in other chapters of this volume, would seem at first sight to provide ideal resources to inform the design and building of a dialogue manager. Yet it has been argued that computers could not possibly be competent conversationalists. One of the reasons for this is that the 'rules' formulated by conversation analysts are not the same kind of rules as the rules which a computer could obey. We shall consider these arguments, using the notion of adjacency pairs as a running example with which to assess the merits of the opposed positions.

11.4. Arguments against a computational approach to conversational phenomena

It is one of the ironies of the development of CA that at its birth it was embroiled in extended and bitter controversies about its epistemological basis and about its practical value.[4]   Now, however, it is being sought out by computer scientists who see its potential for assisting in the design of human-computer interactions, while in turn it is casting epistemological doubts upon the validity of such an enterprise.   We will discuss three arguments used by those who are sceptical about the application of CA findings in the design of computer technology.

11.4.1.   The precision of computer data vs the 'muddiness' of human descriptors

Conversation analysts and, more generally, ethnomethodologists, have stressed the all-pervasive significance of 'indexicality'.   This refers to the idea that the meaning of an expression is relative to such contextual matters as who says it, to whom it is said, where and on what kind of occasion it is said, the social relations between the speaker and hearer, and so forth.   In particular, analysts have argued not just against an empiricist view of language which mechanically associated 'names' with phenomena, but also against more sophisticated views which proposed that naming is carried out using sets of rules associating names with specific fixed criteria (Weider 1971).

In contrast, conversation analysts assert that no description, however detailed, can exhaust the object to be described.   There are always further descriptors which could be applied.   Given this, a speaker has on each occasion to select from available descriptions the one which is going to be used.   The same descriptors can be used in different contexts to indicate different phenomena, and the same phenomena can be described in different ways.   Therefore, there can be no simple correspondence between phenomenon and descriptor, and individual descriptors when considered in abstraction from specific contexts of use seem as a result "muddy" and indefinite (Heritage 1978).

If meanings are indexical, varying from occasion to occasion, it might be wondered how we manage to communicate at all.   The results from conversation analytic studies have shown the range of interpretative resources people employ to identify the sense of any specific utterance.   People's own analyses of co-interactants' talk take into account not only relevant sequential and contextual aspects, but also exhibit an awareness of the interactional tasks for which specific utterances are designed.

---

[4]   One example from an extensive literature is Goldthorpe (1973).

11.4.2. Differences in the ways in which computers and people use rules

The argument about the fundamental indexicality of descriptors certainly implies that a speech understanding system which is to hold a dialogue with people in a 'human-like' way cannot manage by straightforwardly looking up the meaning of words from their dictionary definitions. But the objection is deeper than this. It is further argued that there can be no simple rule-like relationship between context and meaning. That is, the relation between meaning and context cannot be as simple as 'in context C1, this expression means X1, and in context C2 it means X2'. Thus, a dialogue manager whose understanding and generation is based on rules must certainly be inadequate.

Nevertheless, conversation analysts, as a result of their analyses of human interaction, do propose regularities and consistencies in human conduct. Consider, for example, the normatively prescribed expectation that the first part of an adjacency pair is followed by a second part or, more concretely, that questions are followed by answers. There is clearly some merit in this "rule" but, nevertheless in practice not all questions are answered. Moreover, 'answers' do not come with labels attached identifying them as such; not only does the existence of a question provide the 'context' for identifying a particular utterance as 'an answer', but the presence of an identifiable answer can be used in turn to locate its question *as a question* (rather than an assertion, a comment, and so on). Hence a speech understanding system cannot straightforwardly apply the expectation: "whenever you hear a question, generate an answer" as though it were an invariant rule. There are two reasons: it could have trouble identifying what are questions, and there may be no answer to generate.

The regularity that questions are followed by answers does have a use, however. It indicates that, given a first part, a second part is to be expected. The absence of a second part becomes 'noticeable', that is, the absence is something which might be remarked upon by the participants, referred to later in the conversation, used as a warrant for some inference (e.g. "He wasn't listening to me.") and so forth.

11.4.3.   The mechanical execution of a computer program vs the idea that human utterances are social actions

By virtue of being created by a system designer, computer programs are often regarded as deterministic, predictable and mechanical, in contrast to humans who have none of these characteristics. Furthermore, people are social agents, while computer programs are not. And, as conversation analysts have emphasised, people's utterances are actions within sequences of interaction, while the outputs of computers are merely phenomena which, if they are to have any socially significant consequences, have to be interpreted by social actors.

Whether an entity is a 'social being', however, is not a characteristic inherent in the entity, but an ascription by the observer or participant. If we, collectively, choose to regard computers as social beings, then they will be so. The possibility of the ascription of 'sociality' to apparently unpromising material is nicely illustrated in Garfinkel's experiment (Garfinkel 1976), in which he persuaded students seeking advice to visit a new form of counselling service. The students were told that they could ask only questions expecting a 'Yes' or 'No' answer and that their questions should be addressed to a hidden 'counsellor' sitting behind a curtain. Unknown to the students, the 'counsellor' responded to their questions with answers chosen at random, yet almost without exception the students were able to make sense of the answers, did not doubt the competence of the counsellor and professed themselves well satisfied with the session.[5]   A more everyday example is the way that people treat pet cats and dogs (Oldman and Druker 1985).

As we have seen in this section, there is some scepticism about whether the findings of CA could be implemented in a computer-based dialogue manager.   One of the prime objections is that the regularities, or 'rules', which are found in natural language use cannot be implemented in a computer program because they are situated in the specifics of actual sequences of interaction.   Thus, they

---

5   The experiment also raises questions about the adequacy of the Turing test (Turing 1950) which is supposed to indicate whether a computer is intelligent by getting subjects to ask questions through two terminals, one linked to a human respondent and the other to the computer. The computer is judged intelligent if the subject is unable to discover which terminal is connected to the computer. The difficulty with this scheme is that it fails to take into account the intelligence of the subject; in particular, people's ability to make sense of almost anything.

cannot be distilled from those occasions without doing violence to the context sensitive, inferential reasoning processes which people bring to their interactions with others.

The degree to which this argument is conclusive is one which is debated at length by other contributors to this volume. However, it is not one we want to address in this chapter. Our objective is not to try to replicate these inferential procedures, but to try to translate some of their properties into a set of propositions which can be programmed into a computer. This of course means that we are not trying to construct a program that can do what a human can do. We only wish to develop a program which, in its own way, does similar things. This (modest) objective is consistent with our intention, expressed at the beginning of this chapter, to use CA to build computers which facilitate more fluid interactions with their users. The following sections will illustrate one direction in which our work is progressing. This concerns the use of techniques from computational linguistics to address the notion of the adjacency pair.

11.5   A computational approach

The way in which semantics can be embodied in rules has received a great deal of attention in computational linguistics, a field whose primary interest is in formulating theories of language which are amenable to implementation on a computer. Although computational linguists' main focus has been on devising grammars and parsers for language understanding, the techniques which they have pioneered might be relevant to the treatment of dialogue. A fundamental distinction they have made is between a grammar, consisting of a set of rules which specify syntax, and a parser or generator. A parser is a program which acts as an interpreter of the grammar, taking as input a sequence of words and producing a syntactic or semantic representation of the sequence which shows its organisation or structure. A generator is a program which works in the opposite direction, taking a semantic representation as input and producing a corresponding natural language text.

Grammars can be expressed in a number of formalisms. A simple one expresses rules as having two parts, a 'head' and a 'tail', joined by a connector, `--->`, meaning "can consist of". For example, the following rule expresses one way of constructing a simple English sentence at the level of syntax:

```
sentence ---> noun phrase, verb phrase
```

This states that a sentence can consist of a noun phrase followed by a verb phrase (of course, there are other ways of constructing English sentences, which could be covered by other grammatical rules). A full grammar would need to include one or more rules stating what a noun phrase consists of, such as

```
noun phrase ---> determiner, noun
```

(a noun phrase can consist of a determiner, such as "the" or "a", followed by a noun). There would also have to be a 'lexicon', which allocated individual words to parts of speech (e.g. "apple" is a noun, "pear" is a noun, "the" is a determiner, and so on).

Parsers and generators could only be relevant to the management of dialogue if it were possible to construct something that corresponds to a grammar for dialogue. Fortunately, some of the regularities identified by CA can easily be expressed in a grammar formalism. For example, a grammar rule such as the following might express what an adjacency pair can consist of:

```
adjacency pair ---> first part, second part
```

However, this first version of a grammar rule for adjacency pairs fails to specify that the first part and the second part must correspond; if the first part is a question, the second part must be an answer, not a greeting. A better rule would present a number of alternatives for different kinds of pair:

```
adjacency pair ---> question, answer
adjacency pair ---> summons, response
adjacency pair ---> offer, acceptance
                                  etc.
```

These rules also fail to allow for the possibility of insertion sequences. It appears from the rule as we have it so far that the pair can only consist of the first part immediately followed by the second part. We can add a further clause to the rule to allow for insertions between questions and answers:

```
adjacency pair ---> question, answer
adjacency pair ---> question, insertions, answer
```

but we may not want to allow insertions between a summons and a response, so that part of the rule will remain unchanged:

```
adjacency pair ---> question, answer
adjacency pair ---> question, insertions, answer
adjacency pair ---> summons, response
adjacency pair ---> offer, acceptance
```

Only certain kinds of insertion are 'possible': specifically, insertions must themselves consist of question and answer pairs. Hence an insertion may be specified in a rule such as:

```
insertion ---> question, insertion, answer
```

Note that this rule is 'recursive', that is, "insertion" is defined in terms of itself. This is fine if the intention is to represent the idea that within an inserted adjacency pair there may be a further embedded pair, but we also need to allow for the fact that there may be no insertion. This can be done by a further, non-recursive, addition to the rule, which states that an insertion can consist of just a question and answer:

```
insertion ---> question, answer
```

Moreover, insertions can consist of several question and answer pairs, one after the next, so let us define 'insertions' to consist of one or more inserted pairs:

```
insertions ---> insertion, insertions
insertions ---> insertion
```

This rule means that 'insertions' can consist either of a single insertion followed by some insertions, or it can consist of a single insertion.

The rules we have developed so far are:

```
adjacency pair ---> question, answer
adjacency pair ---> question, insertions, answer
adjacency pair ---> summons, response
adjacency pair ---> offer, acceptance
adjacency pair ---> offer, insertions, acceptance
insertions ---> insertion, insertions
insertions ---> insertion
insertion ---> question, insertions, answer
insertion ---> question, answer
```

These simple rules are sufficient to recognise or generate sequences such as

```
q1  q2  q3  q4  a4  q5  a5  a3  a2  a1
```

where 'q' and 'a' indicate questions and answers. They clearly do not constitute anything like a complete set of rules for adjacency pairs, but they are a beginning which we can add to.

Before investigating the behaviour of these rules further, we need to examine how a computer might use them, that is, what the actions of a parser or generator might be. There are many different kinds of parsers, some of which work in ways which are clearly different from what people do in talk. For example, some parsers are designed to process their input from right to left, while others allow for decisions to be taken and later revoked. Real time dialogues cannot be parsed in either of these ways; the order of processing must follow the order of utterance, and a turn in dialogue, once taken, cannot be revoked. What is required, then, is a parser which works from left to right, at every point maintaining as many simultaneous hypotheses as are permitted by the grammar. Although parsers which develop many analyses in parallel tend to be very inefficient, chart parsers are more acceptable because they construct one compact data structure (called a "chart") to record all the structural analyses they discover.[6] A chart can be thought of as encoding all of the alternative understandings of what has gone on in the dialogue so far, together with a set of hypotheses about what will happen next.

Suppose, for the sake of a simple example, that a chart parser is given the adjacency pair grammar introduced above and the sequence q1 q2 q3 q4 a4 q5 a5 a3 a2 a1 as the material to parse (we shall consider

---

[6]   The idea of using a chart-like data structure is due to Earley (1970). For introductions to chart parsing see: Thompson and Ritchie (1984) and Winograd (1983).

below how the parser might come to have such a sequence to work on). The parser's initial task is to unpack this sequence to show that it consists of an embedded collection of adjacency pairs and thus deduce which answers correspond to which questions (note that the question and answer numbers are for the reader's convenience; the parser "sees" only the sequence: q q q q a q a a a a).

The parser works from left to right. First, it considers q1. This could be the start of an adjacency pair or of an 'insertion' (these are the only two possibilities because only the rules for these two items begin with a question). Hence, the parser notes the two hypotheses: that it has the start of an adjacency pair and the start of an 'insertion'. It also notes that if the first hypothesis is correct, it should be able to find 'insertions' immediately following the question, while if the second hypothesis is correct, it should find either 'insertions' or an answer. Notice how the parser, as part of the process of parsing, has generated an expectation of what will come next.

That is all the parser can do until it starts to deal with the second item in the sequence, q2, another question. It generates a similar pair of hypotheses for this and proceeds to the next item, q3, and the next, q4, each time adding two more hypotheses to its collection. It can do more with the fifth item, a4. It already has a hypothesis, generated when processing q4, that q4 will the start of an 'insertion' and will immediately be followed by an answer. There is indeed an answer following q4 and so the parser can mark that the hypothesis is true and conclude that q4 and a4 constitute an 'insertion'. Next it looks to see whether the newly found 'insertion' could be the start of anything else. The rules state that 'insertions' consist of an 'insertion' followed by more insertions or just an insertion alone. Since the parser has an insertion, it can propose the hypotheses that it has found an 'insertions' and can immediately confirm the hypothesis because an 'insertions' can consist of a single 'insertion'. Thus, the parser has now found both an insertion and an 'insertions'. The latter is useful because there is an outstanding hypothesis left from processing q3, that this question forms the first part of either an adjacency pair (from the first rule) or of an insertion (from the last rule). These hypotheses provide expectations that the question will be followed by 'insertions', and the parser has found just such an item. Hence, it can corroborate these hypotheses, although they remain hypotheses because the final item (an answer to q3) has not yet been located.

The example is laborious to follow all the way through in detail. However, the general principle should be clear by now: each time the parser meets a new input item it examines the grammar rules to see whether this item could be the start of a decomposition of a more general category. If so, the parser adds a hypothesis to indicate this. It also examines previous hypotheses to see whether the new item partly or fully confirms one of them. If a hypothesis is confirmed, a new category has been found and the outstanding hypotheses are scanned again to see whether that new category helps any of them. Eventually, if the input corresponds to the grammar, i.e. it is "legal", the parser will yield a parse. The parse for the example sequence, q1 q2 q3 q4 a4 q5 a5 a3 a2 a1 is:

```
adjacencyPair
    question
    q1
    insertions
        insertion
            question
            q2
            insertions
                insertion
                    question
                    q3
                    insertions
                        insertion
                            question
                            q4
                            answer
                            a4
                            insertions
                                insertion
                                    question
                                    q5
                                    answer
                                    a5
                        answer
                        a3
                answer
                a2
        answer
        a1
```

Notice how the questions and answers have been correctly paired by the parser and how the pairing could work over quite long stretches of intervening conversation. The mechanism will, for example, permit initial questions to be tied to their eventual answers, providing the kind of 'long distance coordination' of talk which participants sometimes orient to, as in the example from a flight information service cited earlier.

Another point worth noting about this method of parsing is that it is possible for particular items to satisfy more than one of the outstanding hypotheses. For example, requests for goods can take the form:

```
                      Sinclair, 1976 : 60
        T1:           S: Have   you   got   Embassy   Gold
                      please?
        T2:           H: Yes dear ((provides))
```

Here, T1 can be heard as both a request for cigarettes and a question desiring an informational answer, while T2 provides both an answer to the question and an acceptance of the request.[7] If the parser is given the information that T1 is both a request and a question and T2 is both an acceptance and an answer, it will use the grammar to confirm two hypotheses that the sequence is a request-acceptance pair and a question-answer pair. In the terminology of chart parsing, two 'edges' connecting the same pair of nodes are added to the chart. It is possible to envisage a set of interpretive rules taking the chart as input and marking pairs of edges with the same span as either mutually exclusive or complementary.

Now let us consider what would happen if the final answer in the question and answer sequence, a5, were not forthcoming. An example of such a dialogue has already been discussed in Section 11.2.

In lines 4 to 8, the caller makes a request for the arrival time of a plane from Crete. This is followed by an embedded question and answer pair in which the agent inquires about the approximate arrival time of the aircraft. In lines 29 to 34 the agent informs the caller that she is not able to provide the information requested by the caller: "well I'm sorry I've looked up (.) heraculen which is crete...and chania we don't seem to have any thing". In lines 34 and 35 she provides an account for why she is not able to answer the caller's query: "you may well find it's another carrier". The agent's response is an example of what has come to be known as a 'dispreferred' response, i.e. one that differs from the expectation set up by the prior talk (in this case, the answer expected by the question). Dispreferred responses are characterised, as in this example, by hesitations and/or delays, some preface marking the utterance as dispreferred, such as "well", as in the above extract, and some account of why the preferred response cannot be performed (Levinson 1983, p.307).

In order for the grammar to deal with dispreferreds, one needs to add two further elements. First, the rules have to be augmented with additional ones which take in the organisation of the dispreferred

---

7   Levinson (1983:, p.361) provides a much more detailed analysis of this extract, but one which does not contradict the gloss offered here.

responses. This is easy to do if we extend the concept of 'answer' to include both the preferred and the dispreferred answer:

```
answer ---> preferred answer
answer ---> dispreferred answer
dispreferred answer ---> hesitation, preface, decline
                         to answer, account for decline
```

The second element that needs to be added to the grammar is an indication that the dispreferred response is in some ways 'special'; receipt of a dispreferred has additional consequences for the organisation of the dialogue.

It would thus be possible to write a simple grammar which included rules for both preferred and dispreferred answers. Given a question, competing expectations would have to be set up in the chart, some for a preferred answer, others for a dispreferred answer. But in the parser we have been using, these additional rules could not have the effect of cancelling an overarching adjacency pair when a dispreferred is received. What is needed is for the parser to be able to dispose of some outstanding hypotheses as a side effect of having recognised a particular kind of dispreferred. Some special, and seemingly *ad hoc* facility, would need to be built into the parser to achieve this, and the rule for the dispreferred would need to be marked to indicate that such a cancellation of hypotheses is required. An addition to the parser of this nature is not difficult to design. An incidental advantage of implementing dispreferreds in this way is that it mirrors the fact that dispreferreds are conversationally 'disruptive', requiring the participants to engage in special actions, and tend to be avoided if possible (Levinson 1983, p.333).

If the grammar and parser were being considered for use in a dialogue manager there would also need to be some way of identifying that particular utterances were to be treated as questions or answers, so that the parser could be presented with a sequence of 'q's and 'a's to process. However, it is sometimes difficult to identify a sentence as definitely a question, or an answer, a difficulty which is even more marked with spoken input where the sentences do not come with attached punctuation. Some clues can be obtained from prosody (the inflection of the sentence as it is spoken) and from grammatical form. For example, sentences beginning with 'Wh-' words like 'Who' and 'What' are often questions. But even these clues are no more than indications, for it is possible to be heard to ask a question using a syntactic and prosodic form which would otherwise be categorised as a statement. For instance, one can easily imagine a context in which the statement, "I'm going now" is heard and responded to as though it was the question, "Do you want a lift?".

The implication of this is that although 'lower level' syntactic and semantic parsers may be able to distinguish questions and answers, their categorisation is not necessarily valid as far as understanding the organisation of the dialogue is concerned. Because they rely only on local syntactic and semantic features, lower level parsers cannot assess the effective pragmatic force of an utterance. Nor is the solution to ask these lower level systems to provide a probabalistic assessment, because at these lower levels, there is no evidence available for assigning probabilities. From a syntactic and semantic point of view, "I'm going now" is *certainly* not a question, while "What's the time?" certainly is, although in specific contexts neither utterance may be heard as such.

Thus, a dialogue parser cannot rely on the categorisation of the tokens which form its input, in the way that we have so far assumed. The sequence we have used as an example, q q q q a q a a a a, might have actually been parsed by a syntactic parser as q a q q a q a a a a, and this would have caused the adjacency pair rules to fail (i.e. the rules would treat this sequence as "illegal" input), because they require that questions are matched by answers. We shall investigate how this difficulty may be overcome in the next section.

The adjacency pair example is undoubtedly a simple one and a realistic grammar for a fully-fledged dialogue manager would need to be much more extensive. But it does provide sufficient material to allow us to consider the arguments put forward by conversation analysts against the use of rules to represent conversational organisation and this will be our next task.

11.6 The arguments reconsidered

The arguments against the possibility of building computational models of conversation presented in Section 11.3 fall into three main classes. First, there is the point that it is impossible to build a computer implementation which is capable of dealing with indexicality. Second, there is the argument that computer rules are in some fundamental way different from the rules which conversation analysts have formulated. Third, the argument is made that people are 'members of society' while computers are not. This latter point is one which seems to be committing a category mistake about whether sociality is an inherent feature of an agent or one which is ascribed by other agents, and we shall not consider it further. The former two points deserve much more careful consideration.

The force of the argument concerning indexicality is that the meaning of specific terms or expressions is not fixed, as in a dictionary definition, nor computable using simple rules of deduction, but dependent on the context in which the item is embedded. The hearer has to work actively to find a meaning for the term which makes sense within that context. Moreover, the choice of meanings may not be limited, for example, to a set of pre-established, 'standard' meanings, but may include new meanings developed during the conversation.[8]

The simple dialogue parser we have introduced in the previous section can manage indexicality to a limited degree. It can 'find' which of a pre-defined set of interpretations of an utterance fits its grammar and generate hypotheses from these. For example, we might allow the utterance "It's gone" to be interpreted as a declarative statement of fact, a question, or even an exclamation ("It's gone??!"). On receiving this utterance as input, the parser would choose those interpretations which allow it to extend its current hypotheses. Eventually, further input may constrain the possible interpretations by disallowing some of the hypotheses, so that the apparent ambiguity permitted by having several interpretations of the same utterance is reduced or removed by the cumulative effect of other evidence – the "context".

Such context could include the substantive topic of the dialogue, 'real world knowledge' and past experience, as well as prosodic, syntactic, and semantic features of the utterance. What the simple dialogue parser does not show is how these contextual constraints are generated or applied. In principle, the constraints could be used to disconfirm hypotheses, although in practice a chart parser and grammar which attempted to encompass all these levels simultaneously would be highly inefficient. It may be that a grammar and parser based on the unification of partial information structures (Shieber 1986) from diverse knowledge sources would be more efficient, but this is no more than speculation.

Even if these implementation difficulties were overcome, it has to be admitted that the meanings which the parser considers for an

---

[8]   Garrod (1988) provides a well-documented example, in which two participants in a maze game develop a vocabulary for referring to locations in the maze during the course of the game.

utterance are always strictly limited to those with which it has been pre-programmed; it cannot 'invent' new interpretations as it goes along. Again, in principle, one could imagine a system which could do so, but this is far beyond the state of the art, involving machine learning of subtle patterns. Fortunately, in the kind of information provision applications at which the Sundial system is being aimed, it is possible to make some progress without the system needing to have the capability of creating or learning new interpretations of words or dialogue items.

The notion of indexicality is closely tied to what Garfinkel calls the documentary method of interpretation: the method by which people overcome the potential 'problem' of indexicality. Garfinkel (1967) describes the method in the following terms:

> The method consists of treating an actual appearance as
> 'the document of', as 'pointing to', as 'standing on
> behalf of' a presupposed underlying pattern. Not only
> is the underlying pattern derived from its individual
> documentary evidences, but the individual
> documentary evidences, in their turn, are interpreted
> on the basis of 'what is known' about the underlying
> pattern. Each is used to elaborate the other.
>
> (Garfinkel 1967, p.78)

There are two ways in which one can read this. One could take the passage to mean that, by following the documentary method of interpretation, people are able to induce and then learn entirely new 'patterns'. Alternatively, one can read the passage as indicating that people, already having acquired a set of patterns, use the 'evidences' to select one of these patterns, and simultaneously interpret the evidences in terms of the selected pattern. The latter reading does not call for any discovery or learning. The two are not necessarily exclusive – people could both fit evidence to existing patterns and, when that is not satisfactory, learn new ones – but because the understanding of learning is still in its infancy, there are practical reasons for not going beyond the latter, narrower reading for the purpose of computer modelling.

A computer implementation of the documentary method of interpretation on this more restricted reading is surprisingly straightforward. Indeed, the chart parser we have been examining uses exactly this method for determining the structure of the input it is given. Unless it is a trivial one, the grammar a parser operates on will have alternative 'patterns' against which the input can be matched. Moreover the interpretation assigned to the input by the parser will vary according to which pattern is selected.

11.7 Conclusion

The optimistic message from conversation analysis has been that dialogue between humans is not inchoate and arbitrary, but displays particularly delicate patterns and regularities. The pessimistic message has been that there is something peculiar about these regularities which makes them uncongenial to computer modelling. In this paper, we have argued that while we should not accept the optimistic message with open arms, the pessimistic message is perhaps unwarranted. The idea that the findings of conversation analysis are not susceptible to computer implementation depends on a rather simple-minded notion of what a computer model can do. In particular, it assumes that it is impossible to model the active, 'sense finding' behaviour which people seem to be so good at and which conversation analysts rightly emphasise so strongly. In fact, even a rather simple type of parser can be seen to exhibit these characteristics to some degree. Notions like indexicality and the documentary method of interpretation, which sometimes have been given almost mystical significance as the features which make computational modelling of conversation impossible, seem on closer inspection to be very similar to ideas which have been common currency in the computational linguistics arena for some years.

It would be wrong, however, to conclude that modelling dialogue and, in particular, implementing CA findings in a computer, is straightforward. Major problems remain. As we remarked in the previous section, while humans are capable of induction and learning, computer scientists have made rather little progress in this area. Thus we will have to accept that computational models of dialogue will for the moment have to remain stuck with whatever knowledge their designers initially give them. It is not clear what effect this will have on their ability to converse. For routine activities, where there is little need or opportunity to develop new variations on existing vocabularies, this may not be a major problem, but it is certainly a difficulty which will grow in impact as speech systems become more capable.

The other area where problems can be expected is in integrating the various sources of knowledge to develop an interpretation of an utterance. The human brain seems to be rather good at applying, in parallel, a very large range of interrelated types of knowledge to speech signals. At present, we do not have any clear idea about how we could mimic this within a computer without becoming overwhelmed by the complexity of the interactions between knowledge sources, although architectures such as the 'blackboard' model have been tried with modest success (Erman et al. 1980). Connectionist approaches (McClelland and Rumelhart 1988) may be the most promising in the long term as the way to solve both the learning and the complexity problems, but there is much work to be done before they can be scaled up to handle the requirements of a speech understanding system.

Acknowledgments

Thanks to the rest of the Social and Computer Sciences research group and to Nick Youd and Rod Rivers of Logica Cambridge for their comments. The research on which this paper is based has been supported by the Commission of the European Communities, as part of ESPRIT project P2218, Sundial.

Notes on Transcription Conventions

The structure of these notes is borrowed, in part, from Button and Lee (1987). This is not the full set of symbols; only those to be found in the examples used in the text.

1   Talk

1.1 Sequencing symbols

Overlapping utterances

oo⌐oo   Onset of overlapping utterances.

oo⌐oo   Termination of overlap.

Intervals of no speech or absence of activity

(0.5)   Time of pause to nearest 0.5 second.

(.)   Micropause of less than 0.2 second.

(pause)   Untimed pause.

1.2 Characteristics of speech delivery

Intonation

(a) Simple impressionistic set:

.   Falling intonation.

,   Continuing intonation.

?   Rising intonation.

!   Exclamatory intonation.

(b)   Prosody. Occasionally a linguistic prosodic mark appears, e.g. a tonetic nucleus or contour pattern.

Sound

Standard orthography with occasional pseudo-lexical impressions.

:   Extension of sound beyond normal duration.

The use of colons indicates the stretching of the immediately prior sound. The more colons, the longer the sound is stretched.

```
Nancy:      -A:nd  a- h, .hhh has been with
            them for about fifteen yea:rs.h
            a:nd ah,h So...
```

-           Glottal stop, cutoff.
.t   Mouth click, like in "tch tch" or "tut tut".
.h   Audible aspiration (inbreath).
h.   Audible aspiration (outbreath).

The longer the aspiration, the greater the number of h's.

```
Nancy:      VERY personable VERY SWEET. .hhh
```

=   Two utterances are linked without any discernible space.

```
Nancy:      he's got a real good job with a big
            air conditioning company:,h=
Emma:       =M -m:  h m-
```

Stress and pitch

° °   Passage is quieter than surrounding speech.
CAPS   Passage is louder than surrounding speech.
_   Words, letters or sound particles which are stressed.

```
Sy:         Take up
            m:Metacal er,
            Carnation Slender
            er something like that.
```

_: A drop in pitch.

```
Nancy:      CAPtain in the mari:nes
```

:_   A rise in pitch.

```
Nancy:      having a r:eal good time
```

An increase in emphasis and prolongation indicates that a greater part of the utterance is implicated in the pitch change.

1.3 Transcription difficulties

(transcriptn)   Uncertain speech or person.

( )   Untranscribable speech or unidentified person.

1.4 Transcription descriptions

((descriptn))   Stage directions or comments on the recorded data fragment.

1.5 Presentation symbols

1

2 ...   Line numbering of utterances for referencing in the text.

3

[code]   Reference code for data fragment in the form [Mn: time1-time2], where n is the experiment code, and the fragment is taken from time1 to time2 recorded on the video tape with an electronic clock counter.

2   Special conventions: gaze, keyboard and gesture

2.1 Gaze

These symbols mark a transition in the transcript record.

s   Screen.

k   Keyboard.

m   Map.

e   Eye gaze; eye contact when coincident eye gaze by participants occurs.

Ø   Neutral space.

( )   Potential gaze, but interrupted or incomplete.

2.2 Keyboard display

Standard character set on an Acorn BBC keyboard.

<s>   Space.

<r>   Return.

[]   Character(s) not visible on display – either hidden or not recorded on the display.

// //   Characters within the // are deleted in the reverse order to original typing.

2.3 Gestures

Boundaries of gesture

((Onset of gesture.
))   Close/retraction of gesture.

Acme of gesture

Ps   Point at the screen.
Pm   Point at the map.
gm   Gesture to the map.
gs   Gesture to the screen.
gØ   Gesture in neutral space.

[description]   Describes the place referenced by the pointing
                   gesture, or the movement of the gesture.
L/R prefixes can be subscripted to the above symbols to indicate the
left or right hand.

( )   Incomplete point or gesture.
ſi   Mark map.
Ø   Sharp point or jab.

References

Agre, P. E. (1988). The Dynamic Structure of Everyday Life. Unpublished Ph.D. Dissertation, AI Technical Report 1085. Department of Electrical Engineering and Computer Science, Massachusetts Institute of Technology, Cambridge, Mass.

Agre, P. E. and Chapman, D. (1988). What are Plans For?, AI Memo 1050. Massachusetts Institute of Technology, Cambridge, Mass.

Ainsworth, W. A. (1988). Speech recognition by machine, IEE.

Allen, J. (1983). Reorganising intentions from natural language utterances. In *Computational Models of Discourse* (Eds. M. Brady and R. C. Berwick), 107-166. MIT Press, Cambridge, Mass.

Argyle, M. and Kendon, A. (1967). The experimental analysis of social performance. In *Advances in experimental social psychology* (Ed. L. Berkowitz), Vol. 3. Academic Press, London and New York.

Atkinson, J. M. (1982). Understanding formality: notes on the categorisation and production of 'formal' interaction. *British Journal of Sociology*, Vol. 33, 86-117.

Atkinson, J. M. (1984). Our Master's Voices: the Language and Body Language of Politics. Methuen, London.

Atkinson, J. M. and Drew P. (1979). Order in Court: the Organisation of Verbal Interaction in Judicial Settings. Macmillan, London.

Atkinson, J. M. and Heritage, J. C. (1978). (Eds.) Special Edition of *Sociology*, Vol. 12.

Atkinson, J. M. and Heritage, J. C. (1984). (Eds.) Structures of Social Action: Studies in Conversation Analysis. Cambridge University Press, Cambridge.

Austin, J. (1962). How to do things with words. Oxford University Press, Oxford.

Backer, G. P. and Hacker, P. M. S. (1984). Language Sense And Nonsense. Blackwell, Oxford.

Backer, G. P. and Hacker, P. M. S. (1985). Wittgenstein Rules, Grammar And Necessity. In *An Analytic Commentary On The Philosophical Investigations*, Vol. 2. Blackwell, Oxford.

Balzer, R. (1985). A 15 Year Perspective on Automatic Programming. IEEE Trans. Software Engineering, SE-11, 11, 1257-1267.

Balzer, R. Goldman, N. and Wile, D. (1978). Informality in Program Specifications, IEEE Trans. Software Engineering, SE-4, 2, 94-103.

Bartlett, F. C. (1932). Remembering : a study in experimental and social psychology. Cambridge University Press, Cambridge.

Bilmes, J. (1988). The concept of preference in conversation analysis, Language in Society, Vol. 17, 161-181.

Birdwhistle, R. L. (1971). Kinesics and Context: Essays on Body Motion Communication. Allen Lane, London

Block, N. (1980). What Is Philosophy Of Psychology?. In *Readings In Philosophy Of Psychology* (Ed. N. Block). Harvard University Press, Cambridge, Mass.

Boden, D. and Zimmerman, D. H. (forthcoming). (Eds.) Talk And Social Structure. Polity Press, Cambridge.

Bond, A. H and Gasser, L. (1988). Readings in distributed artificial intelligence. Morgan Kaufman, Los Altos, Ca.

Brand, S. (1988). The Media Lab Book. Penguin, London and Harmondsworth.

Buckland, S., Cordingley, B., Frohlich, D. M., Gilbert, G. N. and Luff, P. (1987). Requirements Specification for the Advice System, Technical Report No. 19. Alvey DHSS Demonstrator Project, University of Surrey.

Button, G. (1981). Comments of Conversation Analysis, Analytic Sociology, Vol. 1, 2, D09-S01.

Button, G. (1987). Moving Out Of Closings. In *Talk and Social Organisation* (Eds. G. Button and J. R. E. Lee), 101-151. Multilingual Matters, Clevedon and Philadelphia.

✓ Button, G. (1989). A Short Review Of Research On Language And Social Interaction In The United Kingdom. Research On Language And Social Interaction, Vol. 22, 327-346.

Button, G. (forthcoming a). Varieties Of Closings. In *Interaction Competence* (Ed. G. Psathas). Lawrence Erlbaum Associates, Hillsdale, NJ.

Button, G. (forthcoming b). Conversation-In-A-Series. In *Talk And Social Structure* (Eds. D. Boden and D. H. Zimmerman). Polity Press, Cambridge.

Button, G. and Casey, N. J. (1984). Generating Topic: The Use Of Topic Initial Elicitors. In *Structures Of Social Action: Studies In Conversation Analysis* (Eds. J. M. Atkinson and J. C. Heritage), 167-190. Cambridge University Press, Cambridge.

Button, G. and Casey, N.J. (1985). Topic Nomination and Topic Pursuit, Human Studies, Vol.8, 3-55

Button, G., Drew, P., and Heritage, J. C. (1986). (Eds.) Interaction and Language Use, Human Studies Special Edition, Vol. 9, Nos. 2-3.

Button, G. and Lee, J. R. E. (1987). Talk and Social Organisation. Multilingual Matters, Clevedon and Philadelphia.

Card, S. K., Moran, T. and Newell, A. (1983). The Psychology of Human-Computer Interaction. Lawrence Erlbaum Associates, Hillsdale, NJ.

Carroll, J. M. and McKendree, J. (1987). Interface designing issues for advice-giving expert systems, Communications of the ACM, Vol. 30, 1, 14-31.

Cawsey, A. (1989a). Explanatory dialogues, Interacting With Computers, Vol. 1, 1, 73-92.

Cawsey, A. (1989b). Generating Explanatory Discourse: A Plan-based, Interactive Approach. Unpublished Ph.D. Thesis. Department of Artificial Intelligence, University of Edinburgh.

Chomsky, N. (1957). Syntactic Structures. Mouton, The Hague.

Cicourel, A. V. (1973). Cognitive Sociology – Language and Meaning in Social Interaction. Penguin, London and Harmondsworth.

Cohen, P. R. and Perrault, C. R. (1979). Elements of a Plan-Based Theory of Speech Acts, Cognitive Science, Vol. 3, 177-212.

Conklin, J. (1989). Design Rationale and Maintainability. In *Proceedings of the 22nd Hawaii International Conference on Systems Sciences,* Vol. 2, 533-539. IEEE CS Press.

Coombs, M. J. and Alty, J. L. (1980). Face-to-face Guidance of University Computer Users-II: Characterising Advisory Interactions, International Journal of Man-Machine Studies, Vol. 12, 407-429.

Cooper, D.E. (1975). Knowledge Of Language. Humanities Press, New York.

Cooper, G. (1989). Ethnomethodology: its potential contribution to HCI. In *Proceedings of the People and Computer Interaction Systems Students Workshop,* May 1989, Open University, (Ed. J. Crellin).

Coulter, J. (1979). The Social Construction of Mind: Studies in Ethnomethodology and Linguistic Philosophy. Macmillan, London.

Coulter, J. (1983a). Rethinking Cognitive Theory. MacMillan, London.

Coulter, J. (1983b). Contingent And *A Priori* Structures in Sequential Analysis, Human Studies, Vol 6, 361-375.

Coulter, J. (1989). Mind In Action. Polity Press, Cambridge.

Coulter, J. (forthcoming a). Ethnomethodology And The Logic Of Language. In *Ethnomethodology And The Human Sciences: A Foundational Reconstruction*, (Ed. G. Button). Cambridge University Press, Cambridge.

Coulter, J. (forthcoming b). Cognition In An Ethnomethodological Mode. In *Ethnomethodology And The Human Sciences: A Foundational Reconstruction*, (Ed. G. Button). Cambridge University Press, Cambridge.

Cutler, A. (1983). (Ed.) Slips of the Tongue and Language Production. Mouton and Walter de Gruyter, Amsterdam.

Dingwall, R. (1980). Orchestrated encounters: an essay in the comparative analysis of speech-exchange systems, Sociology of Health and Illness, Vol. 5, 2, 127-149.

Doran, J. (1988). The Structure and Emergence of Hierarchical Organisations. In *Alvey Workshop on Multiple Agent Systems*. April 1988, Redhill.

Draper, S.W. (1987). A User-centred Concept of Explanation. In *Proceedings of the 2nd Alvey Explanation Workshop*, Guildford, January 1987, IEE, 24-42.

Drew, P. (1987). Po-Faced Responses to Teases, Linguistics, Vol. 25, 219-53.

Drew, P. (forthcoming). Disputes in Courtroom Cross-Examination: Contrasting Versions in a Rape Trial. In *Talk at Work* (Eds. P. Drew and J. C. Heritage). Cambridge University Press, Cambridge.

Drew, P. and Heritage, J.C. (forthcoming). (Eds.) Talk at Work, Cambridge University Press, Cambridge

Durham, T. (1987). Why computers are socially disadvantaged, Computing, 4th June, 26-27.

Earley, J. (1970). An efficient context-free parsing algorithm, Communications of the ACM, Vol. 13, 2, 94-102.

Erickson, F. and Schultz, J. (1982). The Counselor as Gatekeeper. Academic Press, London and New York.

Ericsson, K. A. and Simon, H. A. (1980). Verbal Reports on Data, Psychological Review, Vol. 87, 3, 215-251.

Erman, L. D., Hayes-Roth, F., Lesser, V. R., and Reddy, D. R. (1980). The Hearsay-II Speech Understanding System: integrating knowledge to resolve uncertainty, Computing Surveys, Vol. 12, 213-253.

Farooq, M. U. and Dominick, W. D (1988). A survey of formal tools and models for developing user interfaces, International Journal of Man-Machine Studies, Vol. 29, 479-496.

Fickas, S. Collins, S. and Olivier, S. (1987). Problem Acquisition in Software Analysis: a preliminary study. University of Oregon Technical Report, CIS-TR-87-15.

Finkelstein, A. (1989a). A Structural Framework for the Formal Representation of Cooperation, *5th International Software Process Workshop*. IEEE CS Press.

Finkelstein, A. (1989b). Not Waving but Drowning: representation schemes for modelling software development. In *Proceedings of the 11th International Conference on Software Engineering*, 402-404, IEEE CS Press.

Finkelstein, A. and Fuks H. (1989). Multi-Party Specification. In *Proceedings of the 5th International Workshop on Software Specification and Design*, 185-195. IEEE CS Press.

Foley, J. D. and Wallace V. L. (1974). IEEE Proceedings, Special Issue on Computer Graphics, Vol. 62, 4, 462-471.

Fox, B. A. (1987). Interactional Reconstruction in Real-Time Language Processing. Cognitive Science, Vol. 11, pp. 365-387.

Fraser, H. B. (forthcoming). The Subject of Speech Perception: An Analysis of the Philosophical Foundations of the Information-Processing Model. Ph.D. Dissertation. Department of Linguistics, University of Edinburgh.

Frohlich, D. M. (1986). On the organisation of form-filling behaviour, Information Design Journal, Vol. 5, 43-59.

Frohlich, D. M. (1988). Conversational dynamics for emergent explanations. In *Proceedings of the 4th Alvey Workshop on Explanation*, September 1988, Manchester. IEE, Stevenage, 112-123.

Frohlich, D. M. and Luff, P. (1989). Conversational Resources for Situated Action. In *Proceedings of ACM CHI '89 conference*, 30th April-5th May. Austin, Texas, 253-258.

Fromkin, V. (1973). (Ed.) Speech Errors as Linguistic Evidence. Mouton, The Hague.

Fuks, H. Ryan, M. and Sadler, M. (1989 in press). Outline of a Commitment Logic for Legal Reasoning, In *Proceedings of the 3rd International Conference on Logic, Informatics, Law*.

Gaines, B. R. and Shaw M. L. G. (1984). The Art of Computer Conversation: a New Medium for Communication. Prentice-Hall, Englewood Cliffs, NJ.

Gaines, B. R. and Shaw M. L. G. (1986a). From timesharing to Sixth generation: the development of human-computer interaction, Part I, International Journal of Man-Machine Studies, Vol. 24, 1-27.

Gaines, B. R. and Shaw M. L. G. (1986b). Foundations of dialog engineering: the development of human-computer interation. Part II, International Journal of Man-Machine Studies, Vol. 24, 101-123.

Galliers, J. (1988). Report on a discussion session about Dialogue. In *Alvey Workshop on Multiple Agent Systems*. April 1988, Redhill.

Garfinkel, H. (1967). Studies in Ethnomethodology. Prentice-Hall, Englewood Cliffs, NJ.

Garfinkel, H. and Sacks, H. (1970). On formal structures of practical actions. In Theoretical Sociology (Eds. J. C. McKinney and E. A. Tiryakian), 338-360. Appleton-Century-Crofts, New York.

Garrod, S. (1988). Explanation in dialogue as attempts to overcome problems in coordination. In *Proceedings of the 3rd Alvey Workshop on Explanation*, September 1987, Guildford, 83-93. IEE, Stevenage.

Gazdar, G. and Good, D. A. (1982). On a notion of relevance. In *Mutual Knowledge* (Ed. N.V. Smith). Academic Press, London and New York.

Gazdar, G. and Mellish, C. (1987). Computational Linguistics. In *New Horizons In Linguistics 2* (Eds. J. Lyons, R. Coates, M. Deuchar, G. Gazdar), 225-248. Penguin, London and Harmondsworth.

Genesereth, M. R. (1982). The role of plans in intelligent teaching systems. In *Intelligent Tutoring Systems* (Eds. D. Sleeman and J. S. Brown). Academic Press, London and New York.

Giddens, A. (1976). New Rules of Sociological Method: A Positive Critique of Interpretative Sociologies. Hutchinson, London.

Giddens, A. (1984). The Constitution of Society: Outline of the Theory of Structuration. Polity Press, Cambridge.

Giddens, A. (1987). Social Theory and Modern Sociology. Stanford University Press, Stanford, Ca.

Gilbert, G. N. (1987a). Question and Answer Types. *Research and Development in Expert Systems IV* (Ed. D. S. Moralee). Cambridge University Press, Cambridge.

Gilbert, G. N. (1987b). Cognitive and social models of the user. In *Human-computer interaction – Interact '87, Proceedings of the Second IFIP conference*, (Eds H. J. Bullinger and B. Shackel), Stuttgart, September 1987, 165-172. North Holland, Amsterdam.

Gilbert, G. N. (1987c). Advice, Discourse and Explanations. In *Proceedings of the 3rd Alvey Explanation Workshop* , September 1987, Guildford. IEE, Stevenage, 94-109.

Gilbert, G. N. (1988). Explanation as Process. In *Proceedings of the 4th Alvey Explanation Workshop*, September 1988, Manchester, 67-86. IEE, Stevenage.

Gilbert, G. N., Buckland, S., Cordingley, B., Frohlich, D. M., Hardey, M., Jirotka, M. and Luff, P. (1989). Providing advice through dialogue. Technical Report. Alvey DHSS Demonstrator Project, University of Surrey.

Gilbert, G. N. and Heath, C. (1985). (Eds.) Social Action and Artificial Intelligence. Gower, Aldershot.

Gilbert, G. N. and Jirotka, M. (1989). Planning Procedural Advice. Technical Report 37. Alvey DHSS Demonstrator Project, University of Surrey.

Goffman, E. (1981). Forms of Talk. Blackwell, Oxford.

Goldthorpe, J. (1973). A revolution in sociology?, Sociology, Vol. 7, 449-62.

Good, D. A. (1985). Sociology and A.I.: The lesson from Social Psychology. In *Social Action and Artificial Intelligence* (Ed. G.N. Gilbert and C. Heath). Gower, Aldershot.

Good, D. A. (1989). The viability of conversational grammars. In *Multimodal Dialogue* (Eds. M. Taylor, D. Bouwhuis and F. Neel). North-Holland, Amsterdam.

Goodman, B. (1986). Reference identification and reference identification failures, Computational Linguistics, Vol. 12, 4, 273-305.

Goodwin, C. (1981). Conversational Organization: Interaction Between Speakers and Hearers. Academic Press, London and New York.

Goodwin, C. and Goodwin, M. (1987). Concurrent Operations on Talk: Notes on the Interactive Organisation of Assessments, IPrA Papers in Pragmatics, Vol. 1, 1, 1-54.

Goranzon, B., Florin, M. and Sallstrom, P. (1988). The Concept of Dialogue, AI and Society, Vol. 2, 279-286.

Gorayska, B. and Lindsay, R. (1989). Metasemantics of Relevance. In *Proceedings of the Symposium on Cognitive Linguistics*, March - April 1989, Duisberg.

Gould, J. D. and Lewis, C. (1985). Designing for Usability – Key Principles and What Designers Think. Communications of the ACM, Vol. 28, 300-311.

Gregory, R. L. (1984). Mind in Science. Penguin, London and Harmondsworth

Grice, H. P. (1975). Logic and conversation. In *Syntax and semantics 3: Speech Acts* (Eds. P. Cole and J. Morgan), 41-58. Academic Press, London and New York.

Grosz, B. J. (1986). The Representation and use of Focus in a System for Understanding Dialogs. In *Readings in Natural Language Processing* (Eds. B .J. Grosz, K. Sparck Jones and B. L. Webber). Morgan Kaufmann, Los Altos, Ca.

Grosz, B. J. and Sidner, C. L. (1985). The Structures of Discourse Structure, Technical Report 6097. Bolt Beranek and Newman.

Grosz, B. J. and Sidner , C. L. (1986). Attention, Intentions, and the Structure of Discourse, Computational Linguistics, Vol. 12, 3, 175-204.

Hagerstrand, T. (1975). Space, Time and Human Conditions. In *Dynamic Allocation of Urban Space* (Ed. A. Karlqvist). Saxon House, Farnborough.

Hall, H. (1987). Phenomenology. In *Encyclopedia of Artificial Intelligence*, (Ed. S. C. Shapiro), 730-36. Wiley, New York.

Hamblin, C. (1987). Imperatives. Blackwell, Oxford.

Hauptmann, A. G. and Rudincky, A.I. (1988). Talking to computers: an empirical investigation, International Journal of Man-Machine Studies, Vol. 28, 583-604.

Hayes, P. and Reddy, D. (1983). Steps Towards Graceful Interaction in Spoken and Written Man-machine Communication, International Journal of Man-machine Studies, Vol.19, 231-284.

Heath, C. (1982). The display of recipiency: an instance of a sequential relationship between speech and body movement, Semiotica, Vol. 42, 147-167.

Hebb, D. D. (1949). The organisation of behaviour. Wiley, New York.

Heritage, J. C. (1978), Aspects of the Flexibilities of Language Use, Sociology, Vol. 12, 1, 79-104.

Heritage, J. C. (1984a). Garfinkel and Ethnomethodology. Polity Press, Cambridge.

Heritage, J. C. (1984b). A change of state token and aspects of its sequential placement. In *Structures of Social Action: Studies in Conversation Analysis* (Eds. J. M. Atkinson and J. C. Heritage), 299-345. Cambridge University Press, Cambridge.

Heritage, J. C. (1985). Recent Development in Conversation Analysis, Sociolinguistics Newsletter, Vol. 15, 1, 1-19.

Heritage, J. C. (1988). Explanations as Accounts: A Conversation Analytic Perspective. In *Analysing Everyday Explanation: A Casebook of Methods* (Ed. C. Antaki), 127-144. Sage, London.

Heritage J. C. (1989). Current Developments In Conversation Analysis. In *Conversation: An Interdisciplinary Perspective* (Eds. D. Roger and P. Bull), pp. 21-47. Multilingual Matters, Clevedon and Philadelphia.

Heritage, J. C. and Atkinson, J. M. (1984). Introduction. In *Structures of Social Action: Studies in Conversation Analysis* (Eds. J. M. Atkinson and J. C. Heritage), 1- 15. Cambridge University Press, Cambridge.

Heritage, J. C. and Watson, D.R. (1980). Aspects of the Properties of Formulations in Natural Connection: some Instances Analysed, Semiotica, Vol.9, 181-199

Hinds, J. (1979). Organizational Patterns in Discourse. In *Syntax and Semantics 12: Discourse and Syntax* (Ed. T. Givon). Academic Press, London and New York.

Hoare, C. A. R. (1984). Programming: sorcery or science?, IEEE Software, April, 5-16.

Hobbs, J. (1982). Towards an Understanding of Coherence in Discourse. In *Strategies for Natural Language Processing* (Eds. W. Lehnert, and M. Ringle). Lawrence Erlbaum Associates, Hillsdale, NJ.

Holmes, J. N. (1988). Speech synthesis and recognition. Van Nostrand Reinhold, London.

Horai, H., Saeki, M. and Enomoto, H. (1987). Specification Based Software Development System Pure Tell, IIAS Research Report No. 73.

Hunter, J.F.M (1973). On How We Talk. In *Essays After Wittgenstein* (Ed. J.F.M. Hunter) University of Toronto Press, Toronto.

Ince, D. C. (1988). An Introduction to Discrete Mathematics and Formal System Specification. Oxford University Press, Oxford.

Jefferson, G. (1972). Side Sequences. In *Studies in Social Interaction* (Ed. D. Sudnow), 294-338. Free Press, New York.

Jefferson, G. (1974). Error Correction as an interactional resource, Language in Society, Vol. 2, 181-199.

Jefferson, G. (1983). Notes on a systematic deployment of the acknowledgement tokens "yeah" and "mm hm", Tilburg Papers in Language and Literature no. 30.

Jefferson, G. (1987). In *Talk and Social Organisation*, (Eds. G. Button and J. R. E. Lee), 86-99. Multilingual Matters, Clevedon and Philadelphia.

Jefferson, G. (1989). Preliminary Notes on a Possible Metric which Provides for a 'Standard Maximum' Silence of Approximately One Second. In *Conversation: An Interdisciplinary Perspective* (Eds. D. Roger and P. Bull), pp. 166-196. Multilingual Matters, Clevedon and Philadelphia.

Jefferson, G. (forthcoming). List construction as a task and resource. In *Interactional Competence* (Ed. G. Psathas). Lawrence Erlbaum Associates, Hillsdale, NJ.

Kaiser, G., Feiler, P., Popovich, S. (1988). Intelligent Assistance for Software Development and Maintenance, IEEE Software, May, 40-49.

Kammersgaard, J. (1985). Four Different Perspectives on Human-Computer Interaction, DAIMI PB - 203. University of Aarhus.

Kaplan S. J. (1983). Cooperative Responses from a Portable Natural Language Database Query System. In *Computational Models of Discourse* (Eds. M. Brady and R. C. Berwick), 167-208. MIT Press, Cambridge, Mass.

Kasher, A. (1982). Gricean inference revisited, Philosophica, Vol. 29, 25-44.

Kidd, A. (1987). Cooperative problem solving systems. Paper presented to the HCI '87 Conference, 7-11 September 1987, University of Exeter.

Kidd, A. L. and Cooper, M. B. (1985). Man-machine interface issues in the construction of and use of an expert system, International Journal Man-Machine Studies, Vol. 22, 91-102.

Kiss, G. (1987). High Level Dialogue in Man-Machine Interaction. A survey report commissioned by the Alvey Directorate.

Kiss, G. (1988). High-level Dialogue. In Alvey Workshop on Multiple Agent Systems, April 1988, Redhill.

Labov, W. (1972). Sociolinguistic Patterns. University of Pennsylvania Press, Philadelphia.

Laurel, B. K. (1986). Interface as Mimesis. In *User Centred System Design* (Eds. D. Norman and S. Draper), 67-85. Lawrence Erlbaum Associates, Hillsdale, NJ.

Lave, J. (1988). Cognition in Practice. Cambridge University Press, Cambridge.

Lee, J. R. E. (1987). Prologue: Talking Organisation. In *Talk and Social Organisation* (Eds. G. Button and J. R. E Lee), 19-53. Multilingual Matters, Clevedon and Philadelphia.

Leech, G. (1983). Principles of Pragmatics. Longman, London.

✓ Levinson, S. C. (1983). Pragmatics. Cambridge University Press, Cambridge.

Luff, P. and Frohlich, D. M. (1987). Discourse Dynamics and Dialogue Design, Technical Report No. 38. Alvey DHSS Demonstrator Project, University of Surrey.

Luff, P. and Frohlich, D. M. (forthcoming). Mixed Initiative Interaction. In *Knowledge-based systems and legal applications* (Ed. T. Bench-Capon). Academic Press, London and New York.

Lynch, M., Livingston, E. and Garfinkel, H., (1983). Temporal order in laboratory work. In *Science Observed* (Ed. K. D. Knorr-Cetina and M.Mulkay), 205-237. Sage, London.

Mackenzie, J. (1981). The Dialectics of Logic. Logique et Analyse, Vol. 24, 159-177.

Mackenzie, J. (1985). No Logic before Friday. Synthese, Vol. 63, 329-341.

Maddison, R. N. and Stanczyk (1988). Time in information systems and its impact on modelling processes and data. Information and Software Technology, Vol. 30, 1, 12-22.

Maguire, M. (1982). An evaluation of published recommendations for the design of man-computer dialogues, International Journal of Man-Machine Studies, Vol. 16, 237-261.

Malcolm, N. (1971). The Myth Of Cognitive Processes And Structures. *Cognitive Development And Epistemology* (Ed. T. Mischel). Academic Press, London and New York.

Mallery, J. C., Hurwitz, R. and Duffy, G. (1987). Hermeneutics. In *Encyclopedia of Artificial Intelligence* (Ed. S. C. Shapiro), 362-376. Wiley, New York

Malloch, M. (forthcoming). A Neural Mechanism for Cognitive Representation: Hypotheses on the Evolution, Development and Life of Cortex and Meaning, Ph.D. Dissertation. Department of Artificial Intelligence, University of Edinburgh.

Martin, J. (1967). The Design of Real-Time Computer Systems. Prentice-Hall, Englewood Cliffs, NJ.

Maturana, H. R. and Varela, F. J (1980). Autopoiesis and Cognition: The Realisation of the Living. Reidel, London.

Maynard, D. W. (1987). (Ed.) Special Issue of Language And Social Interaction, Social Psychology Quarterly, Vol. 50, 2.

Maynard, D. W. (1988). (Ed.) Special Issue of Language, Interaction And Social Problems, Social Problems, Vol. 35, 4.

McAllister, K. (1987). The correction of misunderstanding in man-machine dialogue. In *Proceedings of the 3rd Alvey Explanation Workshop*, Guildford, September 1987, 118-131.

McClelland, J. and Rumelhart, D. (1988). Explorations in Parallel Distributed Processing. MIT Press, Cambridge, Mass.

McIlvenny, P. (1989). Communicative Action and Computers. Research Paper No. 444, Department of Artificial Intelligence, University of Edinburgh.

McIlvenny, P. B. (forthcoming). Interactivity and Situated Dialogue: Perspectives on Computational Modelling and Human-Computer Communication. Ph.D. Dissertation, Department of Artificial Intelligence, University of Edinburgh.

McKeown, K. R. (1985). Text Generation. Cambridge University Press, Cambridge.

McTear, M. F. (1985). Breakdown and Repair in Naturally Occuring Conversation and Human-Computer Dialogue. In *Social Action and Artificial Intelligence* (Eds. G. N. Gilbert and C. Heath), 104-123. Gower, Aldershot.

McTear, M. F. (1987). The Articulate Computer. Blackwell, Oxford.

Milner, R. (1986). Is computing an experimental science?. Laboratory for Foundations of Computer Science Report ECS-LFCS-86-1. University of Edinburgh.

Miyake, N. (1986). Constructive Interaction and the Iterative Process of Understanding, Cognitive Science, Vol. 10, 151-177.

Moore, J. D. (1989). Responding to 'Huh': Answering Vaguely Articulated Followup Questions. In *Proceedings CHI '89*, Austin, Texas, April 30-May 1989, 91-96.

Moore, J. D. and Swartout W. R. (1988a). A reactive approach to explanation. In *Proceedings of the Fourth International Workshop on Natural Language Generation*, July 1988.

Moore, J. D. and Swartout W. R. (1988b). Planning and reacting. In *Proceedings of the AAAI Workshop on Text Planning and Generation*, August 25, 1988, St Paul, Minn.

Moran, T. (1981). The command language grammar, International Journal of Man-Machine Studies, Vol. 15, 51-85.

Morris, A. (1987). Expert systems – interface insight. In *People and Computers III* (Eds. D. Diaper and R. Winder). Cambridge University Press, Cambridge.

Nickerson, R. S. (1977). On Conversational Interaction with Computers. In *User-oriented Design of Interactive Graphics Systems*, 101-113. ACM, New York.

Nickerson, R. S. (1981). Some characteristics of conversation. In *Man-Computer Interaction: Human Factors Aspects of Computers and People* (Ed. B. Shackel), 53-65. Sitjhoff and Noordhoff, The Netherlands.

Nickerson, R. S. (1986). Using Computers. MIT Press, Cambridge, Mass.

Norman, D. and Draper, S. (1986). (Eds) User Centered System Design. Lawrence Erlbaum, Hillsdale, NJ.

Norman, M. A. and Thomas, P. J. (1989). Informing HCI Design Practice through Conversation Analysis. Report 1989/1. Department of Computer Science, University of Hull.

Norman, M. A. and Thomas P. J. (in press). Informing HCI Design through Conversation Analysis, International Journal of Man-Machine Studies.

Oldman, D. and Drucker, C. (1985). The non-reducability of ethnomethods: can people and computers form a society?. In *Social Action and Artificial Intelligence* (Eds. G. N. Gilbert and C. Heath), 144-159. Gower, Aldershot.

Orr, W. D. (1968). (Ed.) Conversational Computers. Wiley, New York.

Paris, C. L. (1987). Combining Discourse Strategies to Generate Descriptions to Users along a Naive-Expert Spectrum. In *Proceedings of the 10th International Joint Conference on Artificial Intelligence*, 626-632.

Parnas, D. L. and Clements, P. C. (1985). The rational design process and how to fake it. Lecture Notes in Computer Science 186. Springer-Verlag, Berlin.

Pateman T. (1985). Using and Defending Cognitive Theory. In *Social Action and Artificial Intelligence* (Eds. G. N. Gilbert and C. Heath), 24-39. Gower, Aldershot.

Perrault, C. R. and Allen, J. (1980). A Plan-based Analysis of Indirect Speech Acts, American Journal of Computational Linguistics, Vol. 6, 3-4, 167-182.

Pew, R. W. (1974). Human perceptual-motor performance. In *Human Information Processing : tutorials in performance and cognition* (Ed. B.H. Kantowitz). Wiley, New York.

Pollack, M. E., Hirschberg, J. and Webber, B. L. (1982). User Participation in the Reasoning Processes of Expert Systems. In *Proceedings of the National Conference on Artificial Intelligence*, 358-361.

Pomerantz, A. M. (1975). Second Assessments: A Study Of Some Features Of Agreements/Disagreements. Unpublished Ph.D. Dissertation. University of California, Irvine.

Pomerantz, A. M. (1980). Telling My Side: 'Limited Access' As A 'Fishing' Device, Sociological Inquiry, Vol. 50, 186-196.

Posner, M. I. and Keele, S. W. (1968). On the genesis of abstract ideas, Journal of Experimental Psychology, Vol. 83, 304-8.

Power, R. (1979). The Organisation of Purposeful Dialogues, Linguistics, Vol. 17, 107-152.

Power, R. and Martello, M. F. (1985). Methods of Investigating Conversation, Review article in Semiotica, Vol. 53, 1/3, 237-257.

Preece, J. J. and Robinson H. M. (1989). Report of a workshop entitled 'Integrating evaluation into design', January 24th, Computing Department, Open University.

Psathas, G. (1979). (Ed.) Studies In Ethnomethodology: Everyday Language. Irvington, New York.

Psathas, G. (forthcoming) (Ed.) Interaction Competence. Lawrence Erlbaum Associates, Hillsdale, NJ.

Raudaskoski, P. (1989). Repair Work in Human-Computer Interaction. MSc dissertation. Department of Artificial Intelligence, University of Edinburgh.

Reddy, M. (1979). The Conduit Metaphor: A Case of Frame Conflict in out Language about Language. In *Metaphor and Thought* (Ed. A. Ortony). Cambridge University Press, Cambridge.

Reichman, R. (1985). Getting Computers to Talk like You and Me. MIT Press, Cambridge, Mass.

Reichman, R. (1986). Communication Paradigms for a Window System. In (Eds. Norman and Draper) *User-centered system design: New perspectives on human-computer interaction*. Lawrence Erlbaum Associates, Hillsdale, NJ.

Reilly, R. (1987). Communication Failure in Dialogue : Implications for Natural Language Understanding In *Proceedings of a Workshop on Recent Developments in Natural Language Understanding*, December 1987, London.

Ringle, M. H. and Bruce B. C. (1982). Conversation failure. In *Strategies in natural language processing* (Eds. W. G. Lehnert and M. H. Ringle). Lawrence Erlbaum Associates, Hillsdale, NJ.

Robinson, H. M. (1981). Database Analysis and Design. Chartwell-Bratt, Bromley.

Robinson, H. M. (1989). The capture of meaning in database administration. Unpublished Ph.D. Thesis. Hatfield Polytechnic.

Robinson, K. S. M. (1987). The social construction of health visiting. Unpublished Ph.D. Thesis. The Polytechnic of the South Bank.

Robinson, P., Luff, P., Jirotka, M., Hardey, M., Gilbert, G. N., Frohlich, D. M., Cordingley, B. and Buckland, S. (1988). Functional Specification for the Advice System. Technical Report. Alvey DHSS Demonstrator Project, University of Surrey.

Rochester, and Martin (1977). Crazy Talk. Wiley, New York.

Roger, D. and Bull, P. (1989). (Eds.) Conversation: An Interdisciplinary Perspective. Multilingual Matters, Clevedon, Philadelphia.

Ryle, G., (1963). The Concept of Mind. Penguin, London and Harmondsworth.

Rymaszewski, R. (1987). Negotiating Cooperative Effective Explanations. In *Proceedings of the 2nd Alvey Explanation Workshop*, Guildford, january 1987, IEE Stevenage, 43-49.

Sacks, H. (1964). Transcribed Lecture, Fall 1964, University of California, Irvine.

Sacks, H. (1965). Transcribed Lecture, Winter/2, University of California,Irvine.

Sacks, H. (1966a), Transcribed Lecture, Spring/14, University of California, Irvine.

Sacks, H. (1966b), Transcribed Lecture, Spring/15, University of California, Irvine.

Sacks, H. (1984 [1971]). On doing 'being ordinary'. In *Structures of Social Action: Studies in conversation analysis* (Eds. J. M. Atkinson and J. C. Heritage). Cambridge University Press, Cambridge.

✓ Sacks, H., Schegloff, E. A. and Jefferson, G. (1974). A simplest systematics for the organisation of turn-taking for conversation, Language, Vol. 50, 696-735.

Schank, R. C. and Abelson, R. (1977). Scripts, Plans, Goals and Understandings. Lawrence Erlbaum Associates, Hillsdale, NJ.

Schegloff, E. A. (1968). Sequencing in conversational openings, American Anthropologist, Vol. 70, 1075-1095.

Schegloff, E. A. (1972). Notes on a conversational practice: formulating place. In *Studies in Social Interaction* (Ed. D. Sudnow), 75-119. Free Press, New York.

Schegloff, E. A. (1979). Identification and recognition in telephone conversation openings. In *Everyday language : Studies in Ethnomethodology*, (Ed. G. Psathas). Irvington, New York.

Schegloff, E. A. (1980). What Type of Interaction Is It to Be ?. In *Proceedings of Association of Computational Linguistics 18th Annual Meeting and Parasession on Topics in Interactive Discourse*, 81.

Schegloff, E. A. (1982). Discourse as an interactional achievement: some uses of "uh huh" and other things which come between sentences. In *Analysing Discourse, Text and Talk, Georgetown University Roundtable on Languages and Linguistics* (Ed. D. Tannen), 71-93. Georgetown University Press, Washington D. C.

Schegloff, E. A. (1984). On Some Gestures' Relation to Talk. In *Structures Of Social Action: Studies In Conversation Analysis* (Eds. J. M. Atkinson and J. C. Heritage), 266-296. Cambridge University Press, Cambridge.

Schegloff, E. A. (1986). The Routine As Achievement, Human Studies, Vol. 9, 2-3: 111-152.

Schegloff, E. A. (1988a). Presequences and indirection: applying speech act theory to ordinary conversation, Journal of Pragmatics, Vol. 12, 55-62.

Schegloff, E. A. (1988b). Between macro and micro: contexts and other connections. *The macro-micro link* (Eds. J. Alexander, B. Griesen, R. Munch and N. Smelser). University of California Press, Berkeley and Los Angeles.

Schegloff, E. A. (1989a). Repair and the Organisation of Natural Language. *Invited Address in Association of Computational Linguistics Annual Conference*, June 1989.

Schegloff, E. A. (1989b). Harvey Sacks: a memoir, Human Studies Special Issue Vol. 12, 3-4.

Schegloff, E. A. (forthcoming). To Searle On Conversation: A Note In Return. In (Eds. E. le Pore and R. van Gulick).

Schegloff, E. A., Jefferson, G. and Sacks, H. (1977). The preference of self-correction in the organization of repair in conversation, Language, Vol. 53, 361-382.

Schegloff, E. A. and Sacks, H. (1973). Opening up closings, Semiotica, Vol. 7, 289-327.

Schenkein, J. N. (1978a). (Ed.) Studies in the Organisation of Conversational Interaction. Academic Press, London and New York.

Schenkein, J. N. (1978b). Sketch of the analytic mentality for the study of conversational interaction. In *Studies in the Organisation of Conversational Interaction* (Ed. J. N. Schenkein), 1-6. Academic Press, London and New York.

Schuster, E. and Finin, T. W. (1983). Understanding misunderstandings. Technical Report MS-CIS-83-12. Department of Computer and Information Science, The Moore School, University of Pennsylvania.

Searle, J. R. (1969). Speech Acts : An Essay in the Philosophy of Language. Cambridge University Press, Cambridge.

Searle, J. (1986). Introductory Essay: Notes On Conversation. In *Contemporary Issues In Language and Discourse Processes* (Ed. D. G. Ellis and W. A. Donohue), 7-19. Lawrence Erlbaum Associates, Hillsdale, NJ.

Shackel, B., Eason K., Gardener, A. and McKenzie, J. (1988). Human Factors Guidelines for the design of Computer-Based Systems. HMSO.

Shanker, S. G. (1987). Artificial Intelligence At The Cross-roads. In *Questions In Artificial Intelligence* (Ed. B. Bloomfield). Croom Helm, London.

Sharrock, W. and Anderson, B. (1986). The Ethnomethodologists. Ellis Horwood, Chichester.

Sharrock, W. and Anderson, B. (1987). Epilogue: The Definition of Alternatives: Some Sources of Confusion in Interdisciplinary Discussion. In *Talk and Social Organisation* (Eds. G. Button and Lee), 290-321. Multilingual Matters, Clevedon and Philadelphia.

Shieber, S. M. (1986). An Introduction to Unification-based Approaches to Grammar. CSLI Lecture Notes 4, Stanford.

Sidner, C. L. (1983). Focussing in the comprehension of definite anaphora,. In *Computational Models of Discourse* (Eds M. Brady and R. C. Berwick), 267-330. MIT Press, Cambridge, Mass.

√ Sinclair, J. McH and Coulthard, R. M. (1975). Towards an Analysis of Discourse: The English used by Teachers and Pupils. Oxford University Press, Oxford.

Smith, S. L. and Mosier J. N. (1984). Design Guidelines for user-system interface software. Mitre Corporation Research Report MTR-9420.

Sommerville, I. (1989). Software Engineering, 3rd edition. Addison-Wesley, Norwood, NJ.

Sorgaard, P. (1988). A Framework for Computer Supported Cooperative Work. DAIMI PB - 253. Computer Science Department, Aarhus University, Denmark.

Sperber, D. and Wilson, D., (1986). Relevance. Oxford University Press, Oxford.

Stefik, M. et al. (1987). Beyond the Chalkboard: Computer Support for Collaboration and Problem Solving, Communications of the ACM, Vol. 30, 1, 32-47.

Storrs, G. (1988). Multiple Agent Model of Human-Computer Interaction. In *Proceedings of the Alvey Workshop on Multiple Agent Systems*, April 1988, Redhill.

Suchman, L. A. (1982). Toward a Sociology of Human-Machine Interaction – Pragmatics of Instruction-Following. Draft report. Xerox Palo Alto Research Center, Palo Alto.

Suchman, L. A. (1986). Action in Cognitive Science. ISL Technical Note, April 1986, Xerox Palo Alto Research Center, Palo Alto.

√ Suchman, L. A. (1987). Plans and Situated Actions. Cambridge University Press, Cambridge.

Sudnow, D. (1972). (Ed.) *Studies in Social Interaction,* Free Press, New York.

Tennant, H. R., Ross, K. M. and Thompson, C.W. (1983). Usable natural language interfaces through menu-based natural language understanding. In *Proceedings of CHI '83*, 154-160.

Thimbleby, H. (1988). Delaying Commitment, IEEE Software, Vol. 5, 3, 78-86.

Thomas, P. J. (forthcoming). Conversation Analysis in Interactive Computer System Design. Ph.D. Thesis. University of Hull.

Thomas, P. J. and Norman, M. A. (1989). Interacting with hypertext: functional simplicity without conversational competence. *Proceedings of HyperText II*, 28-30 June 1989, University of York.

Thompson, H. and Ritchie, G. (1984). Implementing natural language parsers. In *Artificial intelligence: tools, techniques and applications* (Eds. T. O'Shea and M. Eisenstadt), 245-63. Harper and Row, New York.

Turing, A. M. (1950). Computing Machinery and Intelligence, Mind, Vol. 59, 433-460.

Turkle, S. (1984). The Second Self – Computers and the Human Spirit. Simon and Shuster, New York.

Turner, R. (1970). Words, utterances, activities. In *Ethnomethodology* (Ed. R. Turner). Penguin, London and Harmondsworth.

van Dijk, T. A. (1977). Semantic Macro-Structures and Knowledge Frames in Discourse Comprehension. In *Cognitive Processes in Comprehension* (Eds, M. A. Just and P. A. Carpenter). Academic Press, London and New York.

van Dijk, T. (1985). (Ed.) Handbook Of Discourse Analysis 3. Academic Press, London and New York.

van Katjwik, A. F. V., van Nes, F. L., Bunt, H. C., Muller, H. F., and Leopold, F. F. (1979). Naive subjects interacting with a conversing information system, IPO Annual Progress Report 14.

Waismann, F. (1965). The Principles Of Linguistic Philosophy (Ed. R. Harre). Macmillan, London.

Walker, T. (1989). What's the use of documentation. Paper presented at an Open University Computing Department Seminar, 4 July.

Wallis, J. W. and Shortliffe, E. H., (1984). Customised Explanations Using Causal Knowledge.. In *Rule Based Expert Systems* (Ed. B. G. Buchanan and E. H. Shortliffe). Addison-Wesley, Norwood, NJ.

Warnock, G.J. (1971). The Object Of Morality. Methuen, London.

Weizenbaum, J. (1976). Computer Power and Human Reason. Freeman.

Wieder, D. L. (1971). On meaning by rule. In *Understanding Everyday life* (Ed. J. Douglas), 107-136. Routledge Kegan Paul, London.

Wilson, J. (1989). On the Boundaries of Conversation. Pergamon Press, Oxford.

Wilson, J. P., Wiemann, J. M. and Zimmerman, D. H. (1984). Models of Turn Taking in Conversational Interaction, Journal of Language and Social Psychology, Vol. 3, 159-183.

Wilson, T. P. (1983). Qualitative "versus" Quantitative Methods in Social Research. Mimeo. Department of Sociology, University of California at Santa Barbara.

Winograd, T. (1983). Language as a Cognitive Process: Syntax. Addison-Wesley, Norwood, NJ.

Winograd, T. and Flores, F. (1986). Understanding Computers and Cognition: A New Foundation For Design. Addison-Wesley, Norwood, NJ.

Wittgenstein, L, (1953), Philosophical Investigations: Second Edition, Blackwell, Oxford.

Wittgenstein, L. (1958), The Blue And Brown Books. Blackwell, Oxford.

Woolf, B. and McDonald, D. D. (1974). Context-dependent Transitions in Discourse. In *Proceedings of the National Conference on Artificial Intelligence.*, 355-361.

Woolgar, S. (1985). Why not a sociology of machines? The case of sociology and artificial intelligence, Sociology, Vol. 19, 4, 557-572.

Woolgar, S. (1987). Reconstructing Man and Machine: A Note on Sociological Critiques of Cognitivism. In The Social Construction of Technological Systems (Eds. Bijker, W. E. et al.), 311-328. MIT Press, Cambridge, Mass.

Wootton, A. (1989). Remarks on the methodology of conversation analysis. In *Conversation* (Eds. D. Roger and P. Bull) , 238-258. Multilingual Matters. Clevedon and Philadelphia.

Wynn, E. (1980). What Discourse Features aren't Needed in Online Dialogue. In *Proceedings of Association of Computational Linguistics 18th Annual Meeting and Parasession on Topics in Interactive Discourse*, 87-90.

Young, R. (1988). (Ed.) Interim Report on The Cosmos Project. Report no 45.5 EXT. Cosmos Coordinators office, Queen Mary College, London.

Zimmerman, D. H. (1980). Special Edition of Sociological Inquiry, Vol. 50.

Index

abstraction 40
action-in-interaction 70
adjacency pair 8, 25, 72, 138, 200, 239
Agre, P. E. 106
algorithms 77
ambiguity 142
analytic mentality 35
analytic strategy 36
anthropologically strange 46
artificial intelligence 1, 3, 151
  distributed artificial intelligence 174
Block, N. 77
Button, G. 74, 87
carbon-based nature of life 125
Carroll, J. M. 162
Casey, N. J. 74, 87
causality 98
  causal mechanism 79
checking move 207, 222
chess 69
clarification 226
closings 64, 73, 75, 88, 214, 223
cognitive science 1
coherence relations 231
collaboration 113
command language grammar (CLG) 44
commitment logic 177

common-sense knowledge 23
communicative competence 10
competing versions 13
computational linguistics 110, 197, 245
computational metaphor 108, 134
computational model 67, 236
  of conversation 2, 76, 89
  of mind 84
computational theory of mind 96
computer conferencing 198
computer-mediated communication 101
computer-supported cooperative work 101
conditional relevance 61, 183, 204
context 143, 243
  context space 197
  relevance context 240
contingency 105, 109
conversation
  multi-party conversation 182
  ungrammatical conversation 136
conversational breakdown 135, 136
cooperation 109, 135
cooperative question-answering 195
Coulthard, R. M. 223